Understanding Social Problems, Policies, and Programs

Social Problems and Social Issues
Leon Ginsberg, Editor

Understanding Social Problems, Policies, and Programs

Third Edition

LEON GINSBERG

UNIVERSITY OF SOUTH CAROLINA PRESS

© 1994, 1996, 1999, University of South Carolina

Published in Columbia, South Carolina, by the
University of South Carolina Press

Manufactured in the United States of America

03 02 01 00 99   5 4 3 2 1

Library of Congress Cataloging-in-Publication Data

Ginsberg, Leon H.
    Understanding social problems, policies, and programs / Leon Ginsberg.
—3rd ed.
        p. cm. — (Social problems and social issues)
    Includes bibliographical references and index.
    ISBN 1-57003-266-1 (pbk.)
    1. Public welfare administration—United States.   2. United States—
Social policy.   3. Social problems—United States.   I. Title   II. Series:
Social problems and social issues (Columbia, S.C.)
HV95 .G518   1999
    361.973—ddc21
                                                                98-25442

Contents

Preface

Among the human services professions, social work is unique in the degree of its emphasis on social policy and services. Among the four traditional areas of the social work curriculum, social welfare policy and services, which this text shortens in name to "social policy," is unique because it is not shared with the curricula of related disciplines. Clinical services, which in social work fall under the curriculum area of social work practice, are central to several other professions such as counseling, clinical psychology, and school guidance. Human behavior and the social environment, a required area of study for social workers, is basically drawn from content developed by other disciplines such as biology, economics, psychology, and sociology. Social research, the final required area of social work study, is always a part of the curriculum for those who study in the social and behavioral sciences as well as other fields.

Although there are subdisciplines in some of the other human services fields which deal with social problems, policies, and services, in none of them is such content so central to the overall curriculum as it is in social work. Social work, which has a different sort of history than other fields that view their mission as that of helping people cope with or overcome personal or social problems, has historically focused on social policy and services.

The roots of social work are in social reform. References are made in ancient religious works to serving the needy and providing for the welfare of the aging, widows, people with disabilities, children, and other groups of people who cannot fully care for themselves. The provision of those services is a rudimentary form of social work. The religious injunctions requiring people to help the less fortunate are the earliest examples of social policies. The more formal, written history of the profession, which can be traced to early-seventeenth-century England, includes examples of the provision of assistance to the disadvantaged as well as the struggles of churches and governments to develop social policies that would achieve social welfare objectives without creating a dependent welfare class.

Although the current primary focus in educating social workers is on helping them learn how to serve communities, individuals, families, and groups, in a variety of circumstances and in a variety of ways social policy precedes any social work practice. For that matter, it may be argued that all human services, including education, mental health, health services, and crime prevention and control, are based upon societal decisions that such services are needed and worthy of financial support. Without such policies there is an absence of legal and social mechanisms for the services to be provided (a process that social work calls "sanction") and no financing for those services. Large numbers of clinical psychologists provide their services within social sanctioned and supported agencies such as schools, mental hospitals and centers, and clinics. Most physicians earn substantial portions of their incomes from programs that result from social policy, such as Medicaid and Medicare, but also from employer-provided health insurance. Hospitals have comparable sources of income.

Before one can speak about educating or employing teachers, policies must be established that provide for the financing of public education and the preparation of students. Before social welfare services are provided, the potential providers must begin with the creation and implementation of social policies that allow such provisions.

The historical reform nature of social work has long led to the recognition of the primacy of the development of policies. Not only are the professional social work organizations involved in the development and advocacy of such policies; the profession also considers it an obligation of each practitioner to engage in policy development and advocacy.

Throughout the history of organized social work the threads of social reform and policy development have been pervasive. For those viewing social work from the outside, however, the social policy orientation can be confusing. Nevertheless, it is of major importance because social work programs are involved with so many external analysts and controllers of their operations. Each agency—local, state, or federal, public or voluntary—is scrutinized and often governed by a board of directors, legislative committee, or executive branch structure that may have only a modest understanding of social workers and social programs. Similarly, viewing the profession from the opposite direction, new students of social work often wonder why they are exposed to social policy courses when their reasons for enrolling have to do with "helping people," not studying the intricacies of problems, policies, and programs.

This book is designed to help two divergent audiences—the board, committee, and executive branch leaders of social work and the students who aspire to membership in the social work profession—understand the social policy dimensions of the discipline. A third audience is, of course, teachers of social policy, who are likely to be the ones who communicate those concepts to leaders and students.

There are already in print several books designed for those with interests in social work's approaches to social policy, many of them quite good. Most could be used in tandem with this brief guide to the overall concepts. This book is designed to help students of social policy understand the array of social policy concepts rather than specific elements of those policies. It is also designed to show how policies emerge from social problems and are translated into programs. It can be used as a stand-alone text for a beginning course, especially if it is supplemented with articles and reference books such as *The Encyclopedia of Social Work* as well as *The Social Work Dictionary* and *The Social Work Almanac*, all of which are published by the largest of the discipline's professional organizations, the National Association of Social Workers. This book, coupled with exploration of those references for detailed information on problems, programs, and policies, as well as the definitions, degrees, and levels of services, ought to help any student better understand the subject.

The original audience for these ideas consisted of doctoral students at the University of South Carolina, College of Social Work. The doctoral program at the college is designed to prepare social work teachers for baccalaureate and master's programs. For years before I taught Theoretical Analysis of Social Policy, the one doctoral course in the subject, I had taught or supervised the teaching of social policy courses for bachelor of social work (BSW) and master of social work (MSW) students in the United States, Colombia, Mexico, and Romania. I had also served on accreditation site-visit teams to many schools in the United States and Canada; had been a member of the Commission on Accreditation of the Council on Social Work Education, which accredits social work programs; and had worked as a social policymaker and consultant in state and federal programs. Perhaps because of that extensive exposure and involvement in social policy theory from a number of perspectives, I realized that the task of educating social policy teachers, who might find themselves on faculties anywhere in the world, was more difficult than it seemed. That is because there is so little unanimity on what the fundamental course content ought to be. Each course, each text, and each of the thousands of social policy teachers seemed to have its own approach to or emphases of the subject matter. The accreditation guidelines are specific enough to help programs determine the content they must include in their teaching, yet they permit (as most educators would agree they should) wide latitude in the design and emphases of the courses.

Therefore, I found it necessary to help those potential social policy teachers understand the broad range of meanings and the variety of approaches used in the field to teach the subject matter. If I focused on historical, descriptive, and social problems approaches to the subject, which are the emphases of the College of Social Work's introductory MSW course, I would not well serve a student who might find employment as a faculty member in a program that emphasizes social policy analysis or the practice of social policy development and implementation. Or if I spent the semester teaching how to convey social policy ideas by tracing and coping with a specific social problem, as some instructors in some colleges and universities do, my students would be baffled when they were required to teach a didactic course that focused heavily on social program descriptions.

I resolved the problem by recognizing and categorizing the hundreds of social policy teaching examples to which I had been exposed. All of the social policy courses I had encountered were organized around one or a combination of several of six components: history, social problems and social issues, public policy, description, analysis, and policy practice. So the framework for my teaching rested on these six components, with lectures, readings, book reports, class preparations, and term papers all organized around them. The students, I thought, needed to understand all six if the course was to be useful to them.

I have taught the course many times, and, so far as I can determine, the six components effectively encompass the current understandings of social policy, the books, and the courses I encounter in accreditation consultations and reviews. Several doctoral graduates have assumed positions as teachers of social policy. All we lacked was access in book form to the model of social policy curriculum which is the basis for the kind of course described.

This is the book. For the spring semester of 1993 the University of South Carolina granted me sabbatical leave to put my ideas into a more formal version than my notes and course syllabi. Although this book is not designed to parallel the many fine social policy texts already in print, it should help students and instructors better understand one or more of those texts. The content is also sufficiently complete to make it useful as a stand-alone text, especially for foundation level—baccalaureate or first-year MSW—courses on social welfare policy and services. With some additional material from classroom lectures, additional readings, research papers, or the use of key reference works, the book could serve as a worthwhile and complete introduction to the subject. It is designed to meet the accreditation requirements of the Commission on Accreditation for the content area and to provide students with sufficient foundation knowledge to understand advanced courses in social policy as well as the social policy underpinnings of other content areas. Readers of the book, whether they are students or board members or other kinds of supervisors of social work programs, should capture a fundamental understanding of the nature and various perceptions of social policy as they are presently taught in social work and social work education.

The book does not present any special ideological points of view. That is, it is not especially oriented to incremental, radical, conservative, or liberal ideologies—although social policy, by its nature, implies some belief that government ought to be involved in serving the needs of citizens.

The book also avoids specific religious orientations, which are important components for many of the social work education programs that are associated with religious denominations. Communicating the social policy components of those religious mandates is an important function for such programs, and this text does not interfere with the capacity of a program to add such orientations to the mix of information provided in social policy courses.

There are ideological differences among existing social policy texts as well as varying degrees of commitment to one or more of the orientations discussed here. Some texts are more historical than others, some are almost exclusively analytical, others focus on social issues and problems, and still others are largely descriptive. Most texts combine two or more of the components offered here, which is also true of most social policy courses. The only specific point of view advocated here is that there are several orientations for understanding and teaching about social policy. This book implies that all those orientations are legitimate and, in many cases, essential to a sound understanding of the subject matter. The book leaves the addition of ideology and specific values to the courses and instructors for whom it is intended. It should be noted here that the term "social policy" is often used in this volume as a shorthand designation for the total subject matter of this book—social problems, policies, and programs.

The first two editions, which this volume updates, filled a gap in the social problems, policies, and programs literature, according to professors and students with whom I talked. People liked the idea of a brief, accessible, but inclusive text that covered the key bases. They also appreciated the low cost of a paperback in the increasingly costly textbook business. Some have found the book useful for introduction to social welfare courses.

To date no reader has insisted that the book missed a seventh or eighth approach to the subject. The six that are included seem capable of encompassing the elements that most students of the subject would include. Therefore, this edition retains the structure of the first. It updates information on some of the literature, makes the historical chapter current, adds additional material on policy analysis, and changes a few examples. In some ways, social welfare has changed significantly since the first edition was published. President Bill Clinton, whose service was beginning when the manuscript for the first edition was completed, was finishing his second term when the third was prepared. The Republican Party had gained control of both houses of the U.S. Congress for the first time in more than forty years and established a clear agenda to make major policy changes, many of which had direct impact on social welfare. They made major changes in social welfare with the president's concurrence which are described in this book.

This edition also discusses the results and some of the implications of the 1998 congressional elections in which the Democratic Party exceeded most historical expectations by adding members to its minority in the House of Representatives and maintaining the same Democratic numbers in the Senate. A Republican move to impeach the president was credited, in part, for the Democratic successes. However, the 1998 results were not generally viewed as a repudiation of the social welfare changes made in 1996 under the Republican Contract with America. More likely, voters who had supported Republicans in larger numbers in 1994 because of their desire to change social welfare policies saw less need to do so in 1998 because their concerns had been resolved.

Other events too had at least an indirect impact on human provisions. Violence again became an inescapable part of the social problems agenda with the bombing of a federal facility in Oklahoma City; the murder trial of football hero and media personality O.J. Simpson, who was accused and acquitted of killing his former wife and her friend; as well as youth gang violence, the murder of employees of health facilities where abortions were performed, and increasing numbers of firearms deaths. But change is the nature of the subject matter and should not surprise anyone familiar with the history of U.S. social welfare, which dates from the 1930s New Deal.

My thanks go to several of my MSW and Ph.D. students in social policy courses who helped me formulate the ideas that are presented here, as well as to my colleagues at the University of South Carolina and my former colleagues at West Virginia University and the University of Oklahoma. I also learned a good deal about teaching social policy from the faculty and students of two universities in Colombia, South America, at the Escuela de Trabajo Social at the Universidad Nacional Autónoma de México, and at social work schools in Romania, where social work had been outlawed—as it had been in many Soviet Union nations, perhaps because of its inclusion of social policy—under the former regime and restored during the 1990s. The 1992 University of South Carolina doctoral students in social policy—Dorothy Callahan, Liz Cramer, Steve Hardin, Debora Rice, and Jean Sullivan—were especially helpful with suggestions when they learned I was working on the first edition of this book. Some of their ideas were cited in the first edition.

This book owes a special debt to David P. Fauri, Ph.D., Professor, School of Social Work, Virginia Commonwealth University, and Barbara J. Ettner, M.Ed. and doctoral candidate, School of Social Work, Virginia Commonwealth University, for their annotated bibliography of policy journals, which is found in appendix 1. Thanks also go to Joyce Shaw of the College of Social Work staff, copy editor Jean W. Ross, and Margaret V. Hill of the University of South Carolina Press for assistance with the manuscript.

Chapter One

Social Policy in Social Work and the Other Human Services Professions

This book is about social welfare policy and services, which is one of the required curriculum areas for people who study social work and other human services fields in colleges and universities. The other areas of study in the human services are usually professional practice, which defines what social workers and others in the human services do in their efforts to help people; human behavior and the social environment, which teaches about the ways in which families, individuals, groups, communities, and societies develop and behave; and research, which covers the methods that are used to better understand and evaluate human services and social welfare programs.

Social welfare is, of course, the total system of programs, services and policies that provides for human well-being. Social Security retirement benefits for older adults, medical care for people with disabilities, and protection against abuse or neglect for children are examples of social welfare, which some call "social services." Social work is the largest profession that works within the social welfare system. The creation of the social work profession a century ago, its growth over the years, and its occasional declines are all products of social policy. So are all the developments of the other human services professions such as gerontology, nursing, rehabilitation counseling and other specialized disciplines that deal with the problems and needs of people. Policies are the sources of all social welfare. Services develop only when there are social policies that create, finance, and provide for administering them. Therefore, all human services workers are educated, employed, and paid because of social policies. Without social policy there would be no workers to carry out those policies.

1

The curriculum areas described earlier—social work practice, social research, human behavior and the social environment, and social welfare policy and services—are all part of the education of the helping professions. Psychology, counseling, nursing, medicine, education, physical therapy, speech therapy, physical education, and virtually all of the other professions that help people overcome their personal, physical, or social problems or needs include those areas in their curricula. Social work, however, is somewhat different because it requires more extensive education about social policy than some other human fields. That is because social workers have always believed that human problems are not simply individual problems, but can often best be solved through social policies. Conversely, social workers have found that many human problems result from the lack of social policies that could prevent those problems. In other cases, social workers believe that some social policies *cause* human problems. Increasingly, all of the human services fields are adopting that point of view and are finding, in the practice of their work, that attention to social policy is crucial to the effective resolution of human problems.

HOW SOCIAL POLICY AFFECTS LIFE

The worst social policy and the starkest example of how influential social policies are have to do with the socioeconomic system of slavery. Slavery was an American social policy prior to the Civil War that allowed some people to own other people. White slave owners could buy and sell black people. They could punish them in any way they wanted. They could kill them if they chose to do so. They could keep them from learning to read or write. During and after the Civil War, President Abraham Lincoln, Congress, and the northern states implemented two new social policies—freeing the slaves; making them citizens; guaranteeing all people, including former slaves, equal rights; and providing the former slaves the right to vote. Those new policies were contained in presidential proclamations, federal laws, and amendments to the Constitution. The treatment of human beings as property and the changes in that treatment—redefining black people as American citizens—were both consequences of social policies.

Although not as brutal as slavery, the segregation in the South that began decades after the end of the Civil War is hard to imagine in today's environment. From the late 1800s through the middle 1950s,

2

there was strict, legal segregation of African Americans from white people in schools, restaurants, hospitals, public transportation, movie theaters, and virtually every other kind of situation in which people might mingle. This was legal, or *de jure*, segregation by color.

Still, there are examples of *de facto* segregation in which, in fact, white and black people are separated from each other—often by choice and even more often by economics that make it difficult for many African-American families to participate in the same activities as many white families. Legal segregation is gone, but realistically, actual segregation continues in many elements of American life.

Until 1920, when the Nineteenth Amendment to the U.S. Constitution was passed, most American women were not permitted to vote, a fact that is unthinkable in the 1990s. Both the denial of the vote to women and the extension of suffrage to them were social policies.

In the 1930s and 1940s, it was the official policy of the Nazi regimes in Germany and its allied European nations to seize, relocate, and kill Jews, Gypsies, homosexuals, people with mental disabilities, and other groups. Another example of social policy is the "ethnic cleansing" in the former nation of Yugoslavia in the 1990s, in which many Muslims were arrested, raped, and murdered.

Almost everything that affects people is a social policy. Social policies determine, in part at least, the ways we marry and divorce, the ways parents may treat their children, the ways we work, the rules under which we employ others in jobs, and our educations. Social policies define what is and is not a crime, how we receive medical care, and the kinds of help we receive when we are unemployed, disabled, or too old to work. Almost anything that influences our lives can be found in social policies.

SOCIAL WORK AND SOCIAL POLICY

Social work's counseling or casework services are somewhat similar to those we find in many of the other helping professions. Our understandings of the ways in which people behave are actually taken from other helping professions and social sciences. Our social research is often indistinguishable from that employed in other helping professions and the social and behavior sciences. In fact, the methods we use were often developed by and are now borrowed by social work from other fields, especially psychology and sociology. Our *Code of Ethics*, when it

3

deals with the ways we treat clients, is, in most respects, similar to those of the other helping disciplines.

It is our extensive involvement with social policy that actually distinguishes social work as a profession. It is what makes it different from related approaches to helping people.

A Definition

Social policy textbooks define *social policy* in various ways, some (DiNitto 1994) emphasizing policies that are developed through government—public policies—and others extending the definition to include policies made by professional organizations such as the National Association of Social Workers and voluntary agencies such as United Way and Family Service Societies. For us the best definition is taken from the *Social Work Dictionary;* according to this widely used and comprehensive source, *social policy* is

> the activities and principles of a society that guide the way it intervenes in and regulates relationships between individuals, groups, communities, and social institutions. These principles and activities are the result of the society's values and customs and largely determine the distribution of resources and level of well-being of its people. Thus, social policy includes plans and programs in education, health care, crime and corrections, economic security, and social welfare made by government, voluntary organizations, and the people in general. It also includes social perspectives that result in society's rewards and constraints. (Barker 1995, 335)

Dear (1995, 2226) defines policy as "just about anything a government does." He says that policies are "principles, plans, procedures and courses of action—established in statute, interpreted in administrative code, spelled out in agency regulation, and supported by judicial decree." By Dear's definition, anything that is formally spelled out, whether by a governmental or nongovernmental agency, about their operations is a policy.

The examples of slavery, segregation, and the Holocaust have to do with the well-being of people. The issue of suffrage deals with society's rewards and constraints. Rules about work and family life are concerned with the ways society regulates relations among people. Clearly, almost anything that has an impact on our lives is a product of a social policy or a group of social policies.

Social Work Ethics and Social Policy

Social work's long-standing professional interest in social policy has been underscored in a number of ways other than, most obviously, the ways it educates its new practitioners. Today social workers are obligated *to do something* about social policy. The 1996 National Association of Social Workers Code of Ethics says that social workers have ethical responsibilities to the broader society. According to the statement, "Social workers should promote the general welfare of society, from local to global levels, and the development of people, their communities, and their environments. Social workers should advocate for living conditions conducive to the fulfillment of basic human needs and should promote social, economic, political, and cultural values and institutions that are compatible with the realization of social justice."

The code goes on to say that social workers should:

1. Facilitate informed public participation in shaping public policies and institutions.
2. Engage in social and political action geared toward gaining equal access to opportunities that help all persons meet their basic needs and develop fully in areas such as employment.
3. Advocate for legislative and policy changes to improve social conditions and promote social justice.
4. Act to expand the choices people have, with special attention to vulnerable, oppressed, exploited, and disadvantaged groups.
5. Promote conditions that will in turn promote respect for cultural and social diversity in the United States and the rest of the world.
6. Work to eliminate discrimination on bases such as ethnicity, sex, race, sexual orientation, religion, age, marital status, political beliefs, and physical or mental disabilities. (*NASW code of ethics, 1996*)

The statement makes it clear that social workers need to learn about social policies not only when they are students; we are also obligated to practice—to do something about—social policy throughout our careers.

Of course, social workers have different routes to being involved in social policies. Some of us are administrators or have other policy jobs in voluntary and government agencies and can propose, implement, or even develop and promulgate social policies that affect the well-being of people. Other social workers carry out their social policy mandates by involving themselves in social action organizations and political campaigns. Others contribute to social policy by writing and speaking to legislators and administrators to influence them to support policies to improve people's lives. Still others of us support social policies by being active in our professional organizations or by simply carrying out policies that make a difference in the lives of people.

No matter what our specific roles, social workers have always known that helping people involves much more than talking to clients or meeting with groups or even providing assistance and other services to those who need them. Helping people requires helpful policies. In the long run a social policy can make much more difference in the lives of those we serve than all of the counseling, economic, or protective services we might provide them. Social policies can change the bases of their lives, prevent future problems, and continue to help them cope with their problems long after they have received the services of a human services agency or professional.

An agency may help a client find a job; a social policy may guarantee that person employment for as long as he or she can work. A human services worker may help a client find ways to pay medical bills; a social policy may guarantee the client medical care. An agency may provide a family with a Christmas basket, but a social policy may provide that family with enough money to support itself and buy its own holiday baskets in the future.

SOCIAL POLICY AND THE PRACTICE OF SOCIAL WORK

In addition to knowing about and working toward improvements in social policy as a professional, ethical obligation, social workers also *use* social policy in their professional work. At times social work students believe that practicing, or "doing," social work is, for most social workers, a process of talking to people about their personal or family problems. Others believe social work practice involved meeting with groups of clients and helping them solve one another's difficulties or helping a community identify and take steps to resolve its social needs. While these examples are clearly parts of the roles of most social workers, many also perform their duties by understanding, explaining, and applying social policies.

For example, parents who visit with a human services worker to help them cope with a troubled child need and receive casework or counseling services of some kind from that worker. The counseling is designed to help them cope with their feelings about the troubled child, develop some strategies for dealing with the child, or even obtain additional help such as group treatment, recreational involvement, or tutoring for the child. The worker, however, would also call upon a fund of knowledge about social policies that might assist the family. If, for example, the child has handicaps or limitations, he or she might be eligible for a program of financial assistance called Supplemental Security Income (SSI) or special health care through the Crippled Children's Program; or transportation to special education classes; or a court action that could "emancipate" a minor child, which in effect helps a child who cannot be kept under control at home to become a legal adult, despite his or her young age. In many cases the contribution of the worker is based upon knowing about and helping clients use social policies that provide necessary services.

Social programs are the real source of help for clients. In the example above, the worker and the client would never have come together had it not been for a social policy that provided a program in which parents with such problems have access to human services workers who can help them. It was social policy that made the whole interchange possible. Little happens in the human services unless there is social policy to authorize, sanction, and pay for it. So, as was suggested earlier, the practice of the human services professions is a product of social policy, and social policy is fundamental to everything else that goes on in human services work.

OTHER DISCIPLINES AND SOCIAL POLICY

None of what has been suggested so far means that social work is the only human services discipline that deals with social policy. All human services workers need to understand and use social policy, and all are, to an extent products of and implementers of social policy. Professional ethics are also taught to students, sometimes with greater emphasis than social work devotes to the subject. In the other disciplines, however, there is usually less attention to and less central role for social policy in

7

educational programs. In some cases social policy is an elective subject rather than a required part of the curriculum, as it is in social work at both the baccalaureate (BSW) and master's (MSW) levels.

Some fields are even more emphatic about the importance of social policy. For example, students of political science, especially those who study in the related field of public administration, may be required to take a number of social policy courses. Some colleges and universities have whole programs, with undergraduate majors and graduate degrees, in policy or public policy, which, of course, include social policy. Political science and public administration are not, however, primarily human services fields, although many students of both often have careers in the human services. Therefore, social work, among the human services professions, is the field that most directly includes and emphasizes social policy in its curriculum.

THE COMPONENTS OF SOCIAL POLICY

Even with the knowledge that social policy is central to social work teaching and practice and even with the clear definition provided by Barker (1995), it is still true that social policy is often a confusing subject for some social workers. Chances are good that they had never heard of social policy before entering a social work major or an MSW program. It is a term not normally discussed in high school or in other undergraduate courses. In fact, it is a term that is not usually heard in the normal course of conversations or even featured in newspapers and magazines. Social policy discussions, unless they are concrete and personal, are not what people pursue at home, at parties, or in classrooms. Many people may have an opinion, say, on the marital relations of the president and his wife, but few will have more than the broadest attitudes about presidential policies. Remarks such as "Get those bums off welfare" are often as close as we get to real policy discussions. Therefore, objective, well-informed analyses of policy issues, books and films about policy, and term paper assignments on social policies may be relatively new or uncommon experiences for students.

Even seasoned human services workers may not know very much or think very much about social policies. I recall a visit with a distinguished hospital social work director many years ago. He had recently interviewed a job applicant and asked what the applicant would like to emphasize if employed at the hospital. The applicant expressed a strong interest in policy. Policy, the applicant hoped, would be the emphasis of her professional career. The social work director told me: "Policy! We don't need policies! We have bookshelves full of policies, and more of them is the last thing we need!" Of course, the applicant was not proposing the writing of more policies. But the hospital social work director's understanding of the term was quite different from the applicant's.

Neither, however, was wrong, despite the clear definition by Barker. *Social policy* has many meanings, and, in the absence of background in the subject, it is a confusing term for many students and practitioners. It is even a confusing term for many social work professors, a group for whom this book was originally designed. Part of the reason for the confusion about the meaning of *social policy* is that the term actually means many things. Educators and authors in the social policy field define the subject in different ways. The textbooks in the social policy field are also quite varied and emphasize different aspects of the term.

As a way of describing the field of social policy and the various approaches taken to it, it is worthwhile to analyze and define these approaches and what they seek to emphasize. Several years of study of the field, review of the textbooks and articles that have been written about it, and consideration of the ways that numerous baccalaureate and graduate social work programs teach the subject suggest that there are six components of social policy as it is studied and taught in the field of social work. These components are the organizing themes of this book.

Sources of the Components

The components of social policy teaching and scholarship come from a number of different sources. Primary among them are the curriculum requirements of the social work accrediting bodies. Accreditation has long been a critical part of social work education, and, historically, social work education programs have aspired to offer degrees that were accredited. According to Frumkin and Lloyd (1995), formal social work education began at the end of the nineteenth century and has continued throughout the twentieth. In the 1930s professional standards were developed, and graduate social work education programs joined together in the American Association of Schools of Social Work (AASSW). For several reasons, the most important being that most people did not enter social work until they had finished their undergraduate studies, social work education was long considered a postgraduate field, despite the fact that undergraduate programs had been

9

offered for many years and finally became eligible for accreditation some twenty years ago. There was even a competing organization to the American Association of Schools of Social Work, the National Association of Schools of Social Work (NASSW), which began in 1942. The conflict between the two organizations was over whether social work, at the graduate level, should be a one- or a two-year program, with the AASSW favoring two years and the NASSW one year. The conflict was resolved with the development of the Council on Social Work Education (CSWE) in 1952, which has continued since then to be the sole organization representing and accrediting social work education. It has accredited master's programs since it began, and in 1974 it began accrediting baccalaureate social work degrees, many of which had existed as long or longer than the master's programs (Lloyd 1987). There are more than fifty doctoral education programs in social work in the United States (Ginsberg 1995).

Throughout these procedures for setting standards for social work education, curriculum materials on social policy have always been required. They have been a necessary component since education for social work practice began. The ideas about social work curriculum were clarified and refined in the thirteen-volume *Social Work Curriculum Study* (1959), which was led by Werner Boehm and involved many of the leading social work educators of the time. Based upon that study, the Council on Social Work Education promulgated, in 1962, a curriculum policy statement (Frumkin and Lloyd 1995). The statement has been updated every few years since then, most recently in 1994, with separate statements provided for baccalaureate and master's education.

The curriculum statements on social policy have changed over the three decades since they began. In some statements, perhaps responding to the activism of the 1960s, it was expected that programs would prepare students to become active participants in social policy development. In later statements such commitments to action were dropped, but the learning content has remained similar. Students have been consistently required to learn about the history of social work, which often includes learning about some of the figures that have influenced its development, about the making of public policy and the political process, and how to analyze and evaluate social policies and programs.

The 1992 *Curriculum Policy Statement,* published by the Council on Social Work Education and revised in 1994, has a variety of requirements for content on social policy. For example, in its statement about the purpose of mater's social work education, the *Statement* says that graduates should be able to "analyze the impact of social policies on client systems, workers, and agencies and demonstrate skills for influencing policy formulation and change" (Edwards et al. 1995, 2653).

In its description of the foundation content (which is required for both baccalaureate and beginning master's programs) on Social Welfare Policy and Services, the *Statement* says:

> The foundation social welfare policy and services content must include the history, mission, and philosophy of the social work profession. Content must be presented about the history and current patterns of provision of social welfare services, the role of social policy in helping or deterring people in the maintenance (or attainment) of optimal health and well-being, and the effect of policy on social work practice. Students must be taught to analyze current social policy within the context of historical and contemporary factors that shape policy. Content must be presented about the political and organizational processes used to influence policy, the process of policy formulation, and the frameworks for analyzing social policies in light of the principles of social and economic justice. (Edwards et al. 1995, 2653)

Scholarship by social work writers and researchers as well as scholarship from other fields, such as public policy and political science, has also made a mark on social policy content. Several books written by social workers have been influential in defining the field of social policy and the knowledge that students are expected to acquire during their studies. Some of those scholars and researchers are oriented to understanding the history of the social work profession, others the systematic analysis of social programs and services, and still others have written about the practice of social policy, an orientation that has consistently involved large numbers of human services professionals, many of them social workers.

Religion has traditionally been an important source of social policy. The original mandates to help the needy and the ethical bases for providing social services are found in sacred books such as the Bible as well as in the oral traditions and holy documents and teachings of various religions.

Government itself has also been influential in defining the social policy information that social workers need. Legislation, government regulations, pronouncements of government officials, and the administration of public programs have all influenced what must be learned, especially in terms of teaching about public policy. During the presidential terms of Ronald Reagan and George Bush (Ginsberg 1987, 1990) and the leadership term of Prime Minister Margaret Thatcher of Great Britain, governments tried to change some of their approaches to social policy from providing services themselves to encouraging the distribution of services through "nongovernmental organizations," which have traditionally been called private, or voluntary, agencies in the United States.

Because so many of the social services are voluntary, the policy-making activities of nongovernmental organizations have a major impact on social policy. For example, the local United Ways are the largest fundraising and allocating organizations in the voluntary social services sector. Their decisions about social services funds are significant, affecting social policy within their own communities. Similarly, social welfare planning councils, or community councils, which operate in many larger communities, have an impact on the policy-making process.

Social welfare agencies define social policies, often in relation to public policies. In the 1980s, when the federal and state governments changed the emphasis of their strategies to delivering many services through nongovernmental, voluntary agencies, these agencies began following policies of seeking contracts with governments as a way of developing their services. Agency executive directors became, in many cases, "presidents," and a corporatelike management style permeated their organizations.

Individual social workers also make policy. In the course of their normal duties, practicing social workers daily make social policies, whether they intend to do so or not. Everything from the most specific, such as the behavior required of children in a youth club affiliated with a YMCA or a Jewish Community Center, to decisions about whether or not to remove a child from the child's parents is a policy, and, although there may be broad policy guidelines covering such issues as well as supervisors who are available for consultation and guidance, many decisions are made by the worker on the spot. Over time these decisions, if they work, are repeated by the individual worker and often replicated by colleagues; thus, they become social policies. The practice of social work, in other words, creates social policy. And, as we will learn, it is the job of some social workers to actually *practice* social policy—to develop, write, and promulgate policies.

The Six Components of Social Policy

Systems theorists tell us that everything is made up of smaller and smaller building blocks, down to such tiny things as electrons, genes, and viruses. A social policy paradigm with ten thousand components would simply not provide a comfortable route for learning about the subject. I highlight six components of social policy; they are interrelated rather than mutually exclusive. That is, each contains some elements of all the others. Each, in turn, could easily be subdivided into smaller parts; another observer could assert, for example, that there are really four or eighteen to twenty-six key components of social policy. After ten years of work defining the field of social policy, I find that these six components are distinct and broad enough to provide an effective range of study and teaching, as well as broad enough to offer students and teachers a useful model, or paradigm.

Historical. Social policy can be understood in terms of its historical roots and developments. As mentioned, all social work students are required to learn about the history of the organized profession. History is the branch of knowledge that records and/or analyzes past events. Chapter 2 discusses the historical component of social policy, the early development of social welfare services, and the modern era, from Social Security to the present.

Social Problems / Social Issues. Another way to study social policy is by studying social problems, or social issues, a subject that is well developed in sociology and, to an extent, in other social sciences. As has already been suggested, social policy is viewed by many as a consequence of social problems. When society determines that a problem is large enough to be considered a problem for large numbers of people, it becomes a social problem. For example, the personal misfortune of having nowhere to live became the social problem of homelessness; the personal misfortune of having a poor or unsafe family life became the social problem of child neglect or maltreatment; and the personal lack of income or resources became the social problem of poverty. Chapter 3 examines the social problems/social issues component of social policy.

Public Policy. One of the most critical of the six components in this model is public policy. Chapters 4 and 5 deal with public policy in detail. The component includes all of the policy decisions made by pub-

13

lic, or governmental, bodies such as legislatures and courts; executives such as governors or the president; executive branch agencies such as state departments of social services of the U.S. Department of Health and Human Services; and independent agencies, which are not executive, legislative, or judicial bodies but do perform some of the same functions.

Descriptive. Part of learning about social policy is simply learning about the programs and services that constitute social welfare. Those programs and services are results of social policy. One classic way of discussing social policy is in the form of a triad: *problem, policy, provision.* In other words, many observers believe that social problems lead to the development of social policies, the ultimate outcomes of which are provisions of social services. Understanding the myriad provisions which arise from social policy—mental health services, financial assistance, job training, day care, and everything else that social agencies and social workers provide—is necessary for understanding social policy. And, of course, being able to help others means, among other things, knowing what services are available to people who face problems.

Analytical. Understanding social policy requires much more than simply knowing what those policies entail. To be an effective professional in the human services one must also know what those policies consist of—who is helped by them most and who is helped by them least, how they are financed, and what alternatives may exist. Chapter 6 covers the analytical approach, the subject of many social policy textbooks.

Policy Practice. Some social workers and other human services professionals practice social policy. That is, they promulgate social policies; write policies for agencies; translate statutes passed by legislative bodies into regulations that agencies and their employees implement; interpret and consult about policies for those who deliver services to clients; and draft legislation for state legislatures and the U.S. Congress. Chapter 9 explains the practice component of social policy.

CONCLUSION

This chapter has offered definitions of social policy and explained why social policy is central to human services professions. It has examined the ways social policy affects people's lives and pointed out its special place in the field of social work as well as its roles in some of the other human services professions. The chapter also introduces the six components of social policy that constitute the basic outline for this book and upon which the subsequent chapters are based.

DISCUSSION QUESTIONS

1. Describe some of the ways in which social policy affects the lives of all people. Provide examples from social services programs you have studied, from your employment in social welfare, or from your field placement or internship.
2. This chapter suggests that social policy is more central to the study and practice of social work than to the other human services professions. Do you agree? If so, explain why you agree, or, if you disagree, explain that position.
3. Based upon your experience or other readings, do you agree with Barker's definition of social policy? If so, explain why you agree. If not, explain how you might want to change it.
4. Do you believe that social policy ought to have a greater or lesser role within the social work curriculum you have experienced? Explain your answer.

REFERENCES

Alexander, C. A. (1995). Distinctive dates in social welfare history. In R. L. Edwards et al. (Eds.), *Encyclopedia of social work*, 19th ed., 2631–2647. Washington, DC: NASW Press.

Barker, R. (1995). *The social work dictionary*, 3d ed. Washington, DC: NASW Press.

Boehm, W. M. (1959). *Social work curriculum study*. 13 vols. New York: Council on Social Work Education.

Dear, R. B. (1995). Social welfare policy. In R. L. Edwards et al. (Eds.), *Encyclopedia of social work*, 19th ed., 2226–2237. Washington, DC: NASW Press.

DiNitto, D. M. (1994). *Social welfare: Politics and public policy*, 4th ed. Englewood Cliffs, NJ: Prentice-Hall.

Frumkin, M., & Lloyd, G. A. (1995). Social work education. In R. L. Edwards et al. (Eds.), *Encyclopedia of social work*, 19th ed., 2238–2247. Washington, DC: NASW Press.

Ginsberg, L. (1987). Economic, political, and social context. In A. Minahan et al. (Eds.), *Encyclopedia of social work*, 18th ed., xxxiii–xli. Silver Spring, MD: NASW Press.

Ginsberg, L. (1990). Introduction. In L. Ginsberg et al. (Eds.), *Encyclopedia of social work,* 18th ed., 1990 supp., 1–11. Silver Spring, MD: NASW Press.

Ginsberg, L. (1995). *Social work almanac,* 2d ed. Washington, DC: NASW Press.

Chapter Two

The Historical Component: Milestones in Social Policy

Although not as well known as other social institutions such as education and religion, social services have a long history. Historians who specialize in the study of social policy history note that as long as there have been civilizations there have also been social welfare services to help people deal with their needs or problems. The earliest forms provided mutual help; that is, when a family was in need because, for example, its crops failed or because of illness or death, other families came to its assistance with food, shelter, and other resources. It is probably true that in modern society mutual help is still the most pervasive form of assistance. Often when parents are temporarily or permanently unable to care for children, neighbors and family members will pitch in to help. Families share food, pass around clothing, help one another with transportation, and make loans or provide cash assistance to those who cannot handle their own requirements.

Any study of social policy history demonstrates that the roots of all current programs and services, such as those discussed in chapters 6 and 7 and elsewhere in this book, can be found in the earliest recorded history. There is nothing really new about most of our social policies. Whatever they are, many have probably been attempted or proposed earlier in some form.

This chapter is not intended to comprehensively cover the total history of social welfare services or social policy. Instead, its purpose is to highlight the fundamental facts about the history of social welfare and social policy and to demonstrate some of the ways in which current as well as proposed social policies are rooted in the past. The goal is to help the reader place social policy in historical context—to learn about the sources of some of the fundamental programs and also how new programs might be better designed and administered with the knowledge available from earlier efforts.

Those who want to embark on a more serious study of social policy history or the histories of social welfare or social work should consult one of the many excellent social welfare histories, such as those by B. S. Jansson (1997), P. J. Day (1997), and J. Axinn and H. Levin (1997). Each has a different emphasis, but each also outlines the fundamental concepts that are important for understanding how social policy has developed throughout history. Another excellent historical analysis of the threat of poverty is M. B. Katz's *The Undeserving Poor* (1989). Noble (1997) wrote a political history of the welfare state, which traces the American experience, in particular.

PERSISTENT THEMES IN SOCIAL POLICY

Studying the history of social policy is a reliable way to confirm the fundamental and persistent themes of social policy, according to this book's point of view. These themes are:

1. Human societies have tended to provide those in need with resources that will help them physically survive.
2. Societies resist helping people more than they need to be helped in order to physically survive.
3. Those who receive society's help are expected to use no more help than they need.
4. Those who receive social help are ideally expected to contribute to the society if they are able to do so—through public service work or through training and rehabilitation activities that will reduce or eliminate their need for help.
5. In some way societies categorize those who seek aid, finding "worthy" and "unworthy" groups, although social workers and other human services professionals believe that this is a false dichotomy. The worthy are typically those who "cannot help themselves," and the unworthy are those for whom having unmet needs is considered to be "their own fault" (see Katz 1989).
6. Assistance benefits should never be as great as or greater than the income of the community or society's lowest-paid workers.

7. The primary responsibility for assistance ought to belong to oneself and one's own efforts. Secondarily, it may fall to family members or neighbors or, if those sources cannot provide help, to an organized charity, church, or other nongovernmental institution. Beyond these sources, responsibility lies with the government.

In these discussions of social work history, as well as those in subsequent chapters, it should be possible to see these fundamental principles at work. Chapter 6 focuses on economic social policy for those whose primary problem is a lack of money, food, housing, and other necessities. Chapter 7 focuses on the services designed to help people with other kinds of needs such as those faced by maltreated children, the aging, and those with physical and mental disabilities.

The division of social programs into economic and noneconomic programs and services is relatively common in the modern social welfare field. In some situations separate agencies are responsible for the two kinds of help. Generally, there is different legislation covering the two kinds of help. The reality is, however, that many of those needing financial assistance and other concrete forms of help also face the kinds of problems addressed by personal, noneconomic social services, and vice versa. Although there is often a distinction made between financial assistance and personal social services, the problems that cause them to be needed are often interrelated.

Social Policy before Nations

Social policy predates the development of the nation-state. Before there were governments there were churches, communities, tribes, and feudal lords. Religious groups, in particular, have always provided some forms of social welfare; although they recognize different doctrines, all of them require their adherents to help the disadvantaged and have done so historically (Reid 1995). Religious involvement in social welfare, which continues has traditionally been central to the history of social welfare. Feudal lords, many of whom attributed their power to God, provided some forms of social assistance to those who were dependent upon them.

Day (1997) provides an excellent discussion of the ways in which social welfare developed in a variety of cultures and regions. She covers ancient as well as modern social welfare development and shows that

China, Greece, and early Roman society, among others, developed social welfare policies. She also describes the Jewish and Christian contributions to such policies as well as later British programs, which are often emphasized in the study of social welfare history.

Among the early biblical injunctions to provide social assistance are those found in Deuteronomy 24:19–22. God orders his people to refrain from going over their fields, olive trees, and vineyards a second time after harvesting their produce because the second harvests should be given to aliens, orphans, and widows. He promises his blessings to those who follow the injunction. The order to help the disadvantaged is a reminder to the Jews that they were once slaves in Egypt and then had been in need themselves.

Religious groups have also governed other elements of family and community life, which have, in turn, affected the social welfare of people. Day (1997), for example, points out that Christianity, a religion that spread throughout the world, supported monogamy and viewed divorce negatively. That Christian social policy was important in securing and extending the well-being and rights of women by providing a social context in which women would not bear the sole responsibility of caring for and raising children. The traditional Islamic law that men could have as many as four wives provided a clear structure to social relations at the family level in the face of an unbalanced population in which there were more women than men.

The Elizabethan Poor Law of 1601

The most important of the laws governing social policy in all of history, especially after the rise of the nation-state, was the English Elizabethan Poor Law of 1601. That law, which was officially called an Act for the Relief of the Poor, is produced complete and in its original form in Axinn and Levin (1997) and contains or implies the seven themes listed previously.

According to Leiby, the 1601 Poor Law:

1. Defined the duty of the parish (which was the local government, comparable to today's counties) to provide relief to the poor.
2. Established overseers of the poor to relieve poverty. These were among the earliest social workers.
3. Gave the overseers the power to raise funds and use them in their poverty relief.

4. Affirmed that government relief was a last resort, after family and friends assisted the poor.
5. Defined helpless (or worthy) people, whose problems included illness, the feebleness of old age, being orphaned, and disability.
6. Established workhouses and other solutions, such as deporting to the colonies "sturdy beggars," often as indentured servants, who asked for help but who appeared capable of providing for themselves. (Leiby 1987)

According to Leiby (1987), the Statute of Charitable Trusts and Uses, which was also enacted in 1601, made possible and established the rules for the creation of charitable trusts and benefits by the wealthy or groups of people with the desire to be helpful and the resources to provide the help.

The Elizabethan Poor Law, compared to earlier statutes, represented humanitarian reforms. Day describes, for example, the punitive 1536 "Act for Punishment of Sturdy Vagabonds and Beggars," which outlawed begging and giving to beggars and penalized violators with "branding, enslavement, and execution" (1997, 109).

Today American and European social policy contains many of these same programs, principles, and services. Although the programs and services have, of course, changed substantially, the basic concepts have had an amazing constancy.

Laws were passed in England to uphold the principles of that country's social policy: the Workhouse Test Act, for example, which forced the unemployed to work for any relief they received (Alexander 1995), was passed in 1697 by the English Parliament. There were some policies in England, and elsewhere, which have not persisted. For example, the Law of Settlement and Removal of 1662 prevented those who needed help from moving from parish to parish to find that help (Alexander 1995). That law and similar policies were designed to make certain that people received no more than they were entitled to receive by preventing them from collecting twice, in two different parishes. The law also helped maintain a labor pool in the parish so that employers could readily employ workers.

Although in our day assistance agencies try to follow careful procedures to prevent clients from collecting from more than one agency or receiving more than they are entitled to receive, aggressive efforts to

21

prevent free movement from place to place have largely been abandoned. In fact, states are no longer permitted to impose residency requirements as conditions for receiving assistance.

Colonial Social Policy

Social policy in the American colonies was based, as might be expected, on the English laws, and during that time there was no central American government. Each colony passed and enforced its own laws. The first of the colonial poor laws was passed in Rhode Island in 1647 (Alexander 1995).

In the colonies as well as in England a variety of methods was used to provide assistance to those in need who could not otherwise benefit from mutual assistance. Orphaned or abandoned children, for example, were often "farmed out" to the lowest bidder—sent to families where they could work for a very low fee: the receiving family would charge the parish for providing them with basic necessities. That practice is something of a forerunner of our system of foster care for children, although foster children cannot be required to work. In the 1536 act, idle children could be taken from their parents and indentured (Day 1997). It is important to remember that these kinds of laws governing children were established before universal, compulsory education and, in fact, before children were viewed as special kinds of humans, with needs that were different from adults' needs, an attitude that persisted until late in the last century. The creation of child labor laws, for example, was a relatively late social policy development in the United States and elsewhere.

Workhouses and poorhouses, which were used to provide lodging and food to those who could not live on their own in return for productive work such as sewing military uniforms or farming surrounding property, were another form of social assistance during the colonial period.

An innovation that has continued to dominate public social assistance was the provision of "outdoor" relief—that is, giving assistance directly to the person, or family, in need, within his or her own home, rather than in an institution. Assistance was also provided in two general forms—cash and kind—which have continued for the centuries during which social policy has been recorded. Cash is simply money, which the person or family can use as they choose in meeting their needs. Kind is assistance in the form of goods or services such as housing, food, clothing, and medical care. Cash and kind remain the methods of assistance in such diverse programs as financial aid, public or community housing, food stamps, and Medicaid, the medical welfare program of the United States.

CRISES

One of the understandings of social policy that arises from the study of history is that human success or need often results not from the good or evil nature of the persons in need but is, instead, a consequence of social, economic, and natural forces, which change human circumstances, sometimes in astounding ways. For example, the Bubonic Plague, or Black Death, in the fourteenth century in Europe caused extensive suffering and need among large populations and created a social policy crisis. Similarly, the end of feudalism there, with its dislocation of the serfs, who had long relied on their feudal lords for support and been tied to them, and the Protestant Reformation, which ended the employment and support of many Roman Catholic people, created the need for help on a broad scale. In colonial America, Indian massacres and smallpox epidemics, among other crises, also caused otherwise self-sufficient people to become needy. More current phenomena, such as the Great Depression of the 1930s, as well as other economic dislocations, wars, droughts, famines, and epidemics such as AIDS are examples of the ways in which forces far beyond the control of individuals and families cause them to experience need.

There is still dispute in social policy debates, however, about the degree of responsibility individuals or families and larger social forces have for handling social problems and needs. How a society thinks about that issue is a significant factor in how that society will cope with its citizens' needs and how it will develop social policy.

Local Responsibility

It is critical to understanding social policy history in the United States to be aware that services were originally local rather than national. Local responsibility for services was reasonable in a time when life was local, economies were largely agricultural, and there were not yet such national innovations as stock exchanges and commodity markets or even provisions for the interchange of funds among localities. Communication and transportation of all kinds—mail, roads, vehicles—were limited. Larger units of government had limited responsibilities and powers, and matters had to be settled on a local level. A major phenomenon in the development of American social policy is the passing of primary social policy responsibility from local governments to increasingly higher levels of government. In the second half of the twentieth century the federal government became the unit with the largest influence over American social policy.

The Role of Voluntary Efforts

In early America, according to B. S. Jansson (1997), a strong tradition of private philanthropy developed rapidly before the American Revolution and continued after the nation was founded. He describes an early series of efforts to develop firefighting services, educational programs, and orphanages, sometimes with private funds and sometimes with partnerships between private donors and governments. Jansson (1997) emphasizes the importance of religious bodies in the development of American social welfare. Churches were among the few voluntary organizations that developed in early times. Protestant churches also incorporated ideas about the religious mandate to share one's blessings with the less fortunate.

Residential Approaches

Throughout the history of social welfare in America, however, there has been a belief that disadvantaged people should not be coddled—that they should be helped only minimally lest they become dependent upon charity. The workhouse concept, the major form of "indoor relief," was a popular way of dealing with the needy. According to Jansson (1997), the Virginia Colony's legislative body decided in 1688 that every county should have a workhouse. New York also created a number of these facilities in the early and middle eighteenth century. Throughout the early years of U.S. history workhouses dotted the landscape. In later years the same facilities became "county farms," "poor farms," and other kinds of institutions for the poor, elderly, or disabled, which were in some ways forerunners of our current residential services for the aged. J. W. Landon (1985) says that these kinds of facilities were the primary means of dealing with poverty in early America. They were overcrowded, and the living conditions were poor. Of course, in a society that believed poverty resulted from the individual's character flaws (Colby 1990), a punitive environment was a reasonable choice. Again, one of the significant developments throughout social welfare history has been the change from institutional care of the disadvantaged—including the poor, the disabled, the elderly, and children who could not live with their own families—to assistance to people in their own homes or to smaller, more homelike group facilities.

The Early Federal Role

Social assistance programs for the disadvantaged, as mentioned, began essentially as local services. The federal government, despite the clause in the preamble of the U.S. Constitution obliging it to "promote the general welfare," was not viewed as the level of government that ought to be involved directly or even indirectly in helping individual citizens. The role of the federal government was historically limited to matters such as international relations, operating the money system and the national banks, and resolving disputes between states. *reconstruc. of the PG.*

That principle was most dramatically clarified by a presidential veto dealing with congressional legislation to provide help to persons with mental illness. A reformer of services to that group, Dorothea Dix, traveled the nation seeking financial support for decent housing and treatment and for the construction of state asylums. She and her supporters persuaded Congress to provide public land for the "insane," which Congress did, in the amount of ten million acres. Their legislation added care for the blind and deaf to services for mentally ill individuals (Axinn and Levin 1997), yet President Franklin Pierce, one of the least-known American presidents, vetoed the legislation in 1854. In his veto message he acknowledged the responsibility of citizens to discharge a high and holy duty of providing for those who "are subject to want and disuse of body or mind." He concluded, however, that providing such help was not the job of the federal government: "I can not find any authority in the Constitution for making the Federal Government the great almoner of public charity throughout the United States" (qtd. in Axinn and Levin 1997, 47).

Both before and after the Pierce veto of the land grants pursued by Dix, charitable services were the province of private charities and state and local governments, not the U.S. government.

People with Mental Disabilities.   Despite the Pierce veto of the Dix advocacy, the federal government later became involved in helping the states with services for people with disabilities in a variety of ways. For example, in a pattern that has been used for many other kinds of efforts, including highways and law enforcement, the federal government gave grants to the states to help provide services to people with mental disabilities, including mental illness and mental retardation. As is discussed in chapter 7, in later years the government became active in providing

25

funds to care for people with such disabilities in their own homes, and in group facilities. Medicaid, the federal health assistance program for low-income people, also provides funding for care. So despite the fact that all of the land grant programs supported by Dix were vetoed and not attempted again, the principle of the federal government helping with the problems of disabled individuals has become and remains a part of federal responsibility and state action. The National Institute of Mental Health, founded in the 1950s, became a research, advocacy, and supportive organization for people with mental illness, under federal auspices and with federal financing.

War Veterans. From early in the nation's history there were federal programs for persons who were in need and who were clearly the responsibility of the federal government. After each war beginning with the Revolutionary War, for example, financial assistance was provided to veterans and their widows and orphans (Axinn and Levin 1997).

Native Americans. In one of the least humane examples of American social policy, the U.S. government also developed social policies regarding American Indians, who were on the continent before the European settlers. At the time the national government was created, and for many years thereafter, U.S. presidents, themselves white males, upheld the idea that white European Americans should control all of North America. When American Indians resisted and defended their territories, the national government responded with legislation, armed action, raids, and murders (Day 1997). By the second half of the nineteenth century the American Indian population had been severely reduced, and those who remained were largely without power.

In 1824, the federal government established the Bureau of Indian Affairs, which was originally under the jurisdiction of the War Department but later moved to the Department of the Interior. The bureau has never been specifically a social welfare agency, but it has always carried out social policies regarding Indians. It is another example of the federal government's direct service relationships with some individuals. It was not until one hundred years after the establishment of the Bureau of Indian Affairs that Native Americans were made citizens of the United States, with passage of the Indian Citizenship Act in 1924 (Lewis 1995).

Alaska Natives have a similar relationship with the federal government, although the issues they face and their cultural groupings are significantly different from those of American Indians. Of course, the relationship between the U.S. government and Alaska Natives began with the purchase of Alaska in 1871 and was modified when Alaska became a state in 1959 (Lally and Haynes 1995).

The Civil War and Former Slaves. Federal policies were necessary after the Civil War to deal with the large number of freed slaves from the southern states whose state governments had been defeated by the federal government and were, therefore, unlikely to be of assistance. The United States established the Freedmen's Bureau, which existed from 1865 to 1872, to assist the former slaves economically, although, according to J. Leiby (1987), the policy itself was better than the execution of the policy. The federal bureau was quickly dissolved, and care of the former slaves was made a function of the local authorities within a few years.

With the exception of war veterans, Native Americans, immigrants upon their arrival to the nation, and former slaves, the U.S. government remained clear of direct helping relationships with individual citizens for most of its history, until the twentieth century. Social policy was the province of state and local governments and charities, which received their funds from contributions by private donors.

The Great Depression. A worldwide economic crisis was the impetus for the development of new national social policies and the greatest changes in the relationship of the U.S. government with its citizens. That crisis was the Great Depression, which began in 1929, under the presidency of Herbert Hoover, a Republican who was known for having organized a food relief program in Europe to help those who were unable to care for themselves at the end of World War I. There were several causes of the Great Depression, but the dramatic incident with which it began was the crash of the stock market. Its results were widespread unemployment, instant poverty for many who had been prospering, and very low prices—although few could purchase even low-priced goods (Jansson 1997). By the time all the effects of the Depression were known, a large proportion of the American population was unable to provide for itself financially. It is difficult for middle- and upper-class Americans today to understand the atmosphere of that era, a time when many people suffered—or had close friends, neighbors, or relatives who suffered—from the crippling economic realities of poverty.

Simply put, the effects of the Depression were so pervasive that human need became a common, no longer an isolated, experience. The poor could no longer be blamed for their poverty; there were simply too many poor. Even among the hardest-working, best-prepared people in

27

the nation there were those who were unable to support themselves. Old means of providing assistance—such as charities, workhouses, and local relief programs financed primarily by donations—as well as the relative isolation of the federal government from its citizens, in terms of addressing social needs, became untenable. Nevertheless, President Hoover continued the policies of Pierce and agreed with the former president's ideology and interpretation of the Constitution on this matter—that social policy issues were the responsibility of local governments and private charities (Jansson 1997).

Local governments, which relied upon local taxes, were, in fact, finding it difficult to survive. Those who were required to pay the taxes had few or no funds with which to pay. Many local governments could not support helping programs and certainly could not add thousands of impoverished citizens to their assistance rolls. Private charities, which relied upon funds from benefactors with sufficient means to make generous donations, could not sustain their services, in many cases, and certainly could not expand them to incorporate large numbers of newly disadvantaged people. The benefactors were as likely to have experienced financial reversals and unemployment as those they once supported.

In short, the entire social and economic structure of the United States was near collapse. The old rules could no longer prevail because new circumstances made them irrelevant.

Franklin Delano Roosevelt

In 1932 Franklin Delano Roosevelt of New York, often referred to as FDR, was elected president. He defeated Hoover under circumstances common to other elections in which an incumbent is not returned to office. When there are economic difficulties U.S. voters tend to defeat incumbent presidents, a situation that Jimmy Carter, in 1980, and George Bush, in 1992, found to be true.

Roosevelt was an exceptionally interesting president for those connected with human services. He was, for example, the only president who had a physical disability; as a consequence of polio, he could not walk and used a wheelchair to get around. He was also the only president to be elected more than twice. Others before FDR had voluntarily limited themselves to two terms. After Roosevelt the Constitution was amended so that no president would be allowed to run for more than two terms. But Roosevelt was elected three more times after his initial election in 1932—in 1936, 1940, and 1944. He died in office in 1945.

Franklin Roosevelt is remembered by social workers for more than those personal and political characteristics. He is best remembered for making major changes in the role and functions of the United States government.

The New Deal.   Roosevelt called his legislative program the New Deal. Several of its elements were economic in emphasis and are, therefore, beyond the direct scope of this chapter. His major programs were directed toward the goals of restoring the U.S. economy, controlling the buying and selling of stocks and bonds, preventing future depressions, and providing the U.S. government with the authority to respond to economic crises such as the Great Depression. His main tools followed the teachings of the economist John Maynard Keynes, whose ideas about economic policy are discussed in chapter 5. Several of his programs, however, had major social welfare connotations.

The New Deal Social Welfare Programs.   Primary examples of the ways in which the New Deal established social welfare programs that dealt directly with individual citizens as means for reducing individual or family economic need were two programs, The Works Progress Administration (WPA) and the Civilian Conservation Corps (CCC). These had been preceded by other efforts such as the Federal Emergency Relief Administration (FERA), which also helped create jobs as well as providing other forms of assistance for promoting economic recovery. The FERA was headed by Roosevelt's top assistant in his social programs, Harry Hopkins, who is widely regarded as one of the most important figures in the historical development of social work.

The WPA was created by Roosevelt's executive order in 1935 and continued until 1943. It eventually provided jobs for eight million people. It provided for the creation of work in many fields, such as construction of public buildings and roads, as well as providing employment for artists and scholars who, for example, painted murals in public buildings and conducted research on social issues (Axinn and Levin 1997). WPA workers received compensation that was greater than they would have received under relief programs. The WPA is the forerunner of many other work programs that followed it and that continue into the current era, such as the Manpower Development and Training Act of 1961, the Comprehensive Employment and Training Act (CETA) of 1973, the Job Training Partnership Act of 1982, and many others. The WPA marked the formal beginning of the federal government's interest and activity in job training, work experience, and employment for those who cannot obtain employment on their own (Jansson, 1997).

Under the program called the Civilian Conservation Corps, which was enacted by Congress in 1933, young, unmarried men ages seventeen to twenty-three were employed and housed in national parks and forests to carry out conservation work. They were provided with food and lodging as well as education and were paid small salaries, which they could send to their families, if necessary. The program continued until 1941 (Alexander 1987).

The Social Security Act of 1935.   For human services workers, and perhaps for the domestic history of the United States, the most important of the New Deal innovations was the Social Security Act of 1935. It was and remains one of the most complex pieces of legislation ever passed in the nation. It established the fundamental social services policy of the United States and continued to govern most of human services provided to the nation's citizens. Although it preserved a major role for the states in the operation of some of its provisions, it established for all time that the U.S. government could have a direct, helping relationship with its citizens. B. S. Jansson (1997) calls the Social Security Act the Magna Carta of American welfare. He has good reason for his conclusion. The act touches or has the potential to touch the lives of all Americans.

Over the nearly forty years I have spent as an active social worker I came to know some of the original architects of the Social Security Act—persons such as Eveline Burns (see chapter 8), Wilbur Cohen, and Ernest Witte. The days when the act was developed must have been exhilarating for those young social reformers. Their goal, and Roosevelt's, was not only to provide aid for people who were suffering from economic disadvantage but to prevent permanently such disadvantage in the future. The basic idea was to finance a system for the permanent security of the American people through an insurance program in which employed people would make contributions while they worked and receive benefits when they no longer worked. It was designed as a massive, low-cost insurance program that could end poverty once and for all. It also provided for those who were in temporary economic need and had provisions for the survivors of employed people who were covered by Social Security. An excellent source of information on the historical development of social policy in the United States is Berkowitz's *Mr. Social Security* (1995), a biography of Wilbur J. Cohen. Cohen was one of the main architects of all the programs in the Social Security Act, which include most of the programs that are associated with American social welfare policy.

30

The Social Security Act is periodically changed by amendments, some of which are far-reaching and others relatively technical. The fundamental nature of the act has remained constant, however, for the many years that it has been part of American social policy.

Provisions of the Social Security Act. Financing of most of the Social Security Act insurance provisions comes from contributions paid by employees and their employers or by self-employed people alone. Virtually all working people in the United States are now covered, although there were many exceptions when the original act was passed. The amounts of the contributions have changed often over the years to reflect inflation and increased benefits.

The major provisions of the Social Security Act are:

1. Old-Age and Survivor's Insurance. This program provides for pensions for employees when they retire and payments to their surviving spouses and minor children should they die.
2. Disability Insurance. This program was added in the 1956 amendments and provides for payments to workers who are physically or mentally disabled and to eligible family members.
3. Medicare. This program was added in 1965 and provides health care insurance for people sixty-five years old and older as well as some younger people who have specific disabling health problems. A related component is Medicaid, another state and federally financed program that provides medical coverage for low-income people who are not old enough for Medicare as well as for Medicare recipients whose medical needs cost more than Medicare pays (Ozawa 1987; Ginsberg 1983).
4. Unemployment Compensation. This program provides cash benefits to people who have lost their jobs and is paid for by a tax on employers. It provides benefits for up to six months in amounts that vary from state to state. In time of great economic problems such as recessions, the period of time is often extended (Day 1997).
5. Family Assistance. The Social Security Act included assistance for families whose members' work histories and contributions did not provide them enough social insurance benefits to take care of themselves if the wage earners grew old, died, or became disabled. Originally called Aid to Dependent Children, or ADC, the program later became Aid to Families with Dependent Children, or AFDC. It provided cash assistance from a combination

31

of federal and state funds to poor families with children. The states determined the benefit levels, and the federal government provided matching funds proportionate to each state's per capita income. The lower the per capita income, the larger proportion the federal government contributed, even though the federal portion was always, even for the richest states, at least half the amount of the assistance checks. The family assistance program, when it was ADC or AFDC, was carefully defined and restricted by the federal government. For example, the money provided had to be in cash—not in forms such as housing, food, or clothing. Until 1981 clients could not be required to work, although since then there has been a steady increase of client work requirements, which are discussed below. In 1996 the AFDC program was replaced by Temporary Assistance for Needy Families, or TANF, a radically different approach to assisting disadvantaged families. The new program is described in more detail in other sections of this book.

6. Supplementary Security Income (SSI). This is a program that, like TANF, is financed by general tax revenues, although in this case they are all federal funds, for low-income, elderly, physically or mentally disabled, or blind people.

Originally, the programs and services of SSI, which was created in 1972, were three federal-state programs for those now served by SSI, which were similar to the AFDC program. SSI placed the administration of the programs with the federal government through the Social Security Administration, which also administers the social insurance programs and sets national payment standards (Ginsberg 1983).

7. The Maternal and Child Welfare Act was also part of Social Security. It established child welfare services in the states for dependent, neglected, homeless, and potentially delinquent children as well as vocational training and rehabilitation programs for physically and otherwise disabled children. It also provided funds for programs to promote the health of children and mothers through prenatal and birthing services for mothers (Day 1997).

Clearly the Social Security Act became the primary source of social and economic assistance in the United States. It provides extensive services that go beyond those enumerated here, although for the most part it follows the persistent themes of social policy described in this chapter.

For example, those who receive services such as retirement benefits and Medicare are people who in all but a small number of cases contributed financially to the Social Security Trust Fund, in which the payments are deposited. The beneficiaries are expect to help themselves through a mechanism established by the government. The principle that those who receive assistance should generally be victims of forces that they cannot control is demonstrated by numerous provisions of many of the programs described here. For example, recipients of unemployment insurance must have been employed and must have lost their jobs through no fault of their own: those who voluntarily quit their jobs or who are fired for good cause are ineligible. Similarly, children are not expected to meet their own needs, and, therefore TANF and the Maternal and Child Welfare Act provide for the young. Even though families are restricted by federal law to no more than five years of assistance (in some states as few as two years), cases in which children alone are served are exempt from those restrictions. In other words, a child who is living in a foster family or with relatives can continue to receive help. It is only the child living with his or her parent or parents who is restricted to five years of assistance from federal funds. The SSI services and the aid programs that were its forerunners are for older adults and persons with disabilities.

There are also features of the assistance provisions of the Social Security Act that require recipients to help themselves. The unemployed must be searching for work, for example, or must be involved in work training or experience programs. The 1996 change in the family assistance program, TANF, requires more work from clients. Most recipients of help have to be working or seeking work or involved in work experience or community service kinds of jobs. Work experience provides clients with a chance to work, often without pay, in public services, schools, and government programs. The clients receive their grants during the experience. The federal legislation sets specific requirements about the percentage of those receiving assistance who must be working if the state is not to be penalized by receiving fewer dollars. By 2002, for example, the state would have to demonstrate that half or more of those receiving assistance are employed in some way. The details of these work requirements and of other provisions of the law are provided in appendix 2 in this book.

If recipients are working at jobs that are not subsidized or have not been created for assistance recipients, they must be paid the minimum wage at least, and they must be protected by the same kinds of labor and employment laws as other workers. Those who are in community service or work experience positions, however, can be paid less and do not have similar protections. Therefore, created jobs pay less than the lowest paid regular work, a principle that can be found in the 1601 Elizabethan Poor Law.

When Roosevelt died in 1945, Harry S Truman, who had been vice president, succeeded him. Truman was also a significant figure for social welfare policy. As discussed in detail later in this book, he introduced legislation to guarantee full employment. He suggested national health insurance, which became a reality twenty years later with Medicaid and Medicare. By executive order, he also ended the segregation of black servicemen, and the military became the most integrated institution in the United States following Truman's bold executive action. He was re-elected in 1948, although he was not favored in the political polls of that time.

Rediscovering and Treating Poverty and the Civil Rights Movement—the Kennedy and Johnson Presidencies

The most notable and active era for social policy development, after the New Deal, was in the 1960s, through programs and legislation introduced and supported by President John F. Kennedy and his successor, President Lyndon Johnson, after Kennedy's assassination. President Kennedy called his program the New Frontier, and President Johnson called his the Great Society. The 1960s was a decade of major social ferment. Two separate but interrelated issues and phenomena marked the era.

Civil Rights. Perhaps most significant in the development of the civil rights movement of the 1960s were events that occurred in the 1950s. Among these were the Supreme Court decision in a case called *Brown v. Board of Education,* in 1954, which brought an end to the South's long-standing policy of separating African American and white schoolchildren, an example of the ways in which courts actually make social policy. Until that decision, states were permitted to have "separate but equal" educational facilities for pupils. The effect of the *Brown v. Board of Education* decision was to decree that separate schools were inherently unequal schools. That decision was accompanied by many others requiring states to allow African Americans to enter formerly white-only colleges and universities and led to legislation guaranteeing such things as equal opportunity in employment and the end to discrimination in public places.

Another event of the 1950s that led to the civil rights change of the 1960s was the Montgomery, Alabama, bus boycott in 1954, led by the Reverend Martin Luther King, Jr., who was assassinated in 1968 and whose birthday is now honored by a national holiday in January. King's boycott and the many other protests, demonstrations, and vigils that followed it were a major part of the impetus for the civil rights executive orders and legislation that followed.

It is difficult to explain the impact of the civil rights movement of the 1960s to those who did not live through the times that preceded it, especially in the South. That is because the changes are largely the elimination of certain acts rather than the development of new programs or structures. Until the 1960s, public facilities such as hotels, restaurants, theaters, and buses maintained strictly separate accommodations for African Americans and whites. Public parks had separate water fountains and bathrooms, one set marked White and another marked Colored. Likewise, buses posted statements that said the front was reserved for whites and the back for African Americans, then commonly called Coloreds or Negroes. Theaters had seats in the balcony for African Americans; main auditoriums were reserved for whites. In some places white and African American professionals were forbidden to hold meetings or have meals together, even in private facilities. White and African American athletes could not, of course, be on the same teams, and they were also forbidden to compete against one another in some sporting events. Some major southern colleges and universities, which now have large numbers of African American athletes, had none, and their sports teams were furthermore forbidden to play against teams that did. Housing was sold and rented in a discriminatory fashion. African Americans were not permitted to live in white neighborhoods, and African Americans and whites were not legally permitted to marry one another in many states.

African Americans protested, lobbied for legislation, sought relief in the courts, and, before the Kennedy-Johnson presidential era was over, had overturned virtually all of the legally sanctioned discriminatory practices that had been the pattern in the South and, in some ways, in the North as well for all of the twentieth century.

Leaders such as Thurgood Marshall, the National Association for the Advancement of Colored People (NAACP) attorney who designed the legal battles that led to the court decisions and, ultimately, much of the legislation that reduced discrimination against African Americans, prompted major social changes for the American population. He was appointed to the U.S. Supreme Court by President Lyndon Johnson and remained a justice until 1991.

The civil rights movement led to federal laws guaranteeing African Americans the right to vote and ending discrimination in education and employment and in "public accommodations" such as restaurants, theaters, and transportation. Of course, federal laws could not deal with all of the individual issues associated with the discriminatory practices in the United States. Many states and local governments passed laws, however, which applied the civil rights requirements of the federal laws to their own governments.

Among the many changes that resulted from the civil rights movement have been the election of large numbers of African Americans to public office, often in places where they might previously have had difficulty voting; affirmative action policies that require employers with histories of discrimination to balance their work forces to include minority workers; and an increased influence of African Americans in the total fabric of American social and economic life.

Ultimately, the civil rights movement also led to changes in the treatment of other population groups including Latinos, Native Americans, gay men and lesbians, and people with disabilities.

A book about the civil rights movement, *Weary Feet, Rested Souls: A Guided History of the Civil Rights Movement* (Davis 1998), provides names, photos, maps, and sites about the major figures and events involved in the civil rights movement.

The Antipoverty Movement. In 1962 Michael Harrington published his landmark book, *The Other America,* which influenced presidents Kennedy and Johnson, legislators, social scientists, and social workers. Harrington documented what Kennedy had discovered during his 1960 campaign for the presidency—that, although the United States was thought to be a prosperous nation that had eliminated poverty with the Social Security Act, there were still large numbers of Americans who did not share that wealth. Kennedy was particularly moved by the poverty he saw in West Virginia, a state that was pivotal in his winning the Democratic presidential nomination. Kennedy made an issue of poverty in his campaign, along with other reform issues.

Early in Kennedy's presidency he established the Peace Corps, a program that has continued into the 1990s and that enrolls Americans in a two-year period of service in nations that seek Peace Corps help, mainly for development projects. Kennedy was also instrumental in arranging for the distribution of surplus food, purchased by the federal government as a means of maintaining farm prices, to low-income people. He also helped to establish the Appalachian Regional Commission, which was designed to provide economic development, education, and other services to help that historically disadvantaged region overcome its poverty.

Other kinds of social policy changes were made in the 1960s, many of them in areas that have long been of concern to social workers. For example, states were required to employ more professionally educated social workers to help people overcome the basic causes of their poverty rather than simply giving them assistance that, the Kennedy administration believed, would tend to perpetuate their dependence on government. Restrictive rules governing recipients of family assistance were liberalized so that families could work and retain a larger part of their earnings. Food stamps were introduced as an alternative to distributing surplus foods. Causes and cures for juvenile delinquency were studied, and some programs were attempted.

Poverty in the United States was not viewed as an ethnic minority problem. In fact, Harrington (1962) and others have continually reminded the nation that most of the American poor are white. However, minorities of color such as African Americans, Latinos, and Native Americans are disproportionately poorer than white Americans. That is, the percentages of minority populations who are poor is much greater than the percentage of whites who are. Therefore, it is assumed that real discrimination could not be overcome so long as minorities were denied social and economic justice or opportunity, even if their legal rights were protected. It was a time of great social unrest among minorities, especially African Americans, whose neighborhoods were the scenes of riots in many large American cities during the 1960s.

It was also a time of mass social action of other kinds, such as the development of the National Welfare Rights Organization, which protested against financial aid programs it considered to be punitive and lobbied for reforms. In general, following the demands for civil rights in the 1960s, there was great social concern and action about poverty and minority rights.

In that context Kennedy outlined, and Johnson worked with Congress to pass into law and implement, the Economic Opportunity Act of 1964, a comprehensive attack on poverty. The act established the Office of Economic Opportunity and put into place a variety of programs and services. Among them were Head Start, a program for preschool children; the Job Corps, a residential and job training program comparable in some ways to the Civilian Conservation Corps; work-study programs for students; and community action programs, which provide funds to local communities to make it possible for them to work on problems they identify themselves. Many of these programs continue to operate. In addition, there were accelerated efforts to place the unemployed and the underemployed in jobs, to develop training programs, and to create new aid programs for colleges and public schools. The federal government created Volunteers in Service to America (VISTA), which functioned in impoverished areas of the United States in a manner similar to the Peace Corps overseas.

Many minorities were involved as participants in these programs and as staff members who helped operate them. While problems still remain, the combination of the civil rights reforms and the antipoverty efforts has made major changes in the socioeconomic status of minorities in the United States.

There were many other social policy changes associated with the Lyndon Johnson presidency, some of which were inspired by the Kennedy presidency. The Social Security Act was amended in 1965 to add Medicare for older adults and Medicaid for low-income families and individuals, two of the most costly and important social programs in American social policy.

From Nixon to Carter

From 1961 until 1981 social policy remained relatively constant. There were some additions to social services, including reforms in services to children. There were also some reductions in budgets and some efforts to reverse social policies that had been previously implemented. Although there were efforts at major social policy reform under President Richard Nixon, who introduced a sweeping welfare reform program called the Family Assistance Plan, and President Jimmy Carter, who introduced a similar plan called the Better Jobs and Incomes Program, through the presidencies of Nixon, Gerald Ford, and Carter the nation did not substantially alter its social policies. Neither Nixon's nor Carter's plan was passed by Congress. Economic conditions that were less satisfactory than they had been in the 1960s led to some reductions in social programs. So did the lengthy, divisive, and expensive Vietnam War.

One of the reasons that the Nixon and Carter reforms failed to gain congressional approval was that they were projected to cost more than the existing programs. (Another was the opposition of the National Welfare Rights Organization, which thought the reform plans were not as generous as they should be.) Under President Nixon the federal government created the Supplemental Security Insurance program.

As discussed earlier, SSI combined the adult categories of assistance from the original Social Security Act. The development of SSI was a partial acceptance and implementation of the principles of Nixon's Family Assistance Plan. It placed responsibility for low-income older and disabled adults directly on the federal government and in the Social Security Administration.

The Reagan Years

In the 1980 presidential election Republican Ronald Reagan, former governor of California, defeated the incumbent, Jimmy Carter. Reagan had campaigned for, and ultimately implemented, policies that reduced social programs. His basic position was to remove the federal government from direct service relationships with citizens, which was the classic position of the Republican Party. Throughout the Reagan presidency, from 1981 through 1988, and, to a lesser extent under his vice president and successor, President George Bush, social programs were viewed largely as inappropriate for the federal government. The enunciated social policy was that the best solution to human problems was a strong economy—in which jobs would be plentiful and lucrative and in which investments would be profitable (Ginsberg 1987, 1990). There were several reactions to and consequences of that policy. For one, Congress insisted on minimizing the reductions in social programs proposed by the presidents and, on its own initiative, added to them. Congress even passed, and President Reagan signed into law, a welfare reform plan, the Family Support Act of 1988, which was somewhat similar to those plans proposed in the 1970s by presidents Nixon and Carter.

The Family Support Act left assistance for families with the state, and the AFDC program remained a federal-state matching program. However, the Family Support Act required states to include families with two parents, an option under the law before 1988. It also increased the requirements of clients for training and work as conditions of receiving assistance.

Although political leaders such as presidents Reagan and Bush might have preferred otherwise, the American commitment to social assistance programs has continued and grown since the major social policy developments of the New Deal. In 1992 the nation elected a new

president, Bill Clinton. When he took office he undertook the establishment of youth services programs, health care reforms, and a number
of other initiatives that resembled programs from John F. Kennedy's
presidency. Among proponents of social policy and social provisions
there was general enthusiasm for the new president.

The Clinton Presidency

The Clinton presidency embarked upon major changes in public
welfare and the financing and structure of U.S. health care (which is discussed in greater detail in a later chapter). The former Arkansas governor took steps to eliminate some of the restrictions on abortion and to
protect those who provided them. He enunciated policies to allow homosexuals to serve in the armed forces so long as they did not speak
openly about their sexual orientation. Early in his term, laws were passed
that provided additional funds to be used by local governments against
crime and that set further restrictions on the sale of guns. Clinton's initiatives on health care reform, which involved task forces led by his wife,
Hillary Rodham Clinton, and hundred of planners and commentators,
did not pass Congress, largely because of opposition to elements of the
health care industry, including health insurance companies and some
providers. Citizens were also reluctant to substitute a system with which
they were often pleased for a new system that might not satisfy them.

In the midterm elections in 1994, the Clinton presidency was unsuccessful in its support of Democratic Party candidates, and the Republican Party won majorities in both houses of Congress for the first
time since the Eisenhower era as well as the governorships of many
states.

The next two years of the Clinton administration were dominated
more by the actions of the U.S. Congress than by the initiatives of the
president. With a Democratic executive branch and Republicans in control of the Congress, there were disputes between the branches about
public policy, especially social policy. In some cases, compromises were
reached. In others, President Clinton vetoed congressional actions. In
yet others, bills were passed by the Congress over the president's vetoes.
In 1995 and 1996 changes to the Medicaid and Medicare programs were
debated in an effort to hold down the increasing costs of health care—
an effort similar in objectives but different in approach from President
Clinton's failed proposals for health care financing reform, discussed
earlier in this chapter. There was the related objective of reducing taxes
as well, another popular idea, also discussed above and later in this chapter.

Some taxes, including taxes on the capital gains earned on property such as homes and stocks, were reduced. Many homeowners whose houses had increased in value and who had formerly been taxed on the increases no longer had to pay those taxes. New Individual Retirement Accounts were developed that allowed many people to save money for retirement and pay no taxes on those savings.

For health care, new legislation was passed and signed by the president that extended government assistance for the health care of children. President Clinton also proposed that people younger than 65 be able to pay for and receive Medicare. For example, men in their 50s who had been laid off from their jobs would be able, under the president's proposal, to cover their health care needs through the Medicare program.

One of the most unusual and memorable events in recent U.S. political history was the preparation and implementation of the Contract with America, which was signed by 367 Republican candidates for Congress and became their platform during the 1994 election (Gillespie and Schellhas 1994). The U.S. Senate, which was less deeply involved in the development of the contract, was also less committed to its principles, although in 1995 it became the document on which much of the action in Congress was based.

In the 1994 election, as noted above, the Republican Party won majorities in the U.S. Senate and the House of Representatives for the first time in forty years and set about to enact its "contract." Much of the Contract with America had special significance for social welfare because, in many ways, it proposed an overhaul of the social welfare systems, a reduction in the size and influence of the federal government, and some major constitutional changes. The program led to efforts for a complete overhaul, as described earlier, of the AFDC program as well as changes in food stamps, Medicaid, and Medicare. One focus of the new Republican congressional majority and others was a change in the federal tax system, often at the higher income levels, in what is described in other parts of this book as a "trickle up" approach to economic development.

Two of the key commitment proposals were a constitutional amendment that would require the United States to operate with a balanced budget and the provision of the line item veto for the president. Both of these failed to pass in 1995. However, the presidential line item veto was passed by Congress in 1996, and President Clinton exercised the new power for the first time in 1997.

The line item veto allows the president to reject parts of bills sent by Congress, even though the balance of the bill becomes law. The president rejected some spending revisions, but his right to do so and the constitutionality of the presidential line item veto were challenged. The federal courts held that the line item veto was unconstitutional, and thus the new legislation and President Clinton's vetoes were invalidated.

The plan also called for a stronger national defense, a reduction in government regulations, and the creation of jobs, legal reforms, and limits on the terms of members of Congress, a proposition that was declared unconstitutional, in the twenty-two states that had already enacted them, by the U.S. Supreme Court in 1995 (*Time,* June 5, 1995).

The plan also called for stern action against violent criminals and steps to strengthen families and protect children. Among the proposals were financial assistance to families who would keep their elderly parents or grandparents at home, cash assistance for people who adopted children, and strong efforts to enforce child support orders and make absent parents pay. The authors of the contract also proposed allowing senior citizens to keep more of their earnings and allowing tax deductions for those who purchase long-term-care insurance. There is an emphasis on reducing paperwork and federal regulations and on eliminating or reducing "unfunded mandates," requirements that the federal government places on states and localities but for which it provides no implementation funds. The Republicans in the House of Representatives worked long hours without breaks to pass and implement as much of their contract as they could within the first hundred days of the congressional session.

The clear leader of the Contract with America, of the Republican successes in the 1994 congressional elections, and of the efforts to change the nation's social policies significantly was Georgia representative Newt Gingrich (Bruck 1995; Gingrich 1995). He had been the leader of the Republican minority in the House of Representatives when the Democrats were the majority. Now that the Republicans were the majority, he became the Speaker of the House, a position second in power only to the presidency. He worked to help obtain funds for Republican congressional candidates, especially those running for the House. Many were grateful to him for their own elections and supported not only his candidacy for leadership but also his policy positions. According to Bruck, by 1995 Gingrich was able to ensure the passage of almost anything he wanted in the House of Representatives. He became one of the most interesting and frequently discussed political leaders in the nation. *Time* magazine named him the man of the year for 1995 (Gibbs and Tumulty 1995–1996).

Despite or possibly because of his prominence and influence, Gingrich was investigated in 1996 and 1997 by the House of Representatives for using for political purposes money he had raised as educational funds. He was ordered to pay a fine of $300,000. In an interesting twist, the Republican presidential candidate defeated in 1996, Robert Dole, loaned Gingrich the money to pay the fine.

Several specific social welfare assistance programs were changed as discussed below, in chapter 6. For example, the Aid to Families with Dependent Children program, which had been strongly controlled by the federal government since its inception in the New Deal, became more of a state-controlled program. States were permitted to impose limits on the length of time that assistance could be received, and federal funds were limited to five years of lifetime assistance to individuals. There was an attempt to eliminate assistance to women who bore children out of wedlock, but that provision was not finalized, in part because of the belief that it would increase the incidence of abortions.

As will be discussed in more detail in chapter 6, the provisions of the Contract with America dealing with public assistance were passed by Congress in 1996 as part of the Personal Responsibility and Work Opportunity Reconciliation Act of 1996. This act was implemented and began affecting low-income people in the United States in 1997. Complete descriptions of the former AFDC program and the new TANF, or Temporary Assistance for Needy Families, program that replaced it are provided in chapter 6 and appendix 2. The details of the new program and its provisions are also discussed in this author's *Conservative Social Welfare Policy* (1998).

By 1998 the Personal Responsibility and Work Opportunity Reconciliation Act of 1996 appeared to be achieving some of its objectives, albeit during a time of economic strength. The South Carolina Department of Social Services, which was not very different than comparable departments in other states, studied 403 clients who had left the public assistance rolls in 1997 and found that two-thirds of them were working a year later (Stroud 1998). Another 24 percent had worked but were not working at the time they were interviewed, and 14 percent had not worked at all since they left the assistance program (Stroud 1998).

An important historical phenomenon tied closely to social welfare policy and services was public resistance to government itself. In the 1990s, many Americans again lost their positive feelings toward government because of what often appeared to be complicated and unreasonable administrative regulations. A best-selling book of 1994, *The Death of Common Sense* by Philip K. Howard, took the position that very little in administrative action is left to the wisdom of government officials. Instead, there are attempts to regulate everything with "self executing" regulations that are so cumbersome as to be almost unreadable. The book's examples of the cost of processing approvals for computer orders that could amount to the cost of the computers themselves; of dozens of steps needed and hundreds of dollars required to change a lock in a public school; of environmental regulations that almost no one can understand but that almost anyone can inadvertently violate at the cost of losing one's business are all popular examples of the kinds of crises facing many people, according to the author. The book hit a chord with governors, legislators, and even the president. Some began trying to eliminate regulations and replace them with the common-sense judgments of well-informed professionals. One story held that the tax return for the Chrysler Corporation was six feet tall, an example of wasteful use of resources that could be better spent improving products or lowering prices.

Social welfare has traditionally been an area characterized by strict regulation. Reductions in regulations tend to have a major impact on social welfare programs and those who administer them.

Public violence was also an issue in the human welfare in the 1990s. For example, some two hundred people were killed in the bombing of the Murrah Federal Building in Oklahoma City. Blocks of public and private property were destroyed, and among the dead were several children who were being cared for in a day-care center in the facility. Timothy McVeigh was tried for the bombing and sentenced to death in 1997. An alleged accomplice, Terry Nichols, was tried for the crime later that year and found guilty of conspiracy and involuntary manslaughter, and sentenced to life imprisonment.

Militia groups and others have strongly protested a 1993 incident in Waco, Texas, in which the headquarters of a religious organization called the Branch Davidians was destroyed in a battle with federal agents. One of the federal government's reasons for confronting the headquarters was the contention that there had been reports of child sexual abuse at the headquarters. Because the Murrah Federal Building was bombed exactly two years after the destruction of the Branch Davidian facility, some assumed that the explosion was an act of retaliation. There is also hostility to the Internal Revenue Service and the income tax that it administers, as discussed earlier. Although it is not unusual for people to complain about taxes, hostility to the income tax has been profound, partly because of the level of taxation and partly because of the complexity of completing tax returns. Although it is probably the case that most Americans have no idea how much they pay each year in income taxes, they think it is a great deal—although the burden is less than it is in many other nations, especially industrialized nations in Europe and Asia. Speaker of the House of Representatives Newt Gingrich said that audiences invariably say yes when asked if they would spent an extra $100 or $200 a year in taxes if the tax system was less complicated and was perceived to be fairer.

Some proposed a "flat tax" instead of a graduated income tax based upon income while others proposed that the idea of an income tax be abandoned completely and replaced with a value added tax, which is the most common form of taxation in much of the world. One of the leading proponents of the flat tax was Steve Forbes, a magazine editor who was a candidate for the Republican nomination for president in 1996 and who is expected to be a candidate again in 2000.

Concerns about taxation were also reflected in 1997 congressional hearings about the Internal Revenue Service, which administers the income tax. There were charges that taxation was unfair, discriminatory, and punitive. Based upon a convergency of various concerns and public policy positions, it seems possible that there will be major changes in the income tax system by the end of the century. Chapter 5 discusses public economic policy, including taxation and various alternative approaches to financing government.

The Contract with America also spoke of getting the federal government "off the backs" of Americans and devolving more and more programs, which had once been state programs, back to the states.

There are many other sources of discontent with government among Americans. Many custodial mothers were distressed that they were not receiving child support payments from their deserting, divorced, or otherwise absent husbands or partners. Strong federal and state government efforts were made, as described in chapter 6, to collect those payments and provide them to mothers and their children. Many fathers, however, equally resented being charged for child support when they felt they were unfairly kept from being with their children and felt that they might be equal or better parents than the custodial mothers.

In other words, there were strong and traditional reasons for many people to dislike the government, a pattern of American thinking that preceded the creation of the nation and the writing of the U.S. Constitution. Distrust and hostility toward government are traditional American attitudes in many ways (Dear 1995).

THE FUTURE OF SOCIAL WELFARE

Dear (1995) says there are many reasons for optimism about social welfare developments in the next century, although he was writing before the major changes inspired by the Contract with America in 1995. His reasons are:

1. Public expenditures for social welfare grew from almost nothing in the 1930s to the second largest government expenditure in the 1990s.
2. So many people are served by the social welfare system, which has become a part of everyday life, that it is not easy to reduce or eliminate any of the programs.
3. Programs for low-income people have continued to grow, despite some cutbacks and some support for totally eliminating them. Programs also cost very little in the total scheme of government expenditures and, therefore, may not appear to be worth bothering to change.
4. Technological progress makes programs both more efficient and more necessary.
5. American society is becoming more tolerant of race and diversity of every kind, a phenomenon that seems to be associated with social welfare programs.
6. There was strong support of the then-current federal administration of President Bill Clinton and Vice President Al Gore for human services.

Dear was correct in many of his projections about social welfare. Clinton and Gore were reelected in 1996.

However, the programs for assistance to families became much more restrictive (as discussed earlier in this chapter, in chapter 6, and in appendix 2, which outlines the new program of Temporary Assistance for Needy Families). Lifetime restrictions on receiving assistance and large reductions in the number of people receiving family welfare aid were experienced in the late 1990s. There was also a much stronger economy and much greater employment opportunity for more Americans, including low-income family members, and these conditions may have contributed to the reason for the reductions in assistance. However, the major changes in the family assistance program indicate a retreat from welfare assistance for low-income families even though overall efforts of the nation to help disadvantaged people may continue to increase.

Most of the criticism of social welfare programs has been about assistance to employment-age adults; there are no serious advocates of large-scale reductions in programs for children or for the elderly. In fact, most programs in some way are associated with providing help to older people and to children. Therefore, any reductions, if they were targeted to other groups, would have to be small because most services are associated with those two most vulnerable groups. There may be differences of opinion about how to care for them, but caring for them will probably remain a high priority.

Although Clinton and Gore were reelected by a large margin in 1996, they were also subjected to public criticism over issues of campaign financing and, in Clinton's case, allegations of harassment by Paula Jones, an employee of the state of Arkansas when Clinton was governor. Therefore, the leading figures in modern social welfare policy, Clinton, Gingrich, and Gore, were all three preoccupied with charges of misconduct in office.

Perhaps the most damaging charges were those against President Clinton, who, along with others in his administration, was investigated for years and at great public financial cost by a special federal prosecutor, Kenneth Starr. A series of investments and financial dealings in Arkansas under the Clinton governorship was called Whitewater, and although neither the president nor his wife was specifically charged, members of the administrations in both Arkansas and Washington were found guilty of crimes. Some were fined and served prison sentences.

In 1998 the president was charged with having sex with a presidential intern, Monica Lewinsky, in the White House, and with lying in courts about that relationship. He ultimately admitted, in some detail, to the relationship but denied having lied to courts about it, which would have constituted the crime of perjury.

The special prosecutor turned his information over to Congress and said that the president had engaged in acts that could lead to impeachment—a process for removing executive branch people, including presidents, from office. The House of Representatives impeached Clinton (sent him to the Senate for a decision on whether he should be removed from office) in 1998. In 1999 he became the first president since Andrew Johnson to be tried by the U.S. Senate for removal from office. A vote of two-thirds for removal ends the career of an executive branch official.

The House considered four charges against the president but only approved two: perjury, for not telling the truth in grand jury testimony, and obstruction of justice, for misleading his staff about his actions. After a lengthy trial in which the Republican members of the House of Representatives Judiciary Committee served as "managers," or prosecutors, the Senate found him not guilty of perjury and split the vote, fifty for guilty and fifty for not guilty, on the charge of obstruciton of justice. The Democratic senators voted against removing the president from office while most of the Republican senators voted for his removal. The Republicans held a majority in the Senate but lacked the two-thirds majority needed to remove President Clinton. Therefore he retained the presidency.

Typically, in American "off-year elections," when there is no election for president, voter turnout is low, and the party that does not have the presidency gains seats in the House of Representatives and Senate. However, in the 1998 elections, in the midst of discussions of impeaching and removing Clinton from office, the Republican Party did not fare well. For the first time in recent history, the party that did not control the White House, the Republicans, lost seats in the House. For 1998 five more Democrats were elected than Republicans when, normally, the Republicans would have gained seats. The Senate balance between Democrats and Republicans stayed exactly the same as it had been before the election. Although the number of state governors remained the same for the Democrats, the Republicans ended the election with one less governor. An independent candidate, Jesse Ventura, a former professional wrestler, was elected governor of Minnesota over his Democratic and Republican opponents.

The failure of the Republicans to add seats in Congress disturbed many Republicans, and within days of the election it became clear that Speaker Newt Gingrich could not be reelected to head the House of Representatives. Some blamed him for pressing for the president's impeachment, which appeared to be unpopular with voters and the reason for the Democratic Party 1998 successes. Others also said that he had authorized and encouraged the use of anti-Clinton television advertisements that had led people to vote against, rather than for, the Republicans. Gingrich now fell from power and even resigned his position as a member of Congress from Georgia, to which he had been re-elected in 1998 by a large margin. Representative Bob Livingston, a Republican from Louisiana, was elected to replace Gingrich as Speaker.

However, Larry Flynt of *Hustler* magazine, who offered cash rewards for proof of sexual affairs with members of congress, revealed that Livingston was identified as one such congressman. Livingston admitted that Flynt was correct and announced that he would later resign from Congress. Instead of Livingston, Fellow Republican J. Dennis Hastert of Illinois became Speaker in 1999. Representative Henry Hyde of Illinois, the leader of the impeachment process, admitted that he had had a romantic liaison while both he and his partner were married in earlier years. Hyde served as chair of the House Judiciary Committee, which is responsible for issues such as impeachment, and as chief prosecutor of the case against President Clinton that was tried in the Senate.

It is possible that welfare was a decisive factor in the 1998 election—because it was no longer an issue. The Personal Responsibility and Work Opportunity Reconciliation Act of 1996, which is described in this chapter and others and detailed in appendix 2, perhaps ended the kinds of concerns that earned support for Republican positions and candidates. Some criticized the Republicans for having no programs to promote in their election efforts.

Whatever all the reasons and issues, 1999 began with major changes in the Republican congressional leadership while President Clinton remained in office.

CONCLUSION

The history of assistance programs for the socially and economically disadvantaged is lengthy. It can be traced to earliest times. That history shows that societies are generally unwilling to see their members go without adequate food, clothing, and shelter and that they typically take steps to prevent or otherwise address such problems.

Certain principles of assistance have long persisted among civilized societies. They provide that assistance ought to be adequate but not so generous that it discourages work; whenever possible, societies insist that those who receive help contribute something to the society through work or training for work. The abiding social policy principles also suggest that societies divide their needy persons into those who appear to be able to help themselves and those who appear to be unable to do so.

DISCUSSION QUESTIONS

1. How fair is the concept that no one should receive assistance that is greater than the lowest-paid worker's earnings? Could family size or special conditions such as age or disability raise questions about the concept?
2. What are some of the primary similarities and differences between the social assistance programs of the New Deal and the programs of the Kennedy and Johnson presidencies?
3. Discuss the ways in which the civil rights movement and the movements for improved social programs were related.
4. Describe what you believe are the underlying differences in the concepts of social policy between presidents Johnson and Reagan and between presidents Bush and Clinton.
5. What indications of protest against government are currently being discussed in the media? Have they changed since that section of the book was written, or are the trends mentioned continuing to grow? Are there new protests?
6. Discuss some of the ways the Personal Responsibility and Work Opportunity Reconciliation Act of 1996 changed the family assistance program created by the Social Security Act.

REFERENCES

Alexander, C. A. (1995). In A. Minahan et al. (Eds.) *Encyclopedia of social work*, 18th ed., 777–788. Silver Spring, MD: NASW Press.

Axinn, J., & Levin, H. (1997). *Social welfare: A history of the American response to need*, 4th ed. New York: Longman.

Berkowitz, E. D. (1995). *Mr. Social Security*. Lawrence: University of Kansas Press.

Brown v. Board of Education of Topeka, Kansas. (1954). 74 SC 686.

Bruck, C. (1995, October 9). Profile: The politics of perception. *New Yorker*, 50–76.

Colby, I. (1990). American social welfare: Miles to go before I sleep . . . . In D. Elliott, N. S. Mayadas, and T. D. Watts (Eds.), *The world of social welfare: Social welfare and services in an international context*, 13–34. Springfield, IL: Charles C. Thomas.

Davis, T. (1998). *Weary feet, rested souls: A guided history of the civil rights movement*. New York: W. W. Norton and Company.

Day, P. J. (1997). *A new history of social welfare*, 2d ed. Englewood Cliffs, NJ: Prentice-Hall.

Dear, R. B. (1995). Social welfare policy. In R. L. Edwards et al. (Eds.), *Encyclopedia of social work*, 19th ed., 2226–2237. Washington, DC: NASW Press.

Dickinson, N. S. (1995). Federal social legislation from 1961 to 1994. In R. L. Edwards et al. (Eds.), *Encyclopedia of social work*, 19th ed., 1005–1013. Washington, DC: NASW Press.

Gillespie, E., & Shellhas, B. (1994). *Contract with America.* New York: Random House.

Gibbs, N., & Tumulty, K. (1995, December 25–1996, January 1). Man of the year. *Time*, 48–87.

Gingrich, N. (1995). *To renew America.* New York: HarperCollins.

Ginsberg, L. (1983). *The practice of social work in public welfare.* New York: Free Press.

Ginsberg, L. (1987). Economic, political and social context. In A. Minahan et al. (Eds.), *Encyclopedia of social work*, 18th ed., xxxiii–xli. Silver Spring, MD: NASW Press.

Ginsberg, L. (1990). Introduction. In L. Ginsberg et al. (Eds.), *Supplement to the Encyclopedia of social work*, 18th ed., 1–11. Silver Spring, MD: NASW Press.

Ginsberg, L. (1995). *Social work almanac*, 2d ed. Washington, DC: NASW Press.

Ginsberg, L. (1998). *Conservative social welfare policy: Description and analysis.* Chicago: Nelson-Hall.

Harrington, M. (1962). *The other America.* New York: Macmillan.

Howard, P. K. (1994). *The death of common sense: How law is suffocating America.* New York: Random House.

Jansson, B. S. (1997). *The reluctant welfare state: A history of American social welfare policies*, 3d ed. Pacific Grove, CA: Brooks-Cole.

Katz, M. B. (1989). *The undeserving poor: From the war on poverty to the war on welfare.* New York: Pantheon.

Lally, E. M., & Haynes, H. A. (1995). Alaska Natives. In R. L. Edwards et al. (Eds.), *Encyclopedia of social work*, 19th ed., 194–203. Washington, DC: NASW Press.

Landon, J. W. (1985). *The development of social welfare.* New York: Human Sciences.

Leiby, J. (1987). History of social welfare. In A. Minahan et al. (Eds.), *Encyclopedia of social work*, 18th ed., 755–777. Silver Spring, MD: NASW Press.

Lewis, R. G. (1995). American Indians. In R. L. Edwards et al. (Eds.), *Encyclopedia of social work*, 19th ed., 216–225. Washington, DC: NASW Press.

Noble, C. (1997). *Welfare as we knew it: A political history of the American welfare state.* New York: Oxford University Press.

Reid, P. N. (1995). Social welfare history. In R. L. Edwards et al. (Eds.), *Encyclopedia of social work*, 19th ed., 2206–2225. Washington, DC: NASW Press.

Stroud, J. S. (1998, November 14). Off welfare, most finding jobs. *State*, B1–2.

Term limits: The fight dies hard. (1995, June 5). *Time*, 25.

Tracy, M. B., & Ozawa, M. N. (1995). Social security. In R. L. Edwards et al. (Eds.), *Encyclopedia of social work*, 19th ed., 2186–2195. Washington, DC: NASW Press.

Chapter Three

The Social Problems and Social Issues Component

Social problems are the targets of social policies. It is impossible to talk about social policy history, analysis, or provisions without referring to the social problems those policies are designed to address. Throughout this book social problems are identified as the sources of social policy and programs. Were it not for the problems and the perception that those problems need to be resolved, there would be no interest in a society's developing these policies and programs.

Some of the scholarship and courses about social policy focus, in large measure, on social problems. In addition to social work courses on social welfare policy and services, courses on social problems are offered in many other fields, especially sociology. Like others of the components discussed in this book, the social problems field is, in some ways, a discipline unto itself with its own specialized scholarship and literature.

This chapter covers the social problems component of social policy. It suggests some conceptualizations of problems and provides methods for distinguishing social problems from more isolated, personal problems. It also includes examples of current social problems as well as analyses of how they came to be identified as such.

WHAT IS A SOCIAL PROBLEM?

Although the term has been used frequently in this book, as if the author and the readers fully understood the term's meaning, there is actually a need to clarify just what is and what is not a social problem. Several authors have provided definitions of the term. R. W. Maris (1988, 6), a sociologist, says, "*Social problems* can be defined as general patterns of human behavior or social conditions that are perceived to be threats to society by significant numbers of the population, powerful groups, or charismatic individuals and that could be resolved or remedied." R. L. Barker (1995, 355) says that social problems involve "conditions between people leading to social responses that violate some people's values and norms and cause emotional or economic suffering."

It is noteworthy that Barker's definition includes social responses, which is another term for social policy, while Maris's definition does not. Barker, a social worker whose 1995 *Dictionary of Social Work* was reviewed and, in some cases, modified by social workers before it was published, appears to take the position that a problem is not really a social problem until society decides to do something about it. Maris agrees, however, that social problems ordinarily, at least potentially, have solutions. It would be difficult to say, for example, that earthquakes and other natural forces are social problems; they are not because they cannot be controlled or stopped. Aspects of the consequences of earthquakes, however, could be defined as social problems. Lack of preparedness to deal with earthquakes in earthquake-prone areas could be defined as a social problem. It meets Maris's and Barker's definitions, and there are possible solutions. Similarly, when people continue to be allowed to build residences along faults, this may also be defined as a social problem.

Among the most important theoreticians of social problems was the sociologist C. Wright Mills (1959), who helped make the distinction, implicit in both Maris's and Barker's definitions, between the private troubles of the individual and the social problems of the broader public and the society. Private troubles—those that impact relatively few people—may be tragic, yet they constitute social problems only when they affect large numbers and when society, as represented by government, sees the troubles as a threat to many people or to the whole society. Threats may be perceived to exist when the consequences of the problem are costly, when others fear they will be injured because of the problem, or when people believe that they might be victims of the problems. There are many humorous and ironic aphorisms that illustrate the differences between private troubles and social problems. One is: "How do you tell the difference between an economic recession and an economic depression?" The answer, which has been attributed to President Harry Truman, is: "It's a recession when your neighbor loses his job; it's a depression when you lose your own" (England & Anderson 1992, 3–D4).

When AIDS, or acquired immunodeficiency syndrome, the disease affecting an alarming number of human beings worldwide, appeared to be a condition that affected small numbers of gay men and intravenous drug users, it was thought of as a private trouble. When it became clear that AIDS affected a wide range of people, including heterosexuals, and that it was quickly spreading, governments and those they represent began to perceive it as a social problem. (According to the Centers for Disease Control and Prevention [1997], by mid-1997 there had been 612,078 people diagnosed with AIDS. Of that total, 379,258 had died by June 1997. These figures include children, as well as adult and adolescent patients.)

There are varying reactions to social problems. What appears to be a solution to a problem to one group of observers is viewed as yet another problem to others. For example, some social workers will say that the major social problem in the United States is poverty. They may cite the low payment levels and time limits for receiving Temporary Assistance for Needy Families. But the earlier AFDC program was eliminated and replaced by TANF because Charles Murray (1994) and others insisted that family welfare programs in themselves were the major cause of poverty. Congress was persuaded that assistance caused poverty rather than curing it and that the best solution to the problem of poverty was eliminating those programs. This author's 1998 book on conservative ideas about assistance describes some of the ways that programs to help eliminate poverty came to be perceived as the causes of the problems they purported to solve.

For some a major social problem is the unwillingness of elected officials to use the death penalty for major crimes. For others the existence of the death penalty is the real social problem.

When President Bill Clinton, in 1993, proposed a social policy to deal with what he perceived as a problem—discrimination against gay men and lesbian women in the military—others said that the real problem was the possibility that the president would revise the discriminatory policies. As we will see, values affect perceptions of social problems. What does and does not constitute a social problem depends upon the values of the observer. Societies define issues as social problems when there is widespread concern about those problems among the citizenry. A classic community organization scholar, Murray G. Ross (1967), helped generations of social workers understand that communities have coalesced only around problems or needs that they themselves have considered significant, not necessarily problems that external experts have identified as social problems. It is the shared belief that the problem represents a serious threat to a community or the larger society which provides people with the will to do something about it.

An interesting means for studying social problems is used by the Fordham Institute for Innovation in Social Policy. Among its efforts is the publication each year of its "Index of Social Health," which translates sixteen social problems into one figure, based upon progress or decline in the statistics governing those problems. The 1995 index, for example, was 41, compared to an index of 75.3 in 1970 (Miringoff 1995). The large decline represents a major decline in the nation's social health. The institute studies indicators such as infant mortality, poverty among the aging, unemployment, and child abuse, among others.

Kingdon (1984) developed a theory about the emergence of social problems onto the policy agenda of government. He notes that people develop concerns about social problems and generate proposals for changes in policies designed to reduce them. They engage in politics and lobbying to make their points. At times, he suggests, people pursue solutions and programs that may or may not be proven to be responsive to the problems they identify. That is, solutions are often sought even before problems are clearly defined.

Kingdon also notes that there are "windows," at which time policy changes are more possible than others. For example, when a program is about to reach the limits of its political authorization and will either be renewed or eliminated, when a new political administration comes into office (often with a desire to make its unique mark on public policy), and at other times of major political shifts. It is true that there are better and worse times for addressing social problems, and Kingdon's identification of "windows" is helpful in understanding those circumstances.

THE NATURE OF SOCIAL PROBLEMS

Dear (1995) suggests four premises which underlie the making of social welfare policy. One might also define those premises as large social problems. The premises or problems he defines are:

Limited resources.   It is simply not possible to address in all ways every social problem or issue that arises. That is true of health care, education, and financial assistance. In the years when health care expenditures in the United States were expanding rapidly, some suggested that if the increases continued at their current rates, health care would eventually overtake the whole Gross National Product. Of course, that could not happen. People would still need to pay for housing, food, transportation, and other basics. Government would still need to provide law enforcement, education, roads, and national defense. So it was obvious that all of the limited resources of American society could not become devoted to only one government function.

When I served as the chief executive officer for a West Virginia higher education system in the 1980s, it was clear that every area of my state wanted its own college or university or at least a branch of one of the existing colleges or universities. Again, that was not possible. Some limits and some concentrations of effort had to take place. Many citizens also wanted to maintain the three medical schools that had been developed, because they found that health care was best in areas where medical schools operated. But spending money on medical education meant spending less on other kinds of education—engineering, social work, and other fields. Limited resources always force policy choices that affect the extent to which social problems will be addressed. Dear says that resources are always going to be limited—ad obvious fact that policy specialists as well as all citizens must comprehend.

Unmet needs. Many social problems are addressed as unmet needs. But, as Dear suggests, there are always more needs or problems than there are resources to overcome them. Chambers (1993) and others suggest that the ranking of needs and decisions about which to address is a manner of society's values.

The problems considered worth addressing often are chosen because they seem to constitute a great evil or public concern or because they are a sources of great fear. Some social scientists point out that society does not become nearly as upset about "white collar crimes" such as stock fraud or embezzlement as it does about violent crimes. However, most citizens would insist that violent crimes threaten their lives and that violent criminals are, therefore, worth more attention than those who steal money—even large amounts of money. One's personal security is viewed as a greater problem than one's financial security, which is a prioritization that is hard to view as incorrect.

Unfairness. Dear's third premise is that societies have persistent and built-in unfairness. Unequal incomes; unequal housing; unequal opportunity, education, health care, and so on are examples of constant and pervasive unfairness. Unfairness is a social problem that most societies attempt to address in one way or another—when there is agreement on the issues. Why should children suffer because of the behavior of their parents? Why should older adults, who have made contributions to the society, sometimes face deprivation in their later years? Why aren't people with mental illness protected from societal neglect and abuse? Or, on another side, why shouldn't productive workers and entrepreneurs be able to retain more of their earnings, since their contributions to the society are great? These issues of unfairness are constant subjects of discussion in the social welfare and public policy frameworks.

Lack of consensus. Dear's fourth premise is perhaps the most significant. Societies as diverse as the United States do not always come to consensus on social welfare policy issues. There may be broad agreement that children and older adults should be provided with dignified and adequate lives, but there is even a lack of consensus on how to achieve that. What is a social problem and what is a social problem that should be addressed by society are complex issues that require a degree of consensus. There is increasing evidence that there are fewer and fewer social welfare policy issues on which there is a large consensus in American life, which means that there is conflict over the limited resources and the selection of unmet needs or unfair circumstances to become the targets of social welfare policy.

PUBLIC OPINION

Public opinion is what synthesizes the four concepts described above and is what M. G. Ross (1967) described. A social problem is what the society, which means the majority of the people or the opinion leaders who can sway a majority, believes is a social problem. Society's beliefs, norms, and values determine what is and is not a social problem, and these are all based in some way or another on public opinion. The opinion leaders may be political figures, the media, or businesses, any of which can mobilize public opinion to define an issue as a social problem. Maris (1988) suggests in his definition that charismatic individuals may also influence the perception that an issue is a legitimate social problem. Television personalities, leading members of the clergy, and leaders of mass organizations may influence what society believes is a social problem.

Segregation of African Americans in the South following slavery was one of the most profound social problems in American history. It may have taken the protests of a few charismatic individuals such as Rosa

Parks, who refused to take a seat in the back of a bus in Montgomery, Alabama, in 1956; Martin Luther King, Jr., who mobilized the movement that arose from Ms. Parks's refusal; and Malcolm X (Branch 1988) to solidify the discontent of African Americans and those whites who opposed segregation and to make it a widely acknowledged social problem that required resolution.

The Self-Fulfilling Prophecy

A special form of public opinion is the "self-fulfilling prophecy," a phenomenon described by students of society, in which people expect something from another individual or a group or a social phenomenon (Merton 1957). When large numbers of people believe something is true, it will become true because they believe it. Of course, the prophecy cannot apply to purely physical phenomena; public opinion does not cause floods. If, however, people believe that the economy is failing, they might take actions because of that belief, such as removing their money from banks, ceasing to make purchases, or avoiding the expansion of their business, any of which weakens the economy and is a potential cause of economic failure. Stock market crashes happen in the same way. If people believe the market is going to decline, they sell their stocks, converting them to cash, and, in doing so, they cause a market decline. Believing that the market will rise has comparable consequences: people buy stocks so they will earn profits, and they attempt to do so before the prices rise too much. Their purchases, which constitute competition for stocks, cause an increase in the market. The self-fulfilling prophecy, here represented as an economic phenomenon, is a major factor in all things social, including the identification of social problems.

IDENTIFICATION OF SOCIAL PROBLEMS

R. W. Maris (1988, 7), in his definitions of social problems, suggests that cancer is considered a social problem because of its magnitude, severity, and primacy, in that cancer causes nearly a half-million deaths each year; while allergies, which are pervasive, cause only five to ten thousand deaths annually. The severity and magnitude of a problem help determine society's willingness to deal with it.

Values and, therefore, perceptions of social problems change over time. In the 1960s President John F. Kennedy suggested that a great social problem was the lack of meat in the diets of low-income Americans.

By the 1990s too much meat (because of the fat and cholesterol) in the American diet is considered a social problem. Lack of exercise is also currently perceived as a social problem, but it was not widely considered a social problem during the 1960s.

For most Americans the most crucial problems are crime and violence or the fear of them. As Walinsky (1995, 44) says, "Our greatest fear is of violence from a nameless, faceless stranger." Public opinion polls and other efforts consistently identify this great concern. And although social scientists can demonstrate that crime rates are declining, they are still high and much higher than they had been decades ago. Similarly, scientific observers say that crimes are not committed by strangers but, most often, by relatives, friends, and neighbors of victims. But, Walinsky (1995) shows that observation applies to crimes that are solved, not, for example to the two of five murder cases that are never solved.

Public attention can lead to public definitions of social problems. For example, one of the most widely read news stories of 1997 was the death in an auto accident of Diana Spencer, the former wife of Prince Charles of the United Kingdom. Spencer, who held the title of Princess of Wales, was killed while riding with a companion in Paris. Although that incident, which occurred in August a long way from the United States, had no direct bearing on the large number of auto accident deaths in the United States, the fact that the accident was somehow associated with photographers' pursuit of the princess for tabloid newspapers aroused interest in the United States for laws that would limit the activities and the access of photographers pursuing celebrities. Many celebrities in the United States spoke out against photographers, who, they said, made their lives difficult through unwanted and aggressive efforts to photograph them. Efforts were mounted to boycott tabloid newspapers and publications that used photographs obtained to exploit public figures.

METHODS FOR STUDYING SOCIAL PROBLEMS

Maris (1988, 99–104) also suggests a series of methods for studying social problems that stresses the study of actual data. He proposes four methodological approaches or sources:

1. Records, documents, and official statistics
2. Case studies and participation in small groups

3. Surveys
4. Experiments

Human services workers use all of these methods for identifying and assessing social problems, especially those who work in the social policy practice area. One of the most popular and widely used means is the "needs assessment," an approach that may involve any one or a combination of Maris's approaches. By conducting such assessments, community planners, administrators, and many other kinds of human services workers determine the course of action they or their agencies may most wisely take.

PROMINENT SOCIAL PROBLEMS

If one were to categorize and rank the problems that human services workers deal with, they might be:

Economic disadvantage. The lack of sufficient income is the basis for most of the social policy expenditures and social programs in the United States. Social Security (or OASDI), food stamps, TANF, child support enforcement, unemployment compensation, worker's compensation, public housing, school lunch programs, Head Start, and many others of the social provisions in this nation arise out of the economic problems of some people (in the case of means-tested programs) and the potential of economic disadvantage for others, in the case of some entitlements, especially those that are preventive in nature. Addressing the problems of economic disadvantage is also fairly straightforward—to provide people with resources they need and lack. Although many critics of such programs assert that it does no good to "throw money at the problem, "many recipients of aid would disagree. Providing money is the initial step in solving economic problems, followed by longer-range solutions.

One author, Mimi Abramovitz (1995), shows that many other nations are much more effective than the United States in reducing the poverty of their citizens. She noted that the now-defunct AFDC reduced poverty by an average of 6.6 percent, while family assistance programs (excluding social insurance programs such as OASDI and Social Security) in Australia, Canada, Germany, Great Britain, and the Netherlands reduced poverty by an average of 16.5 percent. Children who lived in single-parent households in the United States, she found, had their poverty reduced by about 4 percent, while the programs in those other nations brought about a poverty reduction of 30 percent for such children. It seems likely that Abramovitz's conclusions would also apply to income assistance programs such as SSI and TANF.

Inequitable distribution of income. Potentially one of the most disruptive social problems is the decline in the proportion of middle-socioeconomic-class families in the United States while the wealthiest socioeconomic classes have disproportionately increased their incomes (Brimhall-Vargas 1993; Cassidy 1995). According to Cassidy (1995), middle-class families—those between the poorest and richest Americans—have given up about $4,500 per household to the richest fifth of the population. The decline in middle-class incomes from 1979 to 1995 had been about 4.6 percent; before the 1970s, families at all levels had tended to increase their incomes by approximately the same percentages. Wages and incomes for all but the wealthiest have simply been declining. The overall economy has grown, but the middle groups, as well as the lowest, have not been benefiting from the growth.

Cassidy suggests that the changes can be attributed to several factors: international trade (more products made by lower-wage workers overseas are being consumed in the United States); technological progress (workers who use computers and related technology tend to earn more than those who do not, and many workers whose incomes have declined are not prepared to work with computers or lack the opportunities to do so); the declining trade union movement (which had pursued higher wages for workers); and immigration of workers willing to work for lower wages. Cassidy points out that 75 percent of American men do not have college degrees, and generally, those with degrees have prospered more than those without.

Physical illness. Health problems are probably the second most serious social problem, although they too are often really problems of economic disadvantage. Treating illnesses is a technical, professional matter in the province of healing professionals such as practicing nurses and physicians. However, the social problem of physical illness relates to the delivery of and access to health care services and the financing of those services. Of course, some physical illnesses are also social problems because they are communicable and/or affect large numbers of people (such as cancer), resulting in economic hardships within families. Many human services workers are engaged in providing assistance to people who are affected by ill health.

AIDS has created new social problems associated with illness. By 1997 there were almost 600,000 people with AIDS in the United States, most of them young adult men. Their need for basic services such as food, shelter, and medical care and their frequent lack of eligibility for traditional programs are components of a new kind of social problem.

A fundamental issue related to physical illness is the cost of health care. In 1993 President Clinton proposed major changes in the organization and financing of health care designed to hold down costs. However, as is discussed in chapter 2 above, his proposal was not passed by Congress. In 1995 means for dealing with costs by cutting the amounts of money to be spent on Medicare and Medicaid were approved (see below, chapter 6).

Mental illness. Mental illnesses have some of the same dimensions as physical illnesses in addition to threatening institutions or weakening the economic viability of the nation, as some special kinds of mental illness, such as alcohol or drug abuse, may do. Mental health programs are typically the largest employers of social work professionals.

Crime and delinquency. The social consequences of violence, theft, and other misbehavior are great. Social programs designed to deal with crime prevention, apprehension and treatment of offenders, and services in imprisonment, parole, and probation are among the most important tasks of human services workers.

Violence. Violence as a social problem, which had emerged and subsided throughout recent history, again became a high-profile issue in 1994 and 1995, largely because of two absorbing cases. The first was the murder of Nicole Simpson and her acquaintance Ron Goldman in Los Angeles on June 12, 1994. Nicole Simpson was the former wife of actor, TV personality, and former football hero O. J. Simpson. Simpson was accused of the murders, appeared to try to escape in an internationally televised police chase, surrendered, was imprisoned, and was tried, with national television coverage, for months and eventually acquitted.

The case, about which several books were written and which was covered in almost every issue of every newspaper, tabloid, and magazine for more than a year, raised issues of the extent of spouse abuse in the United States—acts of which Simpson was also accused during his marriage—the justice system, and other issues, which are discussed in chapter 4. Some called it the crime of the century (Eliot 1995). One writer who covered the Simpson trial for the media and who is also an attorney (Spence 1997) thought that many Americans had learned about the judicial processes from following the Simpson trial. However, he thought the trial was a poor example of how justice is handled in the United States. He believed that a book authored by Jeffrey Toobin (1996) was the best of the books on the case. Although other crimes, such as kidnapping of the child of aviation hero Charles Lindbergh and his wife, the author Anne Morrow-Lindbergh, have been designated the century's greatest, the murder of Nicole Simpson and Ron Goldman and O. J. Simpson's trial were clearly among the most absorbing events of the decade.

Another case was the bombing of the federal building in Oklahoma City, Oklahoma, on April 12, 1995. (See discussion above, in chapter 2.) Some had initially thought that the bombing was comparable to that of the New York City World Trade Center building in 1993, for which people of Middle Eastern, Islamic backgrounds were accused and eventually convicted.

Maltreatment. The abuse and neglect of the aging population and of children are among the most severe and pervasive social problems in the United States. Large numbers of social and other human services workers are engaged in dealing with that abuse and neglect.

Lack of services to special population groups. Special help for the aging, children, adolescents, and other disadvantaged groups is the focus of many human services workers. Help for people with developmental disabilities and help for those with physical handicaps are among the major assignments of human services workers.

Lack of resources for programs. Human services workers raise funds to finance social programs. The lack of such funds may be viewed as a social problem.

EXAMPLES OF THE EMERGENCE OF SOCIAL PROBLEMS

Dramatic events that are brought to public attention by the media have been critical in a variety of cases in which so-called private troubles have become social problems. In December 1993, for example, an Illinois couple was charged with neglect and other crimes when they went to Mexico on vacation and left their children, aged nine and four, home alone. At nearly the same time, a ten-year-old child in New York was kidnapped and held in a tiny cell for several days, and in this case there were some indications of sexual abuse. These two cases received extensive coverage in the media and became subjects of public concern. Were they of sufficient concern to receive greater attention as social problems in the public mind? Perhaps not. It is likely that most of the many people who became aware of these cases viewed them as fairly singular dramatic events or examples, not as part of a widespread pattern, which they probably are.

In England in February 1993, a two-year-old child, James Bulger, was murdered by two ten-year-old children (Schmidt, February 1993). The story made news all over the world despite the fact that such incidents of children murdering other children occur frequently in many nations, including the United States. It is likely that the story was of special significance because of England's reputation for tranquility and its relatively small number of murders each year as well as because of the young ages of the victim and the perpetrators.

The two ten-year-olds, whose identities were made known to the public after they were convicted, were Jon Venables and Robert Thompson. The abduction and murder took place in Liverpool when Thompson and Venables found Bulger in a shopping mall, persuaded him to join them, and took him to a railroad track, where they murdered him with rocks and beatings.

When they were eleven years old the two boys were found guilty of the murder by a jury and were given indeterminate sentences. They would first serve in secure children's institutions and, when they became legally old enough, would be transferred to secure juvenile facilities. It is also likely that they will serve time in adult prisons, since predictions are that they will stay incarcerated until they are at least young adults (Schmidt, November 1993).

Child protective services workers are all able to describe cases of child sexual abuse, the restriction of children with chains and in locked rooms, and cases of children who are routinely left alone while their parents participate in recreation or work. Perhaps the cases that achieved such broad public recognition seemed different or striking because the families appeared to have middle-class socioeconomic status and thus the means to avoid neglecting or harming children. The parents who left the two children alone did so to vacation in an attractive Mexican resort. (They later relinquished the children for adoption.) Had they been of lower socioeconomic status, say, parents who left their children alone while they spent their time in a local tavern, it is doubtful that the case would have achieved such notoriety. Such events, which occur every day, may reach public attention if, while the parents or guardians are away, there is a fire or other catastrophe in which the children die. There are, however, sufficient numbers of substantiated child neglect cases—518,000 in 1995, according to the Child Welfare League of America (Petit and Curtis 1997)— to clearly make this a social problem to be addressed through federal, state, and local social policies and programs.

Other prominently discussed social problems in recent U.S. history have been illiteracy, domestic violence (assaults against men, women, and children in the family system, by family members), and violence associated with drugs.

HUMAN SERVICES WORKERS AND SOCIAL PROBLEMS

One of the roles of human services workers is to identify and bring to public attention the social problems that they encounter in their daily work. In many ways human services workers are the "early warning system" for social problems. Social workers and their counterparts are among the first to see the development of widespread, disabling problems. This has been true for a number of widely accepted and publicly addressed social problems.

For example, physicians and nurses were among the first to identify the problem of physical child abuse. They began seeing children in emergency situations who were described by their parents as accident victims. In their diagnoses the medical personnel began identifying patterns of broken bones and contusions among large numbers of families. Out of their observations they identified the battered child syndrome, which was a forerunner of the more generally defined category of child physical abuse. Their observations helped child protective services workers and medical personnel learn to discern whether a child was the victim of an accident or actually a victim of abuse by his or her caregivers.

A more recent example is the elevation to the level of a social problem of a phenomenon called the Munchausen syndrome by proxy (Mercer & Perdue 1993). That syndrome, which has been portrayed on television and in other popular media as well as in the professional literature, is one in which a parent causes severe health problems for a child, often through strangling or suffocation, takes the child for emergency health care, and credits him- or herself with heroic steps that saved the child's life. The typical reason for the child's illness is temporary cessation of breathing. Some children who are victims of the syndrome die. Physicians and others began noticing that the same parents were bringing their children to emergency care on a regular basis with difficult-to-diagnose, dramatic, and life-threatening conditions. Hidden camera observations were used to show that parents were actually suffocating their children almost to the point of death. The issue—perhaps so small in its impact that it would be defined as the private trouble of children unfortunate enough to have parents who would harm them in that way—is increasingly being seen as a social problem, largely because the behavior is so deviant and the incidents are so dramatic. The social problem was identified as such by human services workers.

Many other problems—such as the introduction of new, dangerous, and illegal drugs; sniffing glue and other substances by children, which can lead to brain damage and even death; increases in long-term unemployment; and family homelessness—were identified by professionals, who noticed that they encountered repeated examples of them.

SOCIAL PROBLEMS VERSUS PRIVATE TROUBLES

In the human services it is crucial to identify real social problems rather than treat them as repeated examples of private troubles. (Mills 1959). Social problems cannot realistically be solved case by case. Dealing with a widespread, pervasive social problem requires policies and programs. Appropriate policies and programs can resolve the difficulties faced by individuals and, perhaps more importantly, prevent the problems from affecting others in the future. Giving money to a person who requests it on the street will often be followed by another request from someone else. Job training and placement programs, financial assistance, and mental health treatment programs are potential solutions to problems that can have long-lasting and pervasive results.

THE PREVENTION POLICY EQUATION

It is axiomatic in human services that policies, especially preventive policies, along with the programs or provisions that set those policies in motion, are the most efficient and least expensive means for dealing with human need. An example from the health and nutrition fields makes the point. Inadequate childhood nutrition can lead to delays or deficiencies in physical and mental development. Treating physical and mental deficiencies, which may be irreversible, can require hospitalization, institutionalization, and lifelong medical care, all of which may cost thousands of dollars per person per month. Yet a policy designed to prevent childhood nutrition deficiencies and programs such as food stamps or WIC (Women, Infants, and Children Program) provided during the early childhood years can, for a few hundred dollars, prevent the disabling conditions that later can be addressed only through expensive treatment.

Childhood immunizations against several severe illnesses are inexpensive. They are becoming even less expensive under the provisions of new federal policies that purchase serums directly from manufacturers and under programs of universal immunization of all children. Compared to the cost of treating conditions such as polio and the complications of measles, the cost of preventing those conditions through immunization is minuscule.

Preventing severe child abuse or neglect, which could lead to expensive foster or institutional care for many years, is potentially much more cost-effective than identifying and dealing with cases of abuse or neglect after they occur. Prevention in this case can take many forms, including public education, financial assistance to low-income families, and mental health counseling. Early identification by schools or health services can pinpoint the families in which prevention efforts should be pursued.

Clearly, there is an element of efficiency associated with identifying and defining social problems. Doing so can lead to the development of policies and programs that may prevent the problems from spreading.

CONCLUSION

This chapter has presented the social problems component of understanding social policy. To understand social policy and the programs designed to implement policies, one must also understand the phenomenon of social problems. It is from the identification of these problems that social policies are created.

Some of the ways in which private troubles or undiscovered phenomena become described as social problems are discussed in this chapter. The theories that classify social problems are also described, along with some of the means available for studying them. Public opinion and public attitudes about social problems as forces in bringing them to public consciousness and concerted action are also described. In addition, the chapter outlines some of the areas of social problems that are currently crucial to human services professionals and programs. The responsibility of human services workers to identify and deal with social problems is also covered.

Although the social problems component is only one part of the social policy process, it is a central component and one without which the others would have little reason for being realized. Problems—or, as some authors describe them, needs and discontents—are the source of the entire policy process.

DISCUSSION QUESTIONS

1. What do you consider your community's most severe social problem? In your opinion, how did it come to be defined as a social problem rather than a private one?
2. Social policies may play a role in preventing the spread of social problems. Describe a social policy, other than one of those discussed in this chapter, that may have prevented the spread or increase in magnitude of a social problem.
3. Many of those who write about social problems think there may be some ways to use scientific means to gauge problems and agree about what are, in fact, social problems. Discuss the truth or falsity of that point of view. Why might those writers be correct, or why might they be mistaken, based upon what you have learned about the identification of social problems in the United States?
4. This chapter has proposed that social problems arise from public opinion, that the given problems are severe, that they represent need, and that they are sources of discontent. Do you agree with that position, or do you believe that there may be more technical, or positive, ways to identify social problems? If you agree, explain why you do; if you disagree, explain that point of view.

REFERENCES

Abramovitz, M. (1995). Aid to families with dependent children. In R. L. Edwards et al. (Eds.), *Encyclopedia of social work*, 19th ed., 185–187. Washington, DC: NASW Press.

Barker, R. L. (1995). *The social work dictionary*, 3d ed. Washington, DC: NASW Press.

Branch, T. (1988). *Parting the waters: America in the King years, 1954–1963*. New York: Simon & Schuster.

Brimhall-Vargas, M. (1993). *Poverty tables 1991*. Washington, DC: Center on Budget and Policy Priorities.

Cassidy, J. (1995, October 16). Who killed the middle class? *New Yorker*, 113–124.

Centers for Disease Control and Prevention. (1997). *HIV/AIDS surveillance report: U.S. HIV/AIDS cases reported through June, 1997*. Atlanta, GA: Centers for Disease Control and Prevention.

Chambers, D. E. (1993). *Social policy and social programs: A method for the practical public policy analyst,* 2d ed. New York: Macmillan.

Chicago Tribune. (1992, December 29). Parents who left kids arrested aboard plane. *Chicago Tribune,* 364, 1.

Dear, R. B. (1995). Social welfare policy. In R. L. Edwards et al. (Eds.), *Encyclopedia of social work,* 19th ed., 2226–2237. Washington, DC: NASW Press.

Eliot, M. (1995). *Kato Kaelin: The whole truth: The real story of O. J., Nicole, and Kato.* New York: Harper.

England, L. C., & Anderson, S. W. (1992). *The great American bathroom book.* Salt Lake City, UT: Compact Classics.

Ginsberg, L. (1998). *Conservative social welfare policy: Description and analysis.* Chicago: Nelson-Hall.

Jary, D., & Jary, J. (1991). *The HarperCollins dictionary of sociology.* New York: HarperCollins.

Kingdon, J. W. (1984). *Agendas, alternatives, and public policies.* New York: HarperCollins.

Maris, R. W. (1988). *Social problems.* Belmont, CA: Wadsworth.

Mercer, S. O., & Perdue, J. D. (1993, January). Munchausen syndrome by proxy: Social work's role. *Social Work,* 38 (1), 74–81.

Merton, R. K. (1957). *Social theory and social structure.* Glencoe, IL: Free Press.

Mills, C. W. (1959). *The sociological imagination.* New York: Oxford.

Miringoff, M. L. (1995). *1995 index of social health: Monitoring the social well-being of the nation.* Tarrytown, NY: Fordham Institute for Innovation in Social Policy.

Murray, C. (1994). *Losing ground: American social policy, 1950–1980, 10th anniversary edition.* New York: Basic Books.

National Center on Child Abuse and Neglect. (1993). *National child abuse and neglect data system, working paper 2. 1991 summary data component.* Washington, DC: National Center on Child Abuse and Neglect.

Petit, M. R., & Curtis, P. A. (1997). *Child abuse and neglect: A look at the states: 1997 CWLA stat book.* Washington, DC: CWLA Press.

Ross, M. G., with Lappin, B. W. (1967). *Community organization, theory, principles, and practice.* 2d ed. New York: Harper & Row.

Schmidt, W. E. (1993, February 23). Two boys arraigned in Britain in killing of two-year-old. *New York Times,* 142, no. 49, 251, A4.

Schmidt, W. E. (1993, November 26). After murder, Britain asks why? why? *New York Times,* 527, A13.

Spence, G. (1997). *O. J.: The last word.* New York: St. Martin's Press.

Toobin, J. (1996). *The run of his life: The people vs. O. J. Simpson.* New York: Random House.

Walinsky, A. (1995, July). The crisis of public order. *Atlantic Monthly.* 39–54.

Chapter Four

Public Policy: How Governments Make Decisions about Social Policy

Although not all American social policy is public, or governmental, most is. The evolution of social policy from the voluntary sector, especially from religious bodies, is traced in chapter 2. This chapter describes the ways in which public policy is made by government in the United States. Public policies have an impact not only on programs that governments operate but also on the nongovernmental services that are an important part of social policy. Many believe that public policy is the essential activity of government. J. M. Burns, J. W. Peltason, and T. E. Cronin (1995) call public policy the substance of what governments do.

HOW GOVERNMENT POLICY AFFECTS THE VOLUNTARY SECTOR

Social services that are voluntary, such as the American National Red Cross, Boy Scouts and Girl Scouts, YMCAs and YWCAs, family service agencies, church-operated children's homes, and thousands of others in the United States, are directly related to government in several ways.

Taxation Policy

Perhaps the most important of the ways in which voluntary organizations are affected by public social policy is in taxation policy. In the United States most nongovernmental human services are exempt from taxes because they are usually delivered by nonprofit organizations. Their employees, of course, pay taxes on their incomes and sales taxes on their personal purchases. In some states, the organizations pay sales taxes. They do not pay income or business taxes, however, on the funds they raise.

Individuals and corporations who help support the voluntary organizations can make contributions and deduct the contributions from the income on which they pay state and federal taxes. Private foundations, which grant funds from the contributions of individuals and organizations such as corporations, are also exempt from taxes on the earnings of their funds. They use their earnings to support nonprofit activities, many of them human services programs. These tax exemptions are, in most cases, the single most important way in which public policy affects nongovernmental organizations. One writer, Robert Hughes (1995, 65) suggests that the United States has always been a nation with an "extreme loathing of tax," a country built on the tax revolt at Boston Harbor in 1773. However, people in this nation tend to demand the kinds of services for which taxes pay. Decrying efforts to reduce federal funding for the arts and humanities, Hughes also notes that industrialized nations provide funds for the kinds of things that civilize societies.

Public Grants and Contracts

Many nongovernmental organizations today operate with government money through contracts and grants. For example, voluntary organizations seek and often receive government funds. Their policies are made by their own members, or boards, but their real operations may be primarily activities connected with government objectives and supported with government funds.

Perhaps the best example of government-voluntary partnership is in the child care field, which is described in more detail in later chapters. It is important to understand that group child care facilities, or homes, operated by churches or community boards receive much of their financing from government. State departments of human services, mental health, or youth corrections, which are responsible for child care or treatment, place children in those homes and pay a monthly fee for the children's room, board, and services. In some cases specialized programs of treatment for emotionally disturbed children are operated by such voluntary organizations.

Many children's homes are former orphanages. Today there are few orphans in the United States and many fewer than there were when those homes were created. There is still a need, however, for substitute care for children who cannot stay in their own homes for any number of social, economic, and psychological reasons. Therefore, the former orphanages have become today's children's centers, or children's homes, and they operate largely with government money.

There are thousands of other examples of agencies that operate with federal grants to support mental health activities, housing programs, services to the homeless, programs for people with disabilities (including mental retardation), and educational programs for parents and others who are responsible for children with disabilities.

Not all social welfare organizations are either governmental or nonprofit. An increasing number of profit-making organizations provide human services. These include some mental health facilities, alcohol and drug treatment programs, hospitals, organizations that provide information to state agencies on potential adoptive parents, programs for people with developmental disabilities, and youth offender treatment services. Such organizations pay the same kinds of business fees and taxes as any other business might. They are not eligible for and do not seek nonprofit, tax-exempt status.

Licensing and Regulation

Governments also directly control voluntary social services organizations through chartering and licensing them. Even though the organizations may receive little or no financing from government, public policy generally requires that organizations that operate on behalf of people be regulated in some ways by government. Even though they may not be licensed or otherwise sanctioned by government, every organization that seeks tax exemption must receive certification from the government and must make periodic financial reports to government proving that it deserves to continue being exempted from taxes.

A PRIMER OF AMERICAN GOVERNMENT

It is impossible to discuss any human services in the United States without discussing the public policies of which they are a part. Knowing how government in the United States makes social policy requires an understanding of the ways in which American government is organized and operated, although it is beyond the scope of this book to provide a complete description of American government. Textbooks on American government and critiques of it are widely available and cover the subject in depth. Readers who have backgrounds in government or political science or have had thorough introductory or advanced courses in those fields may find much of this chapter elementary and redundant and, therefore, unnecessary.

One central theme that may not be familiar even to students of the general subjects of political science or government is the blurring of the public and the voluntary, or private, sectors, a subject that is addressed in several different contexts in this book. Although there may have been a time in which there were sharp separations between public and voluntary human services, in the 1990s most human services are mixed and contain both public and private elements.

The Federal System

The United States operates under what is called the federal system, or federalism, which is somewhat different from the government structures found in most other nations. The federal system evolved form earliest American history, when the nation did not exist but several states, then called colonies, did. After the Revolutionary War and the adoption of the Constitution, the United States became a nation, and the federal government was organized.

Unlike the United States, many nations have parliamentary governments. The chief executives are prime ministers who are members of the parliament, which is comparable to our Congress. The U.S. government has strict separation of powers. The head of the executive branch, or president, is never a member of Congress when he is president, and no Congress member can serve simultaneously as president. We also use the jury system for trials, which is not the pattern in most of the nations of the world, which rely, instead, on the decision of judges. Some nations have many of the same characteristics as the United States. In fact, much of what the United States does is based on the English government system, but the chief English executive is the king or queen, who is selected through inheritance rather than by election and who has no powers.

In the United States, however, even though there is a national government, it does not hold all of the powers of the nation. The Constitution specifies in the Eleventh Amendment that all of the powers not granted to the federal government in the Constitution are delegated to the states. Therefore, in most ways it is the state government that has always been highly significant in the social welfare of the citizens of the United States.

For the most part, social welfare programs are state programs, although the financial support of the federal government is often the basis for their financing and operation. Understanding the relationship between the state and federal governments is critical, and it is described in this chapter.

Although the federal government is supreme in cases in which there are conflicts, there are also specific powers reserved for each level; the federal government, for example, does not become involved in exercising those powers that belong to the states. A good illustration is law enforcement. With the exception of federal crimes, law enforcement is a state power. The states both make and enforce the laws on crimes as fundamental as homicide, robbery, and embezzlement. Unless federal law has been violated, the federal government is not involved in enforcing local laws.

Yet even that distinction is oversimplified. The federal government has, for example, provided financial assistance to state governments for law enforcement. That is an appropriate, constitutional use of federal power. In some cases a criminal act may violate both state and federal laws. Thus, a murder, which is a state crime, may also involve violation of the victim's civil rights, which is a federal crime. Understanding the details and complexities of state and federal relationships in all areas of government requires extensive study.

Party Politics

In the United States, one of the fundamentals of government is the two-party system. For virtually all of U.S. history, there have been two parties that have dominated government, despite the existence of many other special-interest and specialized parties. Although the parties have no constitutional standing, they are the basis, as is seen later in this chapter, of the organization of legislative bodies and of the executive branch. Party affiliation is also a test for the appointment of members of regulatory or independent agency governing boards.

Parties are strictly voluntary organizations in the sense that people join them and work within them as volunteers. Some financing has been provided to presidential candidates, but that is not limited to the two major parties—Republican and Democratic—but to those who garner sufficient numbers of registrants and voters in elections.

Although there are some general characteristics associated with each of the parties—large business has been traditionally Republican and organized labor traditionally Democratic, for example—there are no hard demarcations of party affiliation. Many wealthy business people are Democrats, and many labor union members are Republicans. The parties have general directions and beliefs, stated in the political platforms they adopt every four years, but parties in the United States are less ideological than parties are in other nations—especially those that have multiple rather than two-party systems and that have proportional representation in their legislative bodies based on the strengths of all the parties and the votes of citizens for candidates of those parties.

In the United States, parties other than the Democratic and Republican are called third parties, although there may be dozens of them at any time. Most receive few votes and elect no more than one or two members to legislative bodies. Some may, at times, garner enough votes to affect the election contests among the major party candidates. However, they are generally not direct and important influences in American politics. On the other hand, their positions often eventually become incorporated into the platforms of the major parties, and their influence is exercised in that way. From time to time, some members of Congress as well as some state legislators are "independents" and not members of any party. Many independents are former members of one party or another and have developed enough support so that they do not need party affiliation to be elected. They, like the third parties, are usually minor influences on government, although some individual independents may exercise significant influence in their legislative bodies. As noted in chapter 2, Minnesota elected a governor who was neither a Democrat nor a Republican.

In some parts of the United States, especially the South, party politics have taken on the characteristics of racial politics. For most of U.S. history after the Civil War, the southern states were dominated by the Democratic Party. Most office holders were Democrats, and the southern states almost always voted for Democratic candidates for president. The region was called "the Solid South." African American citizens joined the Republican Party, which was the party of President Abraham Lincoln, who ended slavery. During those years of racial segregation, in which African American and white people were forbidden by law to sit in the same sections on buses, to drink from the same water fountains, to stay in the same hotels, or to attend the same schools, the Democratic office holders maintained the segregated patterns and resisted any efforts to change them.

Perhaps one of the most profound influences on the membership of the two political parties was the Voting Rights Act of 1965, which ended the post–Civil War practice of denying many African Americans the right to vote. In some states that was accomplished with a poll tax, which required payment of a few dollars to vote. The burden fell disproportionately on African American voters because the African American population was traditionally economically disadvantaged. Many potential African American voters were excluded from voting by the tax on voting. Eventually the poll tax was declared unconstitutional by the Supreme Court, which sharply increased the pool of African American voters.

Some southern states also used other tactics to deny African Americans their right to vote. For example, voting officials in a few states required that people effectively be able to interpret the U.S. Constitution as a condition for registering to vote. White voters were given easy sections and more generous evaluations of their abilities, while African American applicants were given more difficult passages and were failed even when they knew what the passage meant.

The Voting Rights Act of 1965 was a product of Democratic Party presidents and a Democratic Congress, as were many of the other civil rights laws. The Voting Rights Act eliminated impediments to voting for minority group members. Federal monitors were sent to southern states where the offenses had occurred to supervise registration and voting procedures. It was that act that changed the voting patterns and the politics of the South.

For many years, since the New Deal of President Franklin Delano Roosevelt, the African American population had in large measure switched its support to the Democratic Party. When African Americans began voting in large number and also began holding local and state offices in large numbers, they typically did so through the Democratic Party and as Democratic candidates.

Before the 1965 Voting Rights Act, in the 1950s, there were challenges to the state Democratic Party delegations to national Democratic conventions, often led by African American groups. For a while they lost, but by the 1960s African American delegates were a large proportion of the Democratic national conventions and had strong roles in the Democratic Party. One of the consequences, particularly in the South, was a movement away from the Democratic Party by white people who did not want to yield power to African Americans or to support color integration. The evolution in some southern states has been that of the Democratic Party becoming strongly influenced by African American voters and leaders and a departure from the Democratic Party for the Republican Party by some white political leaders at the state and national levels. As the century ended, southern states with large African American populations were becoming increasingly polarized, with large proportions of white office holders in the Republican Party and large proportions of African American office holders in the Democratic Party. In some 1998 elections, however, that pattern did not persist.

Separation of Powers

It is critical for understanding social policy in the United States to recognize that the U.S. government, at every level, operates under a philosophy called the "separation of powers." The three basic powers in American government are executive, legislative, and judicial. None of these is absolutely supreme: each requires the consent, cooperation, and support of the others; each is able, in one way or another, to affect the other two. Some observers call the separation of powers an arrangement of checks and balances, in which no one branch may dominate the others and, therefore, government and the nation. If citizens are unhappy with their state legislature or Congress, they may appeal to the governor or the president to battle for measures that will improve their circumstances. If they believe the legislative or executive branch has acted improperly, they may file suit in the courts. If they are displeased with the courts, they may ask the legislative branch to pass legislation that will negate or reverse court decisions. The separation of powers concept was designed to help avoid the development of a tyrannical government such as the one in England that the earliest English settlers came to American to escape.

The system of separation of powers is critical to policy making, and to making changes in policy, in the United States. Yet most of the nation's citizens are unclear about the separation of powers concept. Many are baffled by, or have misunderstandings about, the ways in which government decisions and policies are made.

The concept of separation of powers in the U.S. Constitution is based on three branches of government—the executive, the legislative, and the judicial. Each branch is generally independent of the others. The Constitution specifies the powers of each branch, incorporating a system of checks and balances that ensures that no branch exceeds its authority. This discussion illustrates the ways in which the three branches interact with and exercise checks and balances on one another.

The separation of powers concept applies to the federal government as well as to the states. In every state there are the same three branches—the executive, legislative, and judicial, as in the federal system. Although there are specific powers that apply in every state, the relationships among the three branches may vary from state to state. It is important for Americans interested in participating in government and social policy to understand how these things are done in their own states because the patterns may be quite different than those in other states.

The state and federal governments constitute the main governing bodies of the United States. While we are attentive to and concerned about cities and towns, they are basically recognized as creations of the states. The powers of the cities are granted to them by the states in which they are located and can be taken away by those same states. The structure of American government is based upon the U.S. Constitution, which is the document that covers the states and the federal government, where the basic powers lie. Counties also exercise significant influence in the United States because they are also convenient subunits and arms of state government. The counties were developed by the states to implement the laws and policies of a state government throughout its territory.

The discussions of social policy in this book focus primarily on the federal and state governments because they are the sources and implementers of U.S. social policy, as opposed to local governments, although there are exceptions. Some states use the county and city governments as the principal operators of social programs.

The Executive Branch

The executive branch of government, as the word implies, executes the nation's laws, or, to state it another way, enforces the laws. In the federal government the executive branch consists of the president and the executive agencies or departments of the government. The president's Cabinet consists of the heads of those executive branch departments such as the Department of State, the Department of Defense, and—more relevant to human services and social policy—the Department of Labor, the Department of Health and Human Services, the Department of Education, the Department of Agriculture, and the Department of the Interior.

Each of these departments at the federal level carries out the laws made by the legislative branch, the U.S. Congress, or orders of the courts, as discussed later in this chapter. It is important to mention here that the executive branch exercises enormous power by deciding how to implement legislative actions. Part of its basis for deciding how to do this is the intention of the legislature, which it studies and cites as it proposes policies regulations.

Personnel. The people who operate the executive branch of government fall into two general classifications. In the United States government there are elected officials and their appointees and permanent "merit," or civil service, employees. The only elected federal officials in the United States government are the president and vice president. The president appoints many of the executive branch employees, especially the department heads or members of the Cabinet, as well as a number of other top officials of each of the government departments.

Presidents also appoint federal judges, and in this way the executive branch has influence over the judicial branch of the government. In addition, the president has appointment power for members of boards and commissions and regulator bodies, as discussed later in this chapter.

The other broad classification of employees is civil service employees. These are people who are appointed to their jobs on the basis of examinations or an evaluation of their qualifications. They stay on the job so long as the job exists or until they voluntarily leave, retire, or are terminated for failure to perform their duties satisfactorily.

Some government scholars refer to those who are appointed by the president as political appointees and the civil service, or merit, staffs as nonpolitical employees. The overall system that governs the selection of nonpolitical personnel is called the civil service system. All but a few of the employees in government are civil service employees.

Many of those appointed by the president serve at the will and pleasure of the president. That is, the president may ask the secretary of Health and Human Services, for example, to leave at any time, and the appointee does so, as was the case in 1979 when President Jimmy Carter terminated the appointment of Joseph Califano, who had been in the position for two years. The same has been true for many other executive branch employees.

Federal judges who are appointed by presidents, on the other hand, serve for life and cannot be removed by the president. The members of regulatory bodies or boards and commissions appointed by the president generally serve for fixed terms—usually longer than the four-year term of the president and vice president.

The U.S. Senate must consent to the presidential appointments of executive and judicial branch officials. A recent example was the appointment of former senator John Tower to the position of secretary of defense by President George Bush in 1989. The Senate refused to confirm the appointment, and Tower did not serve. It is rarer for the Senate to refuse to confirm an executive appointment than a judicial one. Several nominees for the U.S. Supreme Court have been denied confirmation in recent years by the Senate; in 1992 the Senate came close to denying confirmation to current Supreme Court Justice Clarence Thomas, largely over a charge of sexual harassment by former University of Oklahoma law professor Anita Hill.

The States

In the states the separation of powers operates similarly, although the rules and structures change from state to state. It is important for human services workers to understand how their state governments operate. Essentially, the pattern is for the governor to be elected and to appoint most of the executive branch agency heads with state senate consent, much as the president appoints the Cabinet. In the states, however, there is usually more than one elected official. In many states there is a governor and lieutenant governor plus several other executive branch heads, who are chosen by the voters rather than by the governor. Depending upon the state, these may include the state treasurer, state auditor, secretary of state, attorney general, superintendent of education, and secretary, or director, of agriculture. These individuals may not, of course, be removed by the governor. Their responsibility is to the electorate who chose them.

Election or Appointment—a Recurring Issue. A recurring issue in state government is the debate over the best method of selecting key state officials. Is appointing or electing them best for the programs and citizens of the state? Some political science theorists believe that a strong governor system is the best for efficient and effective administration. A strong governor can choose the people he or she wants, direct their work, and hold them accountable for the results of their efforts. If they are not satisfactory, they can be replaced. Electing officials, on the other hand, diffuses authority. They can ignore the governor's directions and may be inclined to take actions that will secure their own political bases and reelections rather than pursuing the best interests of the state. Some of those elected officials have relatively technical jobs, such as the secretaries of state, who issue corporate charters and perform other tasks that could, some argue, be directed by a relatively lower-paid appointed official. Those who favor a strong governor prefer that states elect only one or two officials, much as the U.S. government selects only a president and vice president and lets the others be appointed.

Those who prefer a larger number of elected officials believe that such arrangements provide citizens with more direct control over their officials. If they are unhappy, for example, with the educational program in a state that elects the superintendent of schools, they may replace that superintendent directly by election. Of course, those who prefer a smaller slate of elected officials argue that the same voters can simply turn out the governor at the next election. Nevertheless, the more elected officials there are, the more individuals a citizen can contact directly to pursue specific government objectives. The argument is really over the degree of direct control citizens have over their executive branch officials. Most of the elected positions are spelled out in state constitutions, which are difficult to change; this is why most states have more elected executive branch officials than the experts on public administration would recommend.

Permanent Employees. The states, like the federal government, have merit systems and civil service employment for most of their employees, and the rules are similar to those of the federal government. In fact, many states originally instituted merit systems as a condition for receiving federal funds for human services programs such as AFDC and others established by the Social Security Act, which require the use of merit principles in employing staff. Most states have expanded merit system coverage to a majority of state employees.

The executive branch functions differently in some states, although the trend is toward a powerful governor who performs in many ways as the president does at the national level, making appointments, designing the government's programs through a staff, and taking the lead in financial matters. In a few states the governor is merely part of an executive committee consisting of the governor and other elected executive branch officials, which makes decisions as a team rather than by the work of a single strong executive.

Budget. The basic power of the strong governor and, for that matter, the president, is power over the budget. The governor or president proposes a budget, spends the budget, and administers the finances of the government. Nothing happens in government without money; therefore, the way in which power is exercised is by the control over money.

Generally, in the states the authorization of expenditures and the actual expenditure of money are functions shared by the governor with a state treasurer and perhaps an auditor. Their part, however, is merely to determine that the funds are available and that they are being spent legally. The decisions about how the funds are spent are made by the governor through the executive agencies, based upon the appropriations bills that are passed by the legislative branch.

Over the years the federal and state governments have developed large structures to deal with financial planning and forecasting, such as budget offices and, at the federal level, the Office of Management and Budget (OMB). Each executive agency also has a staff and special units that devote their time and energy to financial management.

HOW THE EXECUTIVE BRANCH INFLUENCES THE LEGISLATIVE BRANCH

In the discussion of the federal system it was noted that the three branches have influence and power over one another. These are three separate, equal, and interrelated branches. The executive branch's influence over the legislative branch is important and not always thoroughly understood. There are several ways in which the executive branch exercises influence over the U.S. Congress in the case of the federal government and the state legislature in the case of state governments.

The most important way in which the executive branch influences the legislative branch is through the development and proposal of legislation. Most of the laws that the legislative branch considers come, in some way, from the executive branch agencies. In other words, when Congress deals with health and human services legislation, the legislation is likely to have originated within the Department of Health and Human Services. Even if the legislation has come directly from the thinking of a legislative committee or individual member of the legislative body, it is usually necessary for the executive branch agency to explain, through consultation with them or formal testimony before committees, how the legislative member or committee can achieve what they desire. Much of the advice given to legislative bodies about proposed legislation comes from the executive branch agencies, which often have to tell the legislative groups what can and cannot be done, how much the legislation will cost, and what impact it will have on citizens. The executive branch agencies prepare "fiscal notes" and other documents to assist the legislative body in making its decisions.

The executive branch also influences legislation by the ways in which it implements a statute or law. In many cases legislation is not as specific as it could be. The executive branch, in implementing legislation, may decide where a building is going to be constructed, how a highway is to be located, or which agencies will receive contracts to operate services. The way in which a piece of legislation is implemented is often as important and influential on the subject of that legislation as is the actual bill that is passed.

There have been examples throughout recent American history of the executive branch refusing to implement laws passed by the legislative branch. In some cases an executive branch has simply refused to spend the money appropriated or to implement the law, particularly when it applies to initiating or expanding programs. Both presidents Richard Nixon and Lyndon Johnson, for example, permitted the withholding of appropriated funds from social programs. They referred to their actions as rescissions, "placing funds in reserve." During his presidency, Ronald Reagan appeared to define some legislation in ways that differed from the intent of Congress. For example, by executive order of the secretary of Health and Human Services, funds that might have been used for providing information on family planning were denied to organizations that provided or informed clients about abortion. In turn, when President Bill Clinton took office, one of his first acts was to reverse that executive action. The ability to do or fail to do what the legislative branch has passed is one of the most powerful influences of the executive branch over the legislative branch. The power of the executive branch in such matters has been tested in the courts and is not absolute. In many cases, however, it is legal.

THE ROLE AND INFLUENCE OF THE LEGISLATIVE BRANCH

The legislative branch of government is a crucial and central part of government operation. Some would suggest that it is the most important and most powerful of the branches, but, as has been suggested already, the three branches in fact influence one another and are essentially co-equal. The legislative branches are different in each of the states and between the states and the U.S. Congress.

The U.S. Congress consists of 535 members, 100 in the U.S. Senate and 435 in the House of Representatives. Each of the fifty states has two senators, regardless of the size of its population. The House of Representatives members, however, are apportioned among the states based on population. Every ten years, after the census, which is required by the Constitution, some states lose members in the House of Representatives and others gain members.

In contrast, each state has a different kind of legislative structure. All have two houses, or chambers, except for Nebraska, which has a one-house, or unicameral, legislature. There is usually a senate, which is called the upper chamber, and a house of representatives, which is called the lower chamber. In many states the original structure was of a senate that represented each of the counties or a grouping of counties, much as the U.S. Senate represents the states. The lower houses represented the population.

The original theory behind these two houses was that there should be two kinds of influence operating in a state government and also in the U.S. government, a built-in form of checks and balances. Property, wisdom, and, perhaps, aristocracy would be the values of the upper chamber's members. The hope was that the members of the senate would not be influenced by the popular passions of the times. Instead, the upper chamber would deliberate carefully, maintain a sense of history, and not allow anything too radical to happen too quickly. In most of the upper chambers, including the U.S. Senate, the members are elected for longer terms than the members of the lower chambers, reflecting that tradition.

Originally in the U.S. government, members of the Senate were not directly elected by the people of each of the states, but, instead, were selected by the state legislatures, which moved them even farther from the popular feelings and passions of the day. That system was changed, and now all senators are elected by the people.

Despite the original designs of the state legislatures, the courts have held that it is unconstitutional for state legislators to represent anything but people: members of the legislatures do not represent trees or cattle or land in a region but only people, the courts have said. Consequently, each state must now base the election of members of both its senate and its house on population alone. Therefore, many rural counties that once had their own representatives in the state senate have now been combined with many other counties for the sake of representation. Because they have small populations, they have less direct voice in the upper and lower chambers than larger metropolitan areas. These issues were decided in the U.S. Supreme Court cases of *Baker v. Carr,* 369 U.S. 186 (1962) and *Reynolds v. Sims,* 377 U.S. 533 (1964) (Plano & Greenberg 1989).

In today's legislative bodies only the U.S. Senate represents something other than population—by representing states. Today every legislator, with the exception of U.S. senators, has to represent approximately the same number of people as other legislators in his or her state. That policy was decided by the courts, which is an example of how the judicial branch exercises profound influence upon the legislative branch.

Operations of Legislatures

Legislative bodies have a number of characteristics that are not well understood by many citizens but are important to comprehend when trying to analyze and influence legislative actions. One important consideration is that only a small portion of all the bills introduced in legislatures ever become law.

The Leadership. Every legislative body has a leadership structure, which is usually a small group of five to ten key members who are selected by their colleagues. That small group makes many of the decisions about the actions of the house or senate. The small groups are necessary because legislatures are bombarded with so much legislation that is highly technical and specialized that not all of the legislators can possibly understand and deal intelligently with everything. One bill may involve complicated issues of environmental pollution which are understood fully by only a few highly trained engineers. Another may deal with complex matters of health care. Still another may deal with the higher education system. Knowing about those systems requires extensive training and years of experience. Therefore, legislators know that they cannot be experts on all subjects. Consequently, they elect and defer to leadership groups.

The leadership usually consists of the top two officers of each house of the legislature. In the senate they are usually a president and a president pro tem. In the house they are typically a speaker and a majority leader. The other members of the leadership group often include chairs of some of the major committees, such as finance, judiciary, or ways and means, the chief financial committee in the house. The election of the leadership is obviously a pivotal issue in the operation of a legislative body. It is also where the political parties come into play. The political party that is dominant in the legislative body selects the leadership; the minority party has a lesser role. In fact, the minority often has no influence on the selection of the leadership. In a private meeting called a caucus, the majority party chooses whom it wants, and because they are the majority, they always win when the entire house or senate votes. Therefore, the chairs and most of the members of the committees are from the majority party. A minority of the members of each committee are from the minority party, which has a parallel structure to the leadership for its own purposes. There are a minority leader, a minority whip, and other leaders who represent the interests of the minority party in the legislative body.

Another factor in leadership selection is seniority. The longer a person has served in some legislative bodies, including the U.S. Congress, the greater his or her prerogatives in assuming committee membership and leadership. In some state legislatures seniority is more important than in others. Ordinarily, however, elected leadership positions such as those described in this section are not based upon seniority, although those who have served longest often build a great deal of support and credibility with their fellow members.

Committees and Their Chairs.   Most of the work of the legislative bodies is done by committees. Once a committee approves a bill, unless it is terribly controversial or important to large numbers of citizens, the bill is likely to pass the entire house or senate. The discussions, debates, and controversy take place in committees. The smaller amount of debate on the floor of the body usually is not truly important to the bill's passage. The subject matter is, as has been suggested, so complicated that members not on the specific committee may not understand the issues well enough to usefully participate in the debates.

Many inexperienced visitors to the U.S. Congress are disappointed and surprised that so few members are actually on the floor engaging in debate. It is not unusual to observe the Senate with one person speaking and only a handful of other senators listening. The same can be seen in the House. The members pour into the chambers for votes but are not likely to be present for debates. Some observers assume, then, that legislators are shirking their duties. In fact, the members are likely to be engaged in committee meetings at the time the debates are going on. That is where the real, detailed work goes on. The committee chairs govern the agendas, in most cases, which gives them a great deal of power. Their appointments emanate from the leadership.

There is at least one important role played by floor debate, however, even when the bill is not controversial, and that is the building of a record about the intentions of the legislative body. Because the legislation does not spell out all the details, the executive branch determines how to implement much of the legislation. It has to justify its decisions, however, by citing the intentions of the legislative body. The floor debates provide a key source of information about what the legislative body intended the legislation to accomplish. Committee minutes are used in a similar way and have similar kinds of influence.

In some cases pieces of legislation have to clear more than one committee. For example, almost every piece of legislation has money attached to it, because it costs money to carry out almost any law that might be passed. Bills have to be taken before a subject matter committee, such as health, education, or human services, and also before a finance or ways and means committee, to make sure there will be money available to implement the law. The financially oriented committee may find that taxes will have to be raised to pay for carrying out the legislation or that the budget may have to be modified to include it.

Similarly, other bills may have impact on several different committees' responsibilities. A bill to license social workers, for example, may change the state laws regarding the practice of professions. Therefore, the bill might need consideration by the judiciary committee as well as the committee that deals with social services or health professions.

The Bill-Passing Process

There are several technical steps involved in turning a bill into a law. They vary among the states and between the states and the federal government. Each state provides information on its own procedures, often through pamphlets describing the flow of a bill from introduction to being signed into law. Such pamphlets can be obtained from the state libraries and from the legislative bodies themselves. The mechanics, however, are themselves only a technical outline and guide to some of the procedures that are followed, such as "reading" a bill three times before it is passed; that typically involves the clerk of the Senate or House reading the name of the bill, publishing it in the daily journal or record of the body, and then voting on it in final form. Rarely is the entire bill actually read aloud. Doing so would, in many cases, require hours. On some occasions members demand the actual reading of a bill, which is a form of filibuster, as a means of delaying action on it or otherwise preventing its passage. Unfortunately, the manuals or pamphlets that outline the bill passage process are not especially informative. They explain how things should happen, but they obviously cannot explain the negotiation, bartering, and conflict that constitute the reality of legislation in U.S. politics. Legislators do favors for one another, support or oppose issues largely on the basis of their own constituent interests without regard to the larger good, follow the lead of their party's governor or gubernatorial candidate, kill a bill by referring it to more committees than might be necessary, or boost or deny the chances of a bill by the way in which they schedule the vote on it—in ways like these the subtle and complex realities of the legislative process come to light. Understanding the dimensions of how a bill does or does not become law requires sophisticated analyses and knowledge of the legislative process such as that found in political science books.

A bill introduced in one house becomes law only after it is passed by the second house and signed by the president or the governor. The president or governor may veto the legislation, but even that is not a final step in the life of a particular bill. If the U.S. Congress chooses to do so, it may pass legislation over the veto of a president with a two-thirds majority, and likewise in the case of state legislatures and governors; most state legislatures, in fact, require a simple majority. If the bill is passed in such a fashion, whether or not it is signed by the governor or president, it becomes law.

Examples of the ways in which the two houses of Congress—the House of Representatives and the Senate—work together on legislation can be seen in the 1995 Contract with America efforts. In many cases, the House first passed legislation on such key items as tax reductions, ending AFDC, and making changes in Medicare and Medicaid. The Senate passed different versions of the same legislation, often with fewer or less dramatic changes in existing programs than the House had supported. In some cases, after the two houses compromised their differences in conference committees, the final legislation was signed by President Clinton, who had in some cases threatened to use his veto if the legislation was presented to him in the form passed by the House of Representatives.

Conflicting values are often a factor in the legislative process. For example, in 1995 some members of Congress wanted to deny states the power to refuse additional assistance to AFDC clients who had additional children while they were already receiving assistance. However, other members of Congress were concerned that such provisions would increase abortions, which they opposed.

Throughout the histories of most states, governors have had the right to exercise "line item vetoes." That is, they can veto parts of bills passed by their legislatures. However, American presidents have lacked that power. In 1996 Congress passed legislation giving the president veto power, and President Clinton exercised his new right in 1997. The legislation giving the president line item veto power was challenged in the courts. Some believe that granting the president the line item veto requires a constitutional amendment, not just a new federal law, a position with which the Supreme Court agreed, as discussed in chapter 2.

Line item vetoes increase the power of the executive branch significantly because they provide the chief executive with the power to reject programs he does not like while approving programs favored. When there is no line item veto, state legislatures and the U.S. Congress can extend their influence by combining legislation that they know the governor or the president wants to see passed with legislation they know that the chief executive wants to avoid. By their bill writing, legislators can attempt to force chief executives to sign bills that only half satisfy them. But the line item veto equals the relationship by letting the chief executive be more selective in what he or she signs. Of course, the legislature or the Congress can still pass the vetoed item over the governor or president's intentions, but success requires more than a majority vote, something that is often difficult to achieve.

Conference Committees. More commonly, there are disagreements between the two houses of the legislature. In those cases "conference committees" are appointed. These committees are representative of both houses. They deliberate and bring forth recommendations to modify the legislation without the objections voiced by either of the two houses. The conference committees meet and make reports, and the House and Senate must vote for the proposal put forward by the conference committee if the bill is to pass. They cannot amend the legislation or otherwise change it. If they do not agree, the bill goes back to the conference committee for another effort.

Most legislation of any consequence goes to conference committees so that even the smallest differences between the two houses can be worked out. A bill is not considered to have been passed and does not go to the president or governor until exactly the same bill is passed by both houses of the legislature.

It is noteworthy that the recent landmark public welfare legislation, the Personal Responsibility and Work Opportunity Reconciliation Act of 1996, is also called Conference Agreement for HR3734. That means the bill was finally drafted by a conference committee of Senate and House members who agreed on a modified version of a House bill. Both the Senate and House finally passed the bill, which the president signed and which therefore became law.

Legislative Staff

A development of more recent years has been the expansion of professional staff within legislative bodies. Both the federal and state legislatures employ large numbers of professionals to write legislation, conduct research, organize hearings, and otherwise administer the legislative process. Again, the complexity and amount of legislation are such that the individual members, on their own, cannot know enough or do enough to deal with it effectively.

State legislatures often centralize their professional staff in organizations called legislative councils or research services. These organizations have teams of professionals, many of them attorneys with expert knowledge in legislation. They are consulted by legislators who have ideas for new statutes. The organization staff converts the ideas into bills, which the legislators then introduce for action.

Professional staff members in Congress and in the state legislatures come from a variety of disciplines. Many, as mentioned, are attorneys with expert skills in legislation and the drafting of bills, which are specialized fields of law. Others have degrees in political science and public administration. In the human services areas many staff members are social workers, psychologists, counselors, or representatives of other human services disciplines. The roles of policy practitioners, which includes legislative staff members, are discussed in more detail in chapter 9. As the legislative process has become more complex, the numbers and responsibilities of legislative staff members have grown. Increasingly, those who want to have some impact on the legislative process in the federal or state legislatures must become acquainted with and work through staff members because they are often the most convenient and effective route to influencing the content of public policy.

It is worthwhile for those who want to understand the legislative process to also know something about the demands on members of Congress and state legislatures. Although the conventional definition of the job is that of studying problems and dealing with statutes about those problems, the reality of legislative work is that the first pressure on a member of Congress or a state legislature is constituent services. Constituent service means intervening with executive branch agencies on behalf of constituents, advising constituents on how to obtain services, often human services such as Social Security, and, on occasion, introducing legislation that will solve the problems of a constituent or group of constituents.

Members of legislative bodies are usually quite responsive to communications from constituents because their ultimate bosses are those constituent voters. Legislators also respond carefully to political party officials, to executive branch officials, particularly the governor or president, as well as to trusted members of their own staffs. That is why it is sometimes more effective for people who have human services legislative concerns to work with and through legislative staff members than with legislators themselves. Staff members have major influence on legislators; obtaining their support for a program or a position can help ensure the action one seeks from a legislative body.

Term Limits

There is apparently strong public support in the United States for limiting the terms of legislators. By 1995 twenty-two states had passed laws denying members of the U.S. Congress unlimited opportunities for reelection. However, in 1995, the U.S. Supreme Court ruled that the U.S. Constitution forbids term limits for elected federal officials such as members of the House of Representatives and the U.S. Senate. The states can, of course, set limits on the careers of their own state representatives and senators. Some state courts have held that voters need to be well informed as to what they are voting on. In some states the courts invalidated term limit laws that placed lifetime restrictions on government service, not because that in itself is unconstitutional but because voters were not informed about the details of the limits when they voted to impose them. The court held that the Constitution sets specific requirements for members of Congress and that in drafting the Constitution, there had actually been a debate about term limits, with the result that there would be none. Therefore, in a 5–4 decision, the Court invalidated all of the state laws that placed limits on the terms of members of

91

the U.S. Congress. Although the voters may support term limits, it would be necessary for the Constitution to be amended if they are to apply to members of the U.S. Congress.

Lobbying and Lobbyists

One of the least-understood issues in the legislative process is lobbying and the roles of lobbyists. Lobbyists are simply people who represent various concerns or interests and who attempt to influence the course (at times the passage, at other times defeat) of legislation or the implementation of legislation through the executive branch. Lobbyists often perform useful services for legislators such as bringing special issues to their attention, conducting research that helps inform legislators, and even drafting bills to deal with special issues for members of legislative bodies. The public stereotype of the lobbyist who spends money on legislators to try to sway a vote or draw attention to a cause is often accurate. Many times lobbyists find that the best way to get the attention of a legislator is to take him or her to lunch or dinner, which may be the only opportunity to capture the legislator's full attention. Many states and the federal government, however, have limitations on the amount of money that can be spent for entertaining legislators. Even when the limits are stringent, lobbyists can influence legislators because they have vast knowledge in special areas and, in fact, represent groups of constituents, who are important to legislators.

Many human services organizations, such as the National Association of Social Workers, the Child Welfare League of America, and the American Public Human Services Association, have lobbyists. They advocate improvements in human services, at least improvements in the organizations that sponsor their efforts, and greater attention to issues of concern to the organization.

There is a variety of techniques used to lobby, aside from having lunch and dinner; others are letter-writing, telegram and telephone campaigns, all of which work best when the correspondence is highly individualized. When individual constituents write to members of legislatures about subjects of particular interest to them, they are more likely to be effective than if they had signed postcards all saying the same thing or sending obviously duplicated letters.

In any case, lobbying is a legitimate and effective practice in the process of influencing legislation. If it had not been for lobbying, there would not have been licensing laws for most of the human services professions, and programs for human services would have been much less generously financed or even maintained without lobbying.

In most state legislatures and in the federal government, those whose role is to try to influence legislation must be formally registered as lobbyists; they also must report on their activities and their expenditures. There is additional discussion of lobbying in chapter 9, which deals with human services workers who are involved in the practice of social policy.

THE JUDICIARY

The judicial branch is the third of the coequal branches of government in the United States. Most people are familiar with the courts and their deliberation in criminal and civil matters, in resolving civil cases such as lawsuits, and in adjudicating domestic matters such as divorce and child custody. The courts also play a role, however, in developing social policy, largely through their decisions about cases that are brought before them.

J. Figueira-McDonough (1993) suggests that the courts are of special importance in shaping current social welfare policy. Many of the reforms of recent years have come through litigation in the courts, especially the federal courts. Litigation has become vital in social policy development, although, according to Figueira-McDonough, the human services literature has not given that route of social change the attention it deserves. Judicial decisions, along with other policy changes, have the capacity to help whole groups of people, not just individuals. Also, as Figueira-McDonough points out, the rights of the most vulnerable individuals can be pursued in the courts more readily than they might through the lobbying process. An individual who contacts a legislator may or may not be taken seriously, depending upon the group he or she represents and its influence. In the courts an individual is heard, and his or her concern must be addressed.

The principles of federalism apply to the courts just as they do to the other two branches of government. There are state and federal courts, each of which handles cases in its own areas of jurisdiction. In general, state courts hear cases about state matters and federal courts about federal matters. In certain situations a case deals with both federal and state laws and can sometimes be tried in both kinds of courts. Usually, however, cases are tried in only one jurisdiction. A federal court typically does not deal with matters of state law and vice versa.

There are different levels of courts. In the federal system there are three basic levels—district courts, circuit courts of appeal, and the U.S. Supreme Court. Similar levels exist in the states, although each state has its own unique arrangements. All but twenty states have no appeals court between the district, or "trial," courts and the supreme appellate courts, also called intermediate courts. Others have specialized appellate courts, and several have more than one supreme court—one for criminal and the other for civil cases, for example.

The lower courts are called trial courts because they are where the cases are actually tried. Trial courts decide issues of fact. Was the person guilty of the crime? Did one party injure another in a civil matter? Who is entitled to the property under dispute? Or how much financial compensation is the injured party entitled to receive? The appellate courts deal only with legal and procedural matters, such as whether or not the evidence used was properly introduced, the judge's instruction to the jury correct, and the indictment properly written. If an appellate court determines that a procedural or legal error was committed, it can order the lower court to try the case again. It cannot determine that a person found guilty by a jury is not guilty. It can, however, say that some element of the trial invalidated the guilty verdict and order that the whole matter be heard again. As a practical matter, many cases are dropped after they are reversed or the decisions invalidated by the appeals courts.

Appellate courts are typically the sources of social policy because they have the power to determine whether a statute passed by a legislature is inappropriate or unconstitutional. They may also invalidate an act of the executive branch by finding that it is improper under the law. The courts may determine that a statute or an act is in conflict with the constitution of the state or the U.S. Constitution. Not all cases of executive acts or statutes being overturned by courts have been done on constitutional grounds. Instead, they may find that another law makes this law invalid or that the implementation of a given statute was improper and outside the intent of the legislation. In general, courts assume that legislative bodies acted properly and that statutes are valid, and they are reluctant to overturn decisions of those who were elected by the people unless the case for doing so is quite strong. The process of reviewing and deciding on the constitutionality of legislation is called judicial review.

Landmark Court Decisions

In making social policy, the courts always make decisions about specific issues in specific cases.

A useful listing of some of the most important cases involving human rights and social policy issues is the following, which was developed by the American Civil Liberties Union. It covers cases before the U.S. Supreme Court, the ultimate source of judicial policy, in which the ACLU was involved.

Many of the cases are about free speech, a particular concern of the ACLU, but others are about the right to travel, the rights of prisoners, segregation (*Brown v. Board of Education* in 1954), and other subjects of concern to human services agencies and workers.

The rights of minorities, both minorities of color and religious minorities, are carefully covered in many of these cases.

ACLU—75 GREATEST HITS

A chronology from 1920 to the present of the most important United States Supreme Court victories that involved the ACLU either as direct counsel or as a friend-of-the-court

1925 Gitlow v. New York

Our first Supreme Court landmark. Though upholding the defendant's conviction for distributing his call to overthrow the government, the Court held, for the first time, that the Fourteenth Amendment "incorporates" the free speech clause of the First Amendment and is, therefore, applicable to the states.

1927 Whitney v. California

Though the Court upheld a conviction for membership in a group that advocated the overthrow of the state, Justice Brandeis explained, in a separate opinion, that under the "clear and present danger test" the strong presumption must be in favor of "more speech, not enforced silence." That view, which ultimately prevailed, laid the groundwork for modern First Amendment law.

1931 Stromberg v. California

The ACLU argued successfully that the conviction of a communist for displaying a red flag should be overturned because it was based on a state law that was overly vague, in violation of the First Amendment.

1932 Powell v. Alabama

This first of the "Scottsboro" cases to reach the high Court resulted in the decision that eight African Americans accused of raping two white women lacked effective counsel at their trial—a denial of due process. In this case, constitutional standards were applied to state criminal proceedings for the first time.

1935 Patterson v. Alabama

In this second "Scottsboro" decision, the Court sent the defendant's case back to state court on the ground that he had been denied a fair trial by the exclusion of African Americans from the jury list.

1937 DeJonge v. Oregon

A landmark First Amendment case, in which the Court held that the defendant's conviction under a state criminal syndicalism statute merely for attending a peaceful Communist Party rally violated his free speech rights.

1938 Lovell v. Griffin

The Court held, in this case involving Jehovah's Witnesses, that a local ordinance in Georgia prohibiting the distributing of "literature of any kind" without a city manager's permit violated the First Amendment.

1939 Hague v. CIO

An important First Amendment case in which the Court recognized a broad freedom to assembly in public forums, such as "streets and parks," by invalidating the repressive actions of Jersey City's antiunion Mayor "Boss" Hague.

1941 Edwards v. California

In this major victory for poor people's right to travel from one state to another, the Court struck down an "anti-Okie" law that made it a crime to transport indigents into California.

1943 West Virginia v. Barnette

A groundbreaking decision, made more resonant by its issuance in wartime. The Court championed religious liberty with its holding that a state could not force Jehovah's Witness children to salute the American flag.

1944 Smith v. Allwright

An early civil rights victory that invalidated, under the Fifteenth Amendment, the intentional exclusion of African Americans from Texas's "white primary" on the ground that primaries are central to the electoral process even though the Democratic Party is a private organization.

1946 Hannegan v. Esquire

A major blow against censorship. The Court severely limited the postmaster general's power to withhold mailing privileges for allegedly "offensive" material.

1947 Everson v. Board of Education

A trailblazer: The Court found school boards' reimbursement of the public transportation costs incurred by parents whose children attended parochial schools constitutional, but Justice Black's statement—"In the words of Jefferson, the clause . . . was intended to erect a 'wall of separation between church and State' . . ."—was the Court's first major utterance on the meaning of the Establishment Clause.

1948 Shelley v. Kraemer

An important civil rights decision that invalidated restrictive covenants—contractual agreements between white homeowners in a residential area barring the sale of houses to black people.

1949 Terminiello v. Chicago

Protection for offensive speech expanded with the Court's exoneration of an ex-priest convicted of disorderly conduct for giving an anti-Semitic speech that "invited dispute." Justice William O. Douglas, for the Court, noted that "the function of free speech under our system of government is to invite dispute."

1952 Rochin v. California

Reversing the conviction of a man whose stomach had been forcibly pumped for drugs by a doctor at the behest of police, the Court ruled that the Due Process Clause outlaws "conduct that shocks the conscience."

1952 Burstyn v. Wilson

Artistic freedom triumphed when the Court overruled its 1915 holding that movies "are a business, pure and simple," and decided that New York State's refusal to license *The Miracle* violated the First Amendment. The state censor had labeled the film "sacrilegious."

1954 Brown v. Board of Education

In perhaps the most far-reaching decision of this century, the Court declared racially segregated schools unconstitutional and overruled the "separate but equal" doctrine announced in its infamous 1896 decision in *Plessy v. Ferguson*.

1957 Watkins v. United States

Under the First Amendment, the Court imposed limits on the investigative powers of the House Un-American Activities Committee, which had found a labor leader in contempt for refusing to answer questions about his associates' membership in the Communist Party.

1958 Kent v. Dulles

The Court ruled that the State Department had exceeded its authority in denying artist Rockwell Kent a passport because he refused to sign a "noncommunist affidavit." The right to travel, said the Court, is protected by the Due Process Clause of the Fifth Amendment.

1958 Speiser v. Randall

Arguing before the Court on his own behalf, ACLU lawyer Lawrence Speiser won his challenge to a California law requiring that veterans sign a loyalty oath to qualify for a property tax exemption.

1958 Trop v. Dulles

An American stripped of his citizenship for being a deserter in World War II suffered cruel and unusual punishment, said the Court, in violation of the Eighth Amendment.

1961 Map v. Ohio

A landmark, in which the Court ruled that the Fourth Amendment's Exclusionary Rule, first applied to federal law enforcement officers in 1914, applied to state and local police as well.

1961 Poe v. Ullman

Though unsuccessful, this challenge to Connecticut's ban on contraceptive sales set the stage for the *Griswold* decision of 1965. In a thirty-three–page dissent, Justice John Harlan argued that the challenged law was "an intolerable invasion of privacy in the conduct of one of the most intimate concerns of an individual's private life."

1962 Engel v. Vitale

In an 8–1 decision, the Court struck down the New York State Regent's "nondenominational" school prayer, holding that "it is no part of the business of government to compose official prayers."

1963 Abingdon School Dist. v. Schempp

Building on *Engel* in another 8–1 decision, the Court struck down Pennsylvania's in-school Bible-reading law as a violation of the First Amendment.

1963 Gideon v. Wainwright

An indigent drifter from Florida made history when, in a handwritten petition, he persuaded the Court that poor people had the right to a state-appointed lawyer in criminal cases.

1964 Escobedo v. Illinois

Invoking the Sixth Amendment right to counsel, the Court threw out the confession of a man whose repeated requests to see his lawyer, throughout many hours of police interrogation, were ignored.

1964 New York Times v. Sullivan

A victory for freedom of the press. Public officials could not recover damages for defamation, ruled the Court, unless they could prove that a newspaper had impugned them with "actual malice." A city commissioner in Montgomery, Alabama, had sued over publication of a full-page ad written by civil rights activists.

1964 Jacobellis v. Ohio

Justice Potter Stewart's famous statement, that although he could not define "obscenity," he "knew it when he saw it," crowned the Court's overturning of a cinema owner's conviction for showing *The Lovers* by Louis Malle.

1964 Reynolds v. Sims

A historic civil rights decision that applied the "one person, one vote" formula to state legislative districts and that was regarded by Chief Justice Earl Warren to be the most important decision rendered during his tenure.

1965 U.S. v. Seeger

In one of the first anti-Vietnam War decisions, the Court extended conscientious objector status to those who do not necessarily believe in a supreme being but who oppose war based on sincere beliefs that are equivalent to religious faith.

1965 Lamont v. Postmaster General

A unanimous Court found unconstitutional, under the First Amendment, a challenged Cold War law that required the postmaster general to detain and destroy all unsealed mail from abroad deemed to be "communist political propaganda"—unless the addressee requested delivery in writing.

1965 Griswold v. Connecticut

Among the twentieth century's most influential decisions. It invalidated a Connecticut law forbidding the use of contraceptives on the ground that a right of "marital privacy," though not specifically guaranteed in the Bill of Rights, is protected by "several fundamental constitutional guarantees."

1966 Miranda v. Arizona

This famous decision established the "Miranda warnings," a requirement that the police, before interrogating suspects, must inform them of their rights. The Court embraced the ACLU's *amicus* argument that a suspect in custody has both a Sixth Amendment right to counsel and a Fifth Amendment right against self-incrimination.

1966 Bond v. Floyd

The court ordered Georgia's legislature to seat the duly elected state senator Julian Bond, a civil rights activist denied his seat for publicly supporting Vietnam War draft resisters. Criticizing U.S. foreign policy, said the Court, does not violate a legislator's oath to uphold the Constitution.

1967 Keyishian v. Board of Regents

A Cold War–inspired law requiring New York public school teachers to sign a loyalty oath fell as a violation of the First Amendment. The decision, capping off a series of unsuccessful challenges to both federal and state loyalty and security programs, rejected the doctrine that public employment is a "privilege" to which government can attach whatever conditions it pleases.

1967 In re Gault

The most important landmark for juveniles, it established specific due process requirements for state delinquency proceedings and stated, for the first time, the broad principle that young persons have constitutional rights.

1967 Loving v. Virginia

A civil rights landmark that invalidated the antimiscegination laws of Virginia and fifteen other southern states. The Court ruled that criminal bans on interracial marriage violate the Fourteenth Amendment's Equal Protection Clause and "the freedom to marry," which the Court called "one of the basic civil rights of man [sic]."

1968 Epperson v. Arkansas

The Court ruled that Arkansas had violated the First Amendment, which forbids official religion, with its ban on teaching "that mankind ascended or descended from a lower order of animals."

1968 Levy v. Louisiana

The Court invalidated a state law that denied an illegitimate child the right to recover damages for a parent's death. The ruling established the principle that the accidental circumstance of a child's birth does not justify denials of rights.

101

1968 King v. Smith

The court invalidated a "man in the house" rule that denied welfare to children whose mother was living with a man, unmarried. The decision benefited an estimated 500,000 poor children who had previously been excluded from aid.

1968 Washington v. Lee

Alabama statutes requiring racial segregation in the state's prisons and jails were declared unconstitutional under the Fourteenth Amendment.

1969 Brandenburg v. Ohio

After the ACLU's fifty-year struggle against laws punishing political advocacy, the Court now adopted our view of the First Amendment— that the government could penalize only direct incitement to imminent lawless action—and invalidated, in one fell swoop, the Smith Act and all state sedition laws restricting radical political groups.

1969 Tinker v. Des Moines

A landmark lift for symbolic speech and students' rights. The Court invalidated the suspension of public school students for wearing black armbands to protest the Vietnam War, writing that students did not "shed their constitutional rights to freedom of speech or expression at the schoolhouse gate."

1970 Goldberg v. Kelly

Setting in motion what has been called the "procedural due process revolution," the Court ruled that welfare recipients were entitled to notice and a hearing before the state could terminate their benefits.

1971 Cohen v. California

Reversed the conviction of a man who allegedly disturbed the peace by wearing a jacket that bore the words "Fuck the draft" while walking through a courthouse corridor. The Court rejected the notion that the state can prohibit speech just because it is "offensive."

1971 U.S. v. New York Times

A landmark among prior restraint cases. The leaking of the Pentagon Papers to the press for publication by Daniel Ellsberg, a former Defense Department official, did not, said the Court, justify an injunction against publication on national security grounds.

1971 Reed v. Reed

A breakthrough women's rights decision that struck down a state law giving automatic preference to men over women as administrators of decedents' estates. For the first time, the Court ruled that sex-based—like race-based—classifications violated the Equal Protection Clause of the Fourteenth Amendment.

1971 U.S. v. Vuitch

The Court's first abortion rights case, involving a doctor's appeal of his conviction for performing an illegal abortion. The Court upheld the constitutionality of the statute used to convict, but expanded the "life and health of the woman" concept to include psychological well-being and ruled that the prosecution must prove the abortion was not necessary for a woman's physical or mental health.

1971 Eisenstadt v. Baird

Extending *Griswold,* this decision overturned the conviction of a reproductive rights activist who had given an unmarried woman in Massachusetts a contraceptive device. The Court held that allowing distribution of contraceptives to married, but not unmarried, people violated the Equal Protection Clause.

1971 Furman v. Georgia

In this seminal case, the Court found that the "arbitrary and capricious" application of state death penalty statutes violated the Eighth Amendment's stricture against cruel and unusual punishment. Hundreds of executions were held up while states tried to fashion new laws that would pass constitutional muster.

1973 Frontiero v. Richardson

Another victory for women's rights. The Court struck down a federal law that would not permit a woman in the armed forces to claim her husband as a "dependent" unless he depended on her for more than half of his support, while a serviceman could claim "dependent" status for his wife regardless of actual dependency.

1973 Holtzman v. Schlesinger

A dramatic lawsuit brought by the ACLU for a New York congresswoman to halt the bombing of Cambodia as an unconstitutional presidential usurpation of Congress's authority to declare war. After a federal order to stop the bombing was stayed on appeal, the ACLU sent a lawyer across country to the remote vacation hideaway of Justice William O. Douglas who vacated the stay and, though later overruled, succeeding in halting the bombing for a few hours.

1973 Roe v. Wade / Doe v. Bolton

One of the Court's most significant decisions, *Roe* erased all existing criminal abortion laws and recognized a woman's constitutional right to terminate a pregnancy. In *Doe,* the companion case, the Court ruled that whether an abortion is "necessary" is the attending physician's call, to be made in light of all factors relevant to a woman's well-being.

1974 U.S. v. Nixon

This test of presidential power involved Nixon's effort to withhold crucial Watergate tapes from Special Prosecutor Leon Jaworski. In the only *amicus* brief filed, the ACLU argued: "There is no proposition more dangerous to the health of a constitutional democracy than the notion that an elected head of state is above the law and beyond the reach of judicial review." The Court agreed and ordered the tapes handed over.

1975 Goss v. Lopez

A victory for students' rights that invalidated a state law authorizing a public school principal to suspend a student for up to ten days without a hearing. The Court ruled that students are entitled to notice and a hearing before a significant disciplinary action can be taken against them.

1975 O'Connor v. Donaldson

The Court's first ruling on the rights of mental patients supported a nonviolent man who had been confined against his will in a state hospital for fifteen years. Mental illness alone, said the Court, could not justify "simple custodial confinement" on an indefinite basis.

1976 Buckley v. Valeo

Freedom of speech and association won a partial victory in this challenge to the limits on campaign spending imposed by amendments to the Federal Elections Campaign Act. The Court struck down the act's restrictions on spending "relative to a candidate" and its required disclosure of $100-plus political contributions.

1978 Smith v. Collin

The peculiar facts of this, one of the ACLU's most controversial First Amendment lawsuits ever, attracted enormous attention: American Nazis wanted to march through a Chicago suburb, Skokie, where many Holocaust survivors lived. The ACLU's challenge to the village's ban on the march was ultimately upheld.

1978 In re Primus

An ACLU cooperating attorney—a sharecropper's daughter and the first black woman to finish the University of South Carolina Law School—was reprimanded for "improper solicitation" by the state supreme court after she encouraged some poor women to challenge the state's sterilization of welfare recipients. Exonerating her, the high Court distinguished between lawyers who solicit "for pecuniary gain" and those who solicit to "further political and ideological goals through associational activity."

1980 Prune Yard Shopping Center v. Robins

A victory for freedom of expression. The Court rejected shopping mall owners' claim that their property rights compelled reversal of the California Supreme Court's requirement that a shopping center allow distribution of political pamphlets on its premises.

1983 Bob Jones University v. United States

The Court rejected two fundamentalist Christian schools' claim, supported by the Reagan Justice Department, that the First Amendment guarantee of religious liberty forbade the denial of income tax exemptions to educational and religious institutions that practice racial discrimination. Instead, the Court held that the IRS is empowered to set rules enforcing a "settled public policy" against racial discrimination in education.

1985 Wallace v. Jaffree

This important church-state separation decision found Alabama's "moment of silence" law, which required public school children to take a moment "for meditation or voluntary prayer," in violation of the First Amendment's Establishment Clause.

1989 Texas v. Johnson

This First Amendment invalidation of the Texas flag desecration statute provoked the newly inaugurated George Bush to propose a federal ban on flag burning or mutilation. Congress swiftly obliged, but the Court struck down the law a year later in *United States v. Eichman*—in which the ACLU also filed a brief. Both rulings were big victories for symbolic political speech.

1990 Cruzan v. Director of Missouri Department of Health

The Court's first "right-to-die" case, in which the ACLU represented the family of a woman who had been in a persistent vegetative state for more than seven years. Although the Court did not go as far as the ACLU urged, it did recognize living wills as clear and convincing evidence of a patient's wishes.

1992 R.A.V. v. Wisconsin

An important First Amendment victory. A unanimous Court struck down a local law banning the display, on public or private property, of any symbol "that arouses anger, alarm or resentment in others on the basis of race, color, creed, religion or gender."

1992 Planned Parenthood v. Casey

A critical, though less than total, victory for reproductive freedom. While upholding parts of Pennsylvania's abortion restriction, the Court also reaffirmed the "central holding" of *Roe v. Wade:* that abortions performed prior to viability cannot be criminalized.

1992 Lee v. Weisman

The Court ruled that *any* officially sanctioned prayer at public school graduation ceremonies violates the Establishment Clause.

1992 Hudson v. McMillian

The Court upheld a Louisiana prisoner's claim that three corrections officers had violated his Eighth Amendment right to be spared cruel and unusual punishment by beating him while he was shackled and handcuffed. The Court held that the unnecessary and wanton infliction of pain is an appropriate standard in prisoners' Eighth Amendment cases.

1993 J.E.B. v. T.B.

In this women's rights victory, the Court held that a prosecutor could not use peremptory challenges to disqualify potential jurors based on their gender.

1993 Church of the Lukumi Babalu Aye v. Hialeah

A religious freedom victory for unusual, minority religions. The Court held that local ordinances adopted by the City of Hialeah, banning the ritual slaughtering of animals as practiced by the Santeria religion but permitting such secular activities as hunting and fishing, violated the First Amendment's Establishment Clause.

1993 Wisconsin v. Mitchell

The Court agreed with the ACLU that Wisconsin's "hate crime" statute, providing for additional criminal penalties if a jury found that a defendant "intentionally selected" a victim based on "race, religion, color, disability, sexual orientation, national origin or ancestry," did not violate the First Amendment because the statute punished racist acts, not racist thoughts.

1994 Ladue v. Gilleo

Unanimously, the Court struck down a Missouri town's ordinance that had barred a homeowner from posting a sign in her bedroom window that said, "Say No to War in the Gulf—Call Congress Now!"

1995 Lebron v. Amtrak

Extended the First Amendment to corporations created by, and under the control of, the government in the case of an artist who argued successfully that Amtrak had been wrong to reject his billboard display because of its political message.

Courts do not simply decide issues that interest them; they deal with cases that are brought to them. Appellate courts, however, can refuse to hear cases that are appealed to them. The U.S. Supreme Court, for example, hears only a small fraction of the cases that are presented to it each year; it must reject many others. When it agrees to hear a case it is usually on a writ of certiorari, the term used when a higher court calls upon a lower court to send up the record of a case for review (Plano & Greenberg 1989). Appellate courts cannot order an action, but they can stop a government from taking actions that are, in the court's decision, illegal. The case of *Roe v. Wade* (410 U.S. 113, 1973), which was decided by the U.S. Supreme Court in 1972, held that a state could not prevent a woman from having an abortion under some specific circumstances, among other things. The Court could not order states that did not permit abortions to do so, yet it invalidated the laws that forbid abortion, which had the same consequences.

The executive branch is legally obligated to carry out the decisions of the judicial branch. Generally, the courts cannot execute their decisions with their own resources. They do not have implementers in the executive branch. They certainly do not command armies or police forces, which are the ultimate enforcers of laws. There have been situations in which the courts have taken steps to ensure the implementation of their decisions. In several school desegregation cases courts appointed administrators to make sure their decisions were implemented because the executive branch agencies of the states in which the cases were heard were reluctant to desegregate the schools. Figueira-McDonough (1993) notes that in many cases judges have been asked to oversee the setting in place of the standards and changes they have ordered, although they have few resources of their own for implementing decisions. In general, it is the responsibility of the executive branch, which is the implementing branch of government and has the resources to enforce the law, to carry out the orders of courts.

In some cases state matters become matters for the federal courts to decide, if the parties think a federal issue is involved. This is true in death penalty cases, almost all of which begin in state trial courts but progress to federal appeals courts because constitutional issues are raised. In a famous 1992–93 case, several Los Angeles police officers were charged in the beating of Rodney King, a private citizen, in Los Angeles. King had been arrested on traffic charges, and the police had difficulty subduing him. A videotape of King being beaten by the police was shown throughout the world. A California jury, however, found the police officers not guilty of improperly using force against King. The verdict caused widespread rioting in Los Angeles, and shortly after it was rendered, federal officials charged the same officers with a violation of King's civil rights. Ultimately, two of the officers were found guilty of the federal charge.

In addition to the state and federal courts described here, there are local courts that deal with more or less minor matters—small claims about financial issues, misdemeanor crimes, and other issues that, while important to the litigants, the accused, or the public, do not often lead to public policy changes.

Criminal versus Civil Cases

The key players in the judicial system depend upon the kinds of cases that are brought. There are two fundamental kinds of cases that come before the courts—civil cases and criminal cases. In some circumstances civil and criminal cases are handled by the same courts; in other cases there are separate courts for the two kinds of cases. Civil cases are those involving disputes between individuals over matters such as property, money, or relationships such as marriage and child custody. Criminal cases are between the government and individuals or groups of individuals who are charged with crimes. The courts resolve disputes, but they also specify actions, as the law requires, against those found guilty of crimes against the people of a state, when they exercise their criminal court functions.

The role of the courts in criminal matters has less importance in the policy-making process than does their role in civil cases. The criminal function is important, of course, in such special cases of human services policy as corrections and juvenile offenses. The nature of the crime, the penalties for it, and decisions about guilt and innocence are, however, typically determined by the legislation dealing with the crime, by juries, and by prosecutors. Although criminal cases occasionally have social policy implications, civil cases usually yield the most important social policy decisions because they deal so often with matters of interpersonal relationships, social programs, and human rights.

The key players in criminal cases are prosecuting attorneys, who are called solicitors or district attorneys in some states. These elected officials and their staffs determine which cases will be prosecuted. In some areas, for example, parents who are delinquent in their child support payments are rigorously prosecuted; in others they are not prosecuted at all. In some places laws against "sodomy" are prosecuted, which has major social policy implications for homosexuals; in others those laws are ignored. In some jurisdictions mothers who give birth to children with drug addictions are prosecuted for child abuse; in others no such cases are tried.

Prosecutors, on their own, do not bring cases to trial. They must present a case to a grand jury, which may choose whether or not to indict a person for a crime. The indictment means that there is sufficient evidence to try the person who is, by constitutional right, presumed innocent unless proven guilty. In practical terms, however, the prosecutor exercises strong influence over the grand jury. If the prosecutor believes a case should be tried, the grand jury typically agrees. The process of sending a case to trial is usually called the process of issuing a "true bill" by a grand jury. If the prosecutor does not believe that the person should be tried, then the grand jury is unlikely to indict that person. There are exceptions, and some grand juries take actions opposite those recommended by the prosecutors. But in the large majority of cases the wishes of the prosecutor and the grand jury are the same.

Readers may remember that Hillary Rodham Clinton, the wife of President Bill Clinton, was called before a federal grand jury in 1996 (Mauro & Phillips 1996). The federal prosecutor and the grand jury investigating a defaulted savings and loan in which Mr. and Mrs. Clinton had some involvement wanted to know about her association with the financial institution, for which she performed some legal work while she was in law practice in Little Rock, Arkansas. Grand jury deliberations are secret, and those who appear before them, including Mrs. Clinton, cannot have their lawyers present when they testify. They can be asked anything and must answer truthfully.

Not all those who are called before grand juries are "targets" of the investigations, as Mrs. Clinton was not. The purpose is to gather information in order to know whether or not it is appropriate to indict someone for a crime or, as is frequently the case, to find there is no basis for indicting anyone.

Perhaps the most important way in which courts influence policy is a result of the way in which law is really made in the United States. Some people believe that court decisions are based upon written laws, or statutes, passed by legislatures. That is true in some cases. Most of the content of the law, however, is based not upon statutes but, rather, upon earlier court decisions. In the American judicial system it is precedent— earlier decisions by courts—that counts. That approach to law is based upon the British judicial system. In fact, early British decisions are built into the law of the United States.

Common law is the name given to the American as well as the British system. In that kind of law each case is argued on the basis of earlier cases that were decided about the same or similar issues. Lawyers are educated by studying cases. They prepare for trials by identifying previous cases that held the position that they are pursuing on behalf of their client. Statutes, of course, take precedence when they are passed, but in many situations there are no statutes, only cases.

The opposite of common law is called Roman, or civil, law, which is used in many Latin American and most European nations. Louisiana law operates under the civil law approach. Under that system the laws are statutory and are modified by statute. Under civil law, judges often have a larger role in determining whether or not the law has been violated than they do under common law, partly because the statutes are more specific in the former case. In practice, however, many common law nations have statutes that define the law, and civil law nations may informally rely upon precedents in making legal decisions.

Selection of Judges

Federal judges are appointed by the president with the advice and consent of the U.S. Senate, which means that the Senate must approve the judges before they can take office. In the states judges may be appointed by the governor, elected by the people for specified terms, or in some cases chosen by the legislature.

In the federal system, judges serve for life or until they choose to retire. They can be removed from office only by impeachment, which is one of the ways in which the Congress exercises power over the courts. In the states there are a number of different patterns, including lifetime appointments, long-term elections, reappointments after periodic evaluations, and a variety of other arrangements.

Social Policy and the Courts

Among the issues decided by the courts are many that deal directly with social policy. For example, the courts may remove children from their homes, finalize adoptions, and take other child welfare kinds of actions. They are also involved in the involuntary commitment of persons with mental disabilities to institutions. They deal with divorces, child support, and many other domestic matters that involve critical social policies. Of course, they are also directly involved in adjudicating juvenile misbehavior cases and in deciding the fates of persons accused of crimes.

The courts enter, at some point, into almost all of the issues of American social policy. In many cases when a court makes a decision it is also making a policy. For example, a child custody case that works its way through the judicial system to the U.S. Supreme Court can impact the ways in which other courts will decide child custody cases. If the Supreme Court were to decide, for example, that courts must presume that a child is best cared for by its mother except in unusual circumstances, that would have an impact on all other U.S. courts deciding similar cases. The Supreme Court would have made a policy. The rights of juveniles who are in conflict with the law, the rights of nonresidents of states who seek public assistance in those states, the rights of clients to hearings when they think they are being mistreated, and many other social policies have been determined by the courts.

Again, one of the most important social policy functions of the courts is judicial review. Recall the Dorothea Dix–inspired federal support for mental hospitals, discussed in chapter 2.

Some Practical Sources and Ideas

One of the most graphic and best illustrations of the ways in which courts actually operate can be found in the writings of John Grisham, an attorney and popular American novelist. In his book *The Client* (1993), there is an instructive discussion of the ways in which government attorneys attempt to compel a child to testify about the murder of a United States senator. The eleven-year-old child is afraid to testify because he has been threatened with harm to himself or his family is he does so. The courts are capable, under some circumstances, of compelling citizens to testify.

In Grisham's novel the legal maneuvering between the government attorneys, who want the information so they can prosecute, and the defense attorneys, whom the boy has hired to help him, provides insight into the ways in which contending parties conflict in legal procedures. Perhaps the most instructive element is the commentary of the judge. This juvenile judge has to work with the child's defense attorney and with the government attorneys to determine whether or not the child must tell what he knows. If he does so, his life will be in danger. If he does not, he could be held in contempt of court and imprisoned in a juvenile facility. The judge rails at the prosecutors and advises the child's defense counsel. Most important, he scrupulously upholds the law, which says that the child has no right to refuse to provide the information that he has about the crime, even if he is in danger.

Judges are immensely powerful within their own purview. Individually, they have greater power than most other public officials in American government. There is very little that can be done to force a change in the mind or the behavior of a judge on a matter within his or her jurisdiction. Judges have great power over sentencing people who are convicted of crimes; in their instructions, they can tell a jury what the law is and is not, and the jury is bound to follow the judge's instructions about legal matters; and they do not tolerate misconduct or lack of respect toward themselves.

Despite comments from some observers such as Gerry Spence (1997), who is quoted below, judges are generally scrupulous about applying the law accurately and correctly. They rarely make decisions that they do not feel are justified by law. And, of course, the law is both the common law decisions that have been passed down over the generations as well as the statutes that are part of the code of laws that the judge applies. Judges resist taking actions that might be counter to the law because of their general desire to be competent, as do all other professionals, but they also dislike being reversed by appellate courts. A reversal of a decision may be considered a mark against the judge's wisdom and professional competence.

Spence, in a chapter analyzing Judge Lance Ito, who presided at the O. J. Simpson trial mentioned earlier, was clear in his assessments of and warnings about judges.

> Judges are untouchable. You are at their mercy, and many have none. Your case is at their mercy. Your client is at their mercy. The only protection you have from a bad judge is an appeal to other judges, who will likely be of the same political bent, who will probably not have read the record, and who may or may not play golf with the tyrant at whose iron hands and stony heart you have suffered. If the judge has committed heinous error, the appeals court is likely to find that it was error, but harmless. I tell you, judges, on the whole—*laudable exceptions admitted*—habitually abuse their power, most often to the detriment of the accused. (Spence 1997, 171)

Spence proposes a lottery system in which practicing attorneys would be chosen to preside at trials, rather than using permanent judges.

Judges are able to have close personal relationships with lawyers from all sides and with clients but also are able to separate their personal sentiments from their professional actions. When I served in state government I had many personal experiences with lawyers and judges. One of the functions of state officials in appointed roles often is to be sued by people who think laws are being improperly applied. Therefore, many state officials have their names attached to important common-law cases, even though they were not directly involved in the cases and may not have even appeared in court when the cases were heard. There is a case dealing with child custody in removal of children from their biological parents called *Gibson v. Ginsberg* that had some notoriety, for example. In that case, Gibson and several other parents charged that the West Virginia Department of Human Services improperly removed children from their homes without guaranteeing families the services they needed to properly care for their children and without giving them opportunity to improve their child care before their children were taken from them. The case was settled after lengthy legal discussions. Changes were made in the child removal policies of the Department of Human Services because of the case. I also testified in other cases, including some of the early Medicaid abortion cases.

One of the more frightening elements of relationships with courts came when our Medicaid fraud investigative unit believed that a pharmacy in a small community was abusing the Medicaid program by substituting low-cost generic medicines for high-priced name-brand medicines and charging the state for the name brands. Our agency, under my name, suspended the man from participation in the Medicaid pharmacy program. He employed an attorney, and I personally conducted a hearing on his charges which was very much like a trial, one of my obligations as a state commissioner. After the hearing, I was persuaded that the man had committed the acts, and, therefore, I implemented his suspension. Within a few hours his lawyer appealed to a judge in their local community, and the judge overruled me and restored the man to the Medicaid program. My lawyers, in turn, went immediately to the State Supreme Court of Appeals, the only appellate court in West Virginia at that time, and it overturned the local judge in favor of the Department of Human Services and allowed the suspension of the man from the program.

Within a few days the judge who had been overruled demanded that I appear in his court, which was some distance away from the state capital, on a routine food stamp abuse case—totally unrelated to the pharmacy case. The Department of Human Services staff around the state regularly brought charges against food stamp recipients and took them to court so that the stamps they took could be recouped. Never before had I been ordered, as the state commissioner, with no special knowledge of the particular case, to appear in court. My lawyers checked with the judge, however, and it was clear that he wanted me there in person, on time, and ready to testify.

I appeared in the court and listened to the case. Every lawyer in the county, it seemed, was also there to witness the judge chastise the department for its handling of the case. After disposing of the case, the judge called me into his office, and we had a friendly conversation.

My concern, knowing about the power of judges, was that the judge could have called me into his county's jail for whatever reason. I traveled to the court with a lawyer and two other staff members. I also took the precaution of notifying a friend in the state police that I might find myself in jail and that I hoped he would find some way to help me get out without spending the night there. I had done nothing wrong, and I was confident that it would not be difficult for me to be released. Yet I had heard of the unsavory kinds of things that can happen to people in jails overnight, and this was not something that I anticipated with pleasure. The problem never occurred, and all I really had to do was show up on time in that court. Nevertheless, the situation was more than slightly intimidating to me.

Conversely, I was friendly with a number of state Supreme Court of Appeals justices when I served as a state commissioner. I attended the wedding of one, socialized with others, and generally found close friendships with the membership. Yet I frequently lost cases in that same court. In one case the Court ordered the Department of Human Services to provide care for homeless people under a statute that, I contended, had not been written to deal with the homeless. It was a statute dealing with adult protective services, and the homeless did not, it seemed to me then, fit the definitions of adults needing protection. Parenthetically, since that time—in reflecting on the case, the law, and the Court's actions—I think they were quite correct. Homeless people are in need of protection and met many of the emotional and mental deficiency definitions that were considered in the statute. At the time, however, because of the immediate demands of my job, I was probably more concerned about maintaining a balanced budget than I was scrupulous about providing services to people who surely needed them. In any case, I lost. Similarly, I lost another case involving services for youthful offenders—expensive services in therapeutic environments. I never noticed the judges providing me with any special kindness based on our friendship. They always sought to read the law the way the law was written; and, although I disliked losing cases, I found their behavior reassuring in the long run.

For a variety of reasons the judicial branch is the least understood part of the federal system and, as Figueira-McDonough (1993) suggests, the least likely to be mentioned in the human services literature. In fact, this branch of government exercises great power and authority as a co-equal with the executive and legislative branches.

INDEPENDENT AGENCIES

In addition to the three branches of government, there are relatively new kinds of organizations in government called independent agencies. These are bodies that are appointed by presidents or governors and approved by senates which typically regulate some highly specialized area of government. They are intentionally separated from the political branches so that they can operate independently and do what is technically most sound without fear of losing their employment or otherwise facing unpleasant consequences because of their decisions; in other words, their jobs are for specified terms. Organizations such as the Securities and Exchange Commission, the Federal Communications Commission, and the Interstate Commerce Commission are examples. They deal with such subject matter as stocks and bonds, the rates that transportation companies may charge, and the licensing of radio and television stations.

These groups are sometimes called quasi-executive, quasi-judicial, and quasi-legislative bodies because they perform the functions of all three branches of government. That is, they may make rules and regulations as if they were an executive branch agency or a legislative group; they administer programs and functions such as licensing, as executive branch agencies do; and they resolve disputes, as the judicial system might do. In some cases they assess penalties for those who violate their own regulations, which makes them comparable to judicial bodies.

116

These organizations are not very active in human services areas at the federal level, but in some states they are directly associated with programs such as social welfare, health services, licensing of human services facilities, and the like.

CONCLUSION

This primer of how government makes policy provides fundamental information on the social policy process that is crucial to a full understanding of that process. Subsequent chapters, as they discuss social policies and programs, all require an understanding of the executive, legislative, and judicial branches of the federal and state governments, which are the main actors in the making of public policy.

The next chapter talks about economic policy, which is a special case in the U.S. policy process, and it describes some of the ways in which social policy is impacted by the economic policies of the federal government.

DISCUSSION QUESTIONS

1. Discus some of the ways in which executive policy making and legislative policy making differ.
2. Visit an attorney's office or a law library and read a human services case decided by the U.S. Supreme Court. There are cases in the areas of child welfare, adoption, mental health, and other fields that you will be able to find with the help of the attorney or a librarian. Try to determine what the issues in the case were and note what the Supreme Court decided. Was there any invalidation of existing department or federal law on constitutional grounds? Did the Court uphold or reverse a lower court decision?
3. What are some of the virtues, in your opinion, as well as some of the deficits of the federal system followed in the United States? Why do you think the United States has continued that historic arrangement, even though transportation, the size of the population, and communications have changed so much since the system was first developed over two hundred years ago?
4. Discuss the ways in which the three branches of government are co-equal. How does each exercise authority over each of the others?

REFERENCES

American Civil Liberties Union. (1995, Spring). ACLU 75 greatest hits. *Civil Liberties*, 1–4.

Burns, J. M., Peltason, J. W., & Cronin, T. E. (1995). *Government by the people*, 16th ed. Englewood Cliffs, NJ: Prentice-Hall

Figueira-McDonough, J. (1993, March). Policy-practice: The neglected side of social work intervention. *Social Work*, 38 (2), 179–188.

Grisham, J. (1993). *The client.* New York: Doubleday.

Hughes, R. (1995, August 7). Pulling the fuse on culture. *Time*, 61–68.

Mauro, T., & Phillips, L. (1996, January 24). First lady to be "witness vs. world in there." *USA Today*, 1–2.

Plano, J. C., & Greenberg, M. (1989). *The American political dictionary.* New York: Holt, Rinehart, and Winston.

Roe v. Wade, 410 U.S. 113 (1973).

Spence, G. (1997). *O. J.: The last word.* New York: St. Martin's Press.

Much of the content in this chapter has come from the author's study of and personal experiences in politics. For a detailed review of information on the structure and function of American government, readers are encouraged to consult current introductory texts in the field of government or political science. The most widely consulted and comprehensive of these texts is Burns, J. M., Peltason, J. W., & Cronin, T. E. (1995). *Government by the People,* 16th ed., Englewood Cliffs, NJ: Prentice-Hall. Earlier editions of this work contain basic information on the public policy process which is sufficiently current to explain some of the concepts discussed in this chapter.

Chapter Five

Public Economic Policy

The ways in which a national government operates its economy—in general, the total of all the nation's goods, services, and wealth—is a complicated subject that ought to be studied in depth by anyone engaged in social policy analysis and development. The components of social policy can be understood only by grasping the fundamental ideas of political science and economics.

Government economic policy has an impact on all social policy. Public economic policy in the American system is made primarily by the executive and legislative branches. It is also made by some of the independent agencies, especially the Federal Reserve Board, which runs the American banking system and which, in large measure, governs the U.S. economy.

BASIC ECONOMIC CONCEPTS

Classic Free-Enterprise Economic Theory

There are several economic theories underlying American government. Among the most important and pervasive are the classic economic theories of Adam Smith (1910). They include the belief in capitalism and free enterprise as fundamental to a viable economic system. Among Smith's classic theories is the belief that the government that governs best is the government that governs least. Smith's laissez-faire (the French term for "to leave it alone") economic theory, in particular, suggests that government should let the economy operate through the activities of individuals who are trying to maximize their own gains and avoid losses. The desire to maximize one's wealth is, according to this classic theory, the essence of economic development. It is the philosophy that has been followed for much of the history of the

119

United States, from early American times through the Great Depression era of presidents Herbert Hoover and Franklin D. Roosevelt. It was also the predominant theory of Ronald Reagan and, to an extent, informed the presidency of George Bush. Although other theories have been added to fundamental American economic practices, the basic ideas remain those of Adam Smith's classic economics.

Many classic American economic practices and beliefs follow the nation's commitment to free enterprise. The requirement under American policy that business avoid collaborating and work, instead, to compete directly and aggressively with one another comes from the thinking and writings of Smith, as well as other economic thinkers who share his beliefs. These convictions about the wisdom of government staying out of the economy were the basis, during much of American history, for the nation's refusal to deal with problems such as poverty and national health care. It was only the crisis of the Great Depression that turned the nation in a new direction, toward undertaking to solve pressing social problems as a nation.

The capitalist tradition in the United States is so strong that it is almost taken for granted. One author, E. S. Greenberg (1989), has written a complete descriptive text on American government that asserts that the whole system—executive, legislative, and judicial—is set up to support and maintain the capitalist tradition in the nation. His text emphasizes the maldistribution of wealth in the nation; the use of government to keep workers in line and capitalists on top; and the clear, although often unstated, premise that American democracy and capitalism are inseparable.

A nation that totally believed in Smith's classic approach would make little room for social welfare programs that promote social justice through the redistribution of wealth. Instead, classically oriented policy makers believe, the economy ought to be left alone and allowed to flourish; when it does, everyone will be better off, and social and economic justice will prevail. The American commitment to avoiding involvement by the national government in the economy is also a product of the federal system. Under the Constitution, before it was amended, most government activities directly affecting individuals came from the states. The national government dealt only with major national concerns, such as the money system, international relations, and defense (Ginsberg 1987). Direct contacts between the federal government and individual citizens were rare. Over the years, however, through amendments to the

Constitution, there have been more and more direct connections built between the federal government and its citizens.

Again, the fundamental concept underlying our economic system is free enterprise capitalism, and with it comes dislocation, which may, for example, cause people to lose their jobs, require them to move, or otherwise force them to endure changes that they would prefer not to make. In the classic economic philosophy such disruptions are essential to a healthy economy: those within the labor force who are situated where they are not needed ought to relocate to places where they are needed. Unemployed people, if left alone, the theory states, will make rational decisions that provide for their economic well-being. It is that pursuit of economic advantage by all the actors in the economy which builds economic viability. Any interference drags the economy downward, the classic theory asserts.

Adam Smith was writing in the eighteenth century, at a time when small merchants, shopkeepers, and tradespeople dominated economic activity. The notions of unbridled free enterprise and competition made good sense in such times, before there was instantaneous international trade and communications and before giant conglomerates, the antithesis of classical theory, could dominate large segments of the market.

Competition could, Smith envisaged, benefit everyone. Shoemakers, for example, would sell their shoes at the best price they could get. They would also compete with other shoemakers for quality production. Customers would flock to those with the best products and prices, and, thus, consumers and producers alike would benefit. The producers would use their earnings to expand their businesses or embark on other economic ventures, which would employ still more consumers. The free market, if left alone to pursue its own activities and values, would make everyone prosperous.

Although P. R. Popple and L. Leighninger (1993), among others, call the adherence to the classic ideas of free market economics a "conservative" approach, it is probably the case that this model is central to the U.S. economic system. Most national economies, including that of the United States, are mixtures of several different economic theories; nevertheless, belief in the value of the free market guides and colors many elements of American economic policy. American policy generally supports such principles as the virtue of competition, the negative consequences of fixing prices, and the belief that businesses must earn profits or fail. Many Americans believe in these ideas, elements of a strong national tradition, although they may do so without thinking of themselves as advocates of the philosophy of Adam Smith.

Marxism and Social Control of the Economy

A second approach is the planned, or socialist, economy, in which government controls and attempts to manage all economic activity. The theories behind these concepts are many, but most of them emanate from the concepts of Karl Marx and Friedrich Engels (Hirsch 1993). Marx was born in Germany. His father was a lawyer and a Jew who converted to Christianity. Marx also spent much of his adult life in England and studied economic works such as those of Adam Smith in the British Museum almost daily for years. Marx's ideas laid the basis for the political system of communism as well as the economic system of socialism. Other philosophers, such as Claude Henri de Saint Simon (Bullock & Stallybrass 1977) contributed to theories supporting an economic system based on socialist, or cooperative, ideals.

Under socialist economies, governments own the basic tools of production such as manufacturing, transportation, and utilities of various kinds. The former communist nations of Europe and parts of Asia have followed this philosophy, which is often attractive because it emphasizes the fair distribution of resources and wealth, fairness in the economy, the desire that no one suffer, universally adequate housing, and so forth. Most of these economic concepts have been rejected by the former communist governments, many of which are trying to develop free market, or capitalist, economies along the lines of that in the United States.

Of course, Marx's theories were more complex than what has been stated here. He and Friedrich Engels, his close associate for many years, believed that market economic systems exploited workers for the advantage of capitalists, who in fact "stole" the labor of their workers; profits, in this view, actually belonged to the workers. When a product is produced the owner might provide the tools and the materials, but the real value is the labor that goes into making the materials into something worthwhile. Workers are never paid the full value of their work, according to this theory, and the difference between what they earn and the price of the product goes to the owner in the form of profits; therefore, labor was exploited by capitalists, who enriched themselves through the work of others. Marx envisioned an ideal society in which all of the people owned all of the tools of production; in which people received what they were entitled to, based on their needs; and in which

122

everyone worked as well as he or she could, because society belonged to everyone. A classless society without needs and a people with plenty was the Marxist ideal (Hirsch 1993).

Popple and Leighninger (1993, 15) call those who support these Marxist approaches "radicals" who "would prefer an economic system where workers have control over the conditions of their work; where goods are produced for genuine need and not to satisfy whims created by advertising; where money is not the measure of worth; and where basic rights, such as medical care and housing, are not reduced to commodity status and sold in the marketplace to the highest bidder." They add that some such radicals want a government that organizes and delivers medical care, housing, and social welfare benefits for all citizens. Of course, it is not just these so-called radicals who seek such changes. So do many liberals and conservatives and others who support what is termed by some the pursuit of social justice.

Current Critiques of Nonmarket Economies. Socialist, or planned, economies, in theory, appear to have the advantage of distributing resources satisfactorily, providing essential services, and making sure there are no absolute poor. On the other hand, critics of planned, or nonmarket-based, economies demonstrate that in truth in such economies everyone is relatively disadvantaged, people tend to lose incentive and entrepreneurial spirit, and, generally, everyone has subsistence earnings and resources but not much more than that.

In my own experience in communist countries there does appear to be a sort of shared misery rather than a shared prosperity. When I visited Cuba in 1990 I was astonished at how poor virtually everyone was. That was, as likely as not, however, a consequence of the U.S. boycott of Cuba as much as of the communist system under Fidel Castro. When I visited Romania in 1992 and 1993 I saw the remnants of communist government; here again there were certain basic advantages of the system which were quite humane. People were well educated, medical services were readily available, and there was plenty of food, although the variety and quality were poor. Prices were low; people had places to live, although they were often unattractive dwellings in large apartment houses, which some of the people said they did not enjoy. But, of course, there are variations among Marxist nations. In Cuba, for example, which has remained communist at a time when many such countries have rejected communism, citizens are permitted to own their own homes, which was not always so for those living in the former Soviet Union.

Other critics insist that capital is necessary for the operation of a national economy, and they believe that without the profit incentive there will not be sufficient investment in capital. Capitalists make a vital contribution, they say, by investing their wealth in new or expanding enterprises.

Of course, a society that has no economic problems, which is the Marxist ideal, probably would have no other problems to be addressed by human services workers. Generally, Marxists believe that most social ills are economic and that, if the economy is just, there will be a just society. In many of the former communist countries, therefore, psychology, social work, and some other human services professions were eliminated. By the 1990s many of those countries (my own experiences have been in Romania) had no social work and psychology schools nor professors and practitioners. I was pleased to be part of the efforts to help Romania reestablish its human services professions.

Some point to the Western European socialist nations, which seem to combine some of the more humane elements of socialism with some of the virtues of free enterprise economics so that life is relatively good for most people—in, for example, the Netherlands, Scandinavia, and Germany—as worthy models. Although few are terribly rich, taxes are high, and the population is not fully satisfied with every aspect of its economic life, basic needs are met.

At the same time, the nations with a fundamentally free enterprise system also seem to be doing well. Many are in Asia. For example, *Newsweek* reported on what it called the "Saigon Virus" (Moreau 1993), which is the name being used for the strong, free-enterprise economy of the former capital of what was South Vietnam. Saigon, which has been called Ho Chi Minh City since the Vietnam War, is a city of four million inhabitants, which is only 7 percent of the Vietnamese population; they account, however, for one-third of the country's industrial production, much of it based on small, family-run businesses that would have fit the definitions of a proper economy developed by Adam Smith. Much of Southeast Asia follows similar patterns. Hong Kong, Japan, Singapore, and Taiwan are among the most prosperous economies of the world, yet in some of these nations the people work long hours and lack the wage and hour protection and other labor law advantages that those in more mixed economies have. There is little doubt that strong capitalist, free-enterprise operations helped Asian nations become economically powerful.

A good bit has to do with those nations' resources. Wealthy nations with abundant natural resources, well-educated people, and capital appear to function well under free enterprise economics. Overpopulated, impoverished nations of the world, on the other hand, have sometimes pursued socialist, central planning as a means of preventing great economic need.

However, the Asian economic strength and some of Marx's critiques of capitalism came to mind in the late 1990s, when several Asian economies neared collapse. Indonesia, Japan, Korea, and Thailand, among others, were suddenly in economic decline. Some thought that the inherent desire of capitalist economies to grow had led to excessive growth—production of more goods than could be sold. In order to prevent a worldwide economic catastrophe (many non-Asian nations had invested in Asian economies and were likely to lose those investments), an organization called the International Monetary Fund loaned large amounts of money to several Asian nations. Those nations, in turn, laid off employees and otherwise cut back their economic activity such as production of goods. Perhaps the Asian experience illustrated, when Asia was growing miraculously, the truth of Adam Smith's theories. But the Marxist critiques also came into play when that miracle turned to economic disaster for many Asians.

Some modern economists are reassessing the contributions and theories of Marx. Although major discussions of his influence have been about the communist systems that were attributed to him and by and large failed, others such as Cassidy (1997) view Marx as an effective and cogent student of capitalism. Marx's basic theory is that history can best be understood by studying economics, which is all pervasive. Cassidy points out that nations, political trends, and lifestyles are influenced by nothing more than their economic circumstances. He notes that Marx shows that capitalism had achieved miracles greater than any in precapitalist history. When we compare air travel, railroads, electricity, television, and skyscrapers to the Egyptian pyramids and the Gothic cathedrals, it is easy to see what he means.

Marx also wrote about the inherent unfairness of capitalism—of the tendency for the owners to take more than the workers. In 1978, Cassidy says, typical chief executives of American corporations earned about 60 times more than their average workers. By 1995, after years of economic growth, chief executives earned 170 times more than their workers. Increasing amounts of money that might have gone for better wages go instead to company profits. And money in America continues to be redistributed from the poorest to the richest. In the 61 years from 1980 to 1996, the amount of total income that went to the top 5 percent of households grew from 15.3 percent to 20.3 percent, while the money going to the bottom 60 percent of households dropped from 34.2 to 30 percent (Cassidy 1997).

So although Marx's ideas of what societies—especially the poorest people—might do to make the society fairer were not especially viable, his analyses of and predictions about capitalism may have been largely on target.

MANAGING THE ECONOMY—
THE INFLUENCE OF JOHN MAYNARD KEYNES

The theories of government's ability to manage the economy—cooling it off when it is too hot, growing too fast, and becoming too inflationary, or heating it up and making it more effective and more responsive to economic needs—come in part from the works of John Maynard Keynes (Pennant-Rea & Emmott 1983).

In the U.S. system, Keynesian economic theory has governed American thinking for much of the time since the presidency of Franklin D. Roosevelt, which coincided with Keynes's writing and the popularization of his theories. In fact, even the free-enterprise-oriented, capitalist administrations of Ronald Reagan and George Bush tended to follow some of the fundamental teachings of Keynes. Despite the fact that authors such as Popple and Leighninger (1993) call supporters of Keynesian economics liberals, the reality is that most public officials appear to embrace Keynesian approaches, treating them as valid economic principles rather than aspects of some political point of view.

Keynes, who was from England, visited the United States during the Great Depression of the 1930s (Burns, Peltason, & Cronin 1995). He insisted that if people did not consume or invest enough, the national income would fall. He proposed that government find ways to increase expenditures on consumer goods and also investments in heavy industries such as steel and shipping facilities. If private business could not do it, government must, he said.

In many ways the 1930s New Deal programs were based upon Keynesian economic theory. Rapidly injecting money into the economy was one of the purposes of such employment and training programs as the

Works Progress Administration and the Civilian Conservation Corps. After World War II the U.S. Congress passed the Employment Act of 1946, which was designed to provide mechanisms for managing the economy but also to stimulate the economy and to pursue high levels of employment (Dolgoff, Feldstein, & Skolnik 1993). The act created the Council of Economic Advisors, one of the federal executive branch's primary mechanisms for monitoring and fine-tuning the economy. President Harry S Truman, recognizing the need for the government to take steps to maintain the health of the economy and high levels of employment, proposed the legislation (Burns, Peltason, & Cronin 1995). The policy of trying to guarantee employment to all employable people was reaffirmed in 1978 through the passage of the federal Humphrey-Hawkins Full Employment Act (Dolgoff, Feldstein, & Skolnik 1993). The goal of full employment, by requiring the government to create jobs and employ those who would not otherwise be employed, has not been implemented or seriously pursued, according to Dolgoff, Feldstein, and Skolnik (1993).

The *multiplier* and *leverage* effects are among the concepts provided by Keynes. They are discussed in more detail in a following section on the money supply. The emphasis on consumption to stimulate economic growth, referred to above, is an example of the multiplier effect, and the emphasis on investment is an example of the leverage effect. Keynes also was one of the first to show how deficit financing can help government grow—that by borrowing in the short term, governments can expand their economies. He also showed the other side of the lesson—that when things are moving along well in an economy and the economy is close to inflation, governments best serve their people by contracting the money supply, by making it more difficult to borrow, and by reducing economic activity. Keynes was one of the first to show how governments, by public policy, are able to tune an economy in ways that make it possible to keep the economy in balance, so that most people are employed, goods and services are equitably distributed, there is sufficient growth, and there is only modest inflation.

As suggested earlier in this section, it appears that conservative and liberal politicians alike concur about the value of the Keynesian approach. His findings constitute something of a law in economics, a law that is operational. Historically, as discussed in chapter 2, the most severe economic crisis ever to hit the United States was the Great Depression of the 1930s. It was the policy of the New Deal, which began in 1933, to apply Keynesian theory to modern government. The economy did, in fact, expand, and the Depression did end, and since the 1930s there has never again been as severe an economic crisis as that one. Whether or not such economic disaster will occur in the future, despite efforts to prevent it, is still unknown.

These discussions of Keynesian economic theory and government spending are crucial because many times government's expenditures are for social welfare programs. Programs for creating jobs, providing housing and financial assistance, and improving education are among the solutions to social problems; at the same time they serve those in need, these solutions add money to the economy and thus stimulate it along the lines suggested by Keynes.

The tendency throughout the world is toward mixed economies that follow the Keynesian model, provide the humanity and protection of the socialist and communist approaches, and allow the relatively free activity of economic markets under the free enterprise system. In truth, most governments, particularly Western governments and especially the U.S. government, use a mixed approach. That is, in the United States, for example, there is a high degree of emphasis on capitalism, competition, and other manifestations of Adam Smith's free enterprise approach to government. At the same time, governmental attempts to improve the economy by speeding it up or slowing it down, following the theories of John Maynard Keynes, have been encouraged. There are also many examples of government involving itself directly in human services and the redistribution of wealth, which are in some ways Marxist ideas. Government in the United States is, thus, largely mixed—although the fundamental tenets underlying it support free enterprise and capitalism.

A contemporary Harvard University economist, John Kenneth Galbraith, who is in his 90s, presented some original ideas in his works on economic principles (Cassidy 1998). Perhaps his most significant book is The Affluent Society (Galbraith 1998). Galbraith wrote about the importance of public expenditures for the common good in such examples as roads and schools. The classical capitalist objective of making profit can readily disregard public expenditures for larger social objectives.

TAXATION

One of the ways in which government affects social policy is through tax policy. By giving special advantages, for example, to social agencies and those who support them, government supports social welfare programs.

By definition, all taxation is a means for distributing the cost of government in ways that are considered just and fair by the government and its people. Taxes are not primarily a means for raising revenue, although that is typically the way we think of them. Instead, they are a way of raising revenue in a manner that citizens may believe to be rational and equitable (Snider 1965).

Governments may simply take—and have taken—the property of citizens and use it for governmental operations. It may take people and force them to labor on behalf of the government. Taxes are simply a way of making the rules explicit and of trying to find a way that distributes the burden fairly and in line with beliefs of the society. In many ways taxes reflect the values of a nation's population. When we provide tax deductions for charities and charitable contributions, for health care expenditures, and for older people, we are expressing our belief in their worth over other kinds of activities and people.

Governments always make sure they have the money to do what they want to do. The questions are simply over how they will obtain that money, from whom they will obtain it, and in what amounts.

There are three general classifications of taxes—*proportional, progressive, and regressive.* R. Pennant-Rea and B. Emmott (1983), among others, claim that a proportional tax is blind to income, that it takes the same proportion of a wealthy person's funds as a poor person's. A flat 10 percent tax on all incomes, without regard to the circumstances of the taxpayer, would be a proportional tax, which is seldom used. It has been strongly supported by Steve Forbes, who has sought the presidency of a Republican. He calls his plan a "flat tax," which is proportional and which is discussed below.

Progressive taxes require people to pay on the basis of their wealth. The more money they have, the larger share of their money is paid in taxes, and, similarly, the lower their incomes, or wealth, the lower the taxes they pay. The U.S. federal personal income tax is a progressive tax. It charges higher rates at the upper levels of income and lower rates at the lower levels; in fact, people with the lowest incomes pay little or no personal income tax. The earned income tax credit gives money to low-income families through the tax system.

There is a bias in the income tax toward those who earn their money from working as opposed to those who earn their money from investments. Those who earn money from investments may pay a larger tax on their earnings than those who earn money from working. There is also a bias in favor of families. Those who support children and other family members pay fewer dollars in taxes than those who support only themselves. As noted, too, there is a bias in favor of those who give money to charitable causes. They pay lower taxes because they do not pay taxes on the amounts that they contribute to charitable causes. Thus, the income tax, like all taxes, reflects a variety of values and government goals.

A regressive tax is one that places its burden more heavily on lower-income people than on upper-income people. The favorite example used by those who write about tax policy is the sales tax, which is charged at a certain rate—5 percent is a common amount—on purchases. Some say that the sales tax is fair because it charges everyone the same amount, that everyone faces an equal burden. In reality, however, the sales tax is regressive, because the lower one's income, the larger the percentage of one's earnings that is spent on items for which sales taxes are paid, such as food and clothing. People with great wealth spend smaller proportions of their entire wealth on items that they purchase in retail stores. They use much of their money for savings, investments, insurance, and the like, on which sales taxes are usually not charged. Therefore, there is a great difference in the percentage of one's income that is paid in sales taxes, based upon one's overall income. In some states sales taxes are not applied to necessities such as food, clothing, and shelter, which mitigates against the regressive nature of the sales tax; the lower-income families, who spend the largest parts of their incomes on such necessities, are not taxed on them, thus making the sales tax less regressive.

A taxation idea that became popular during the 1996 presidential campaign was the "flat tax," which was supported most strongly by candidate Steve Forbes but also had other adherents. The idea was to replace the progressive income tax, which is complicated and requires extensive effort to calculate for many people, with a single-rate tax for all taxpayers. Different supporters had different ideas about its amount and variations in its administration, but generally it was suggested that the rate be 15 or 20 percent. The inherent lack of progressivism in the tax would be compensated for with an exclusion for all taxpayers who earned less than a specified amount per year. Most calculations of the impact of the Forbes plan, at least, showed that it would greatly benefit the higher-wage earners and cost middle-income taxpayers more than the system that was in existence (Gibbs 1996).

In 1993 President Bill Clinton said that his administration was considering using a Value Added Tax (VAT) as a means of financing his new health care reforms. The VAT, according to Pennant-Rea and Emmott (1983), is widely used in European nations, Mexico, and other nations but, thus far, not in the United States, Canada, and Japan. The VAT is somewhat akin to the Marxist notion of the value of labor. When a raw material is turned into a finished product, it is taxed every step of the route, from beginning to end, but ultimately only the consumer pays the tax. For example, a rancher sells a head of cattle to a packing house. That rancher pays the VAT of 10 or 20 percent but passes it along as part of the price to the packing house. The packing house sells the meat that it takes from the head of cattle to a food store and also pays the VAT and passes the tax cost along to the food store. The food store sells the product to the consumer, who pays the VAT and is the only participant who does not pass along the tax.

Ultimately, the VAT can quickly and easily raise extensive revenues for the government. The consumer pays what amounts to a large national sales tax. Is the tax regressive? Perhaps it is, because it is applied to products at all stages of their manufacture. Lower-income people spend disproportionately more for products than upper-income people. This tax, however, is supposed to be easy to administer and raises revenues efficiently, and it could, in theory, replace all or part of the income tax.

Some suggest that the Social Security tax is regressive. Everyone pays the same rate on his or her earnings up to a maximum salary. The lower-income person pays his or her percentage, matched by a comparable amount from the employer, up to that maximum. The amount of one's earnings does not affect the rate paid, only the amount, thus the wealthier person pays only to the maximum and nothing above that. Social Security benefits, however, are related to one's earnings and the amount of one's contributions over time. Therefore, the lower-income worker can expect benefits upon retirement or if he or she ever becomes disabled, which are related to the amount paid into the system.

Some assert that Social Security is not a tax at all. They view it as an insurance premium that protects one against retiring in poverty, early death, or disability. Participants receive the amount they should, based upon their contributions. Benefits are based on money paid in, not on the special needs of the beneficiaries.

There are many other kinds of taxes. Some are called sin taxes.

These taxes are placed on alcohol and tobacco, for example. The assumption is that government wants to discourage the use of these products and, therefore, makes them more expensive by applying extra taxes. There are also luxury taxes on such things as jewelry, expensive vehicles, boats, and other costly items. Taxes of this kind are based on the notion that people who can afford such luxuries ought to pay more in taxes than those who cannot afford such luxuries.

There are fuel and energy taxes as well. Governments that want to control the use of fuel and energy will raise the taxes on these commodities as a way of discouraging people from wasting energy. In some European nations gasoline costs three times as much as it does in the United States.

There are also a number of tax incentives, special breaks in tax structures, to encourage some kinds of purchases or behaviors and to discourage others. For example, some states exempt food and clothing from sales taxes. Others exclude medical care and prescriptions from the sales tax. These, again, are means for making the sales tax more progressive.

There are a number of ways in which government expresses its policies and preferences through the tax structure.

THE MONEY SUPPLY

The amount of money in circulation and the value of that money are also products of governmental policy. When government wants more money in circulation, it makes it easier for banks to borrow money from the federal government and make loans to citizens. The loaning of money by banks actually creates money and expands the money supply. The more money banks loan, the more money there is in the economy. When government wants to reduce the money supply and cut down the amount of money in circulation, it makes it more expensive and difficult for banks to make loans (Snider 1965).

Government needs to control the money supply as a means of controlling inflation, which occurs when there is more money in the economy than there are available good and services, or to spur economic growth when there is not enough money being invested in the economy. Increasing the interest rate slows down the economy and helps prevent or at least control inflation. Lowering the rate tends to lead to economic investment and growth.

In the United States the executive branch of government influences the money supply, often based upon the advice of the Council of Economic Advisors, a group of three members appointed by the president with the consent of the Senate. In addition, the president annually must report to Congress on the nation's economy. The establishment of that report and the creation of the Council of Economic Advisors resulted from the passage of the Employment Act of 1946 (Burns, Peltason, & Cronin 1995). Other entities, such as the Federal Reserve Board and the Department of the Treasury, also play significant roles in studying and molding the economy.

The process of creating money works by consumers and businesses borrowing money from banks and from investment in capital growth. Banks are able to loan money, based upon their assets and their reserve requirements. For example, if the bank has a current reserve requirement of 10 percent and it makes a loan of $10,000, it must have $1,000 in assets to back the loan. The other $9,000, however, is new money, and when the borrower pays back the loan, plus the interest, the bank now has greater assets. It actually created the $9,000 by the use of its account with the Federal Reserve Bank, an independent agency which is, in essence, a bank for banks. The banks can borrow more money from the Federal Reserve, which increases its assets, and make more loans. The Federal Reserve makes it more costly for banks to borrow when it wants to restrict the money supply and less costly when it wants to expand the money supply.

Parenthetically, paper money and coins have very little to do with the amount of money in circulation. There is a great deal more money in circulation than there are bills or coins to cover it. Cash is simply a convenience that is used for some transactions. Most of the money in circulation is simply numbers in checking accounts which are transferred from one account to another (Snider 1965). Little of the money people spend is cash. Instead, it is spent through writing checks. With the widespread use of credit cards there is even less need for cash. People charge their expenditures to their credit cards, they are billed for those expenditures, and they write checks to pay the credit card bills. In the whole process no cash ever changes hands. Again, money is created by banks when they make loans; the loans are generally made in the form of credit to a customer's checking account.

One of the ways in which the money supply increases is through expenditures. Government is a major spender of funds, along with businesses. Businesses spend to increase their profits. Governments spend most often to carry out their programs; however, they sometimes spend to improve the economy. When governments and businesses spend money on anything, they increase the supply of money in the economy. When governments spend money at the lower levels of the economy, by providing assistance to low-income people, for example, the money is spent almost immediately. As it circulates through the economy—to the stores in which the people spend the money, the banks where the stores deposit their receipts, the manufacturers or farmers who make the products that are purchased or grown—the amount of money is multiplied. Therefore, government jobs programs, cash assistance programs, and food stamp programs, in addition to improving the lives of people, are means to introduce more money into the economy. Putting money into the hands of any people puts money into the hands of all people. The effect of putting money into the economy through assistance programs stimulates what is referred to as the multiplier effect, a concept developed by Keynes, as discussed below.

The leverage effect (also a Keynesian concept), on the other hand, occurs when money is introduced into the economy "at the top"—by providing financial assistance, contracts, and other benefits to large corporations and to wealthy individuals. The money, once used, again moves through the economy, although not always as rapidly as when it is introduced at the lower levels of the economy. One of the approaches tried for increasing the resources at the top of the economy has been "supply side economics" (Pennant-Rea & Emmott 1983), a central tenet of Reagan's early 1980s policy. When a major manufacturer or a very wealthy person is provided with a government contract or a tax cut or any other means of providing relief to the top of the economy, the theory goes, the money circulates and provides employment, and money in other forms, to everyone else.

Some people refer to the leverage effect as "trickle down" economics: provide money to the top earners in the economy, and they will invest it in new production, purchases, and home construction, among other things; eventually those funds will trickle down to reach everyone else. Conversely, if you put the money into the base of the economy, such as assistance programs for disadvantaged people, the money will eventually "trickle up" to the wealthiest. Spending money simply adds to economic activity and wealth.

Of course, when governments spend more than they have or more than they can justify based upon the wealth of their nation, they cause inflation. That is, if they spend money that is not worth very much— given that the wealth of the nation determines what the money is worth—they cheapen the money and stall the economy. Inflation is simply devaluation of money; it is too much money chasing too few goods. When on a given day $100 purchases only half of what it would have been able to purchase a day or month earlier, the cost has been inflated and the money has lost half its value.

Inflation typically results when money no longer reflects the value of the nation's wealth. Simply printing money, without an adequate economic base to back the amount that is printed, leads to inflation.

Social policy is affected by monetary policy in many ways, and social policies influence the money system. In the simplest terms, when there is a large supply of money available, there are more resources for social services of all kinds, and governments are more likely to appropriate those funds for such services than they are when money is in short supply. Similarly, social programs usually benefit the lowest-income individuals and families in the nation most directly. Those individuals and families, of necessity, spend nearly all the money available to them. In some cases, through borrowing, they spend more money than they have available. The multiplier effect comes rapidly into play when the money is spent, and the trickling up through the economy is often dramatic. The ultimate result is often a stronger or at least more active economy as well as increases in tax revenues, often larger in amount than the social services expenditures were.

When the money supply contracts and interest rates increase, there is less investment by businesses, which often results in reduced employment. This, in turn, can cause greater social needs. In many ways social policies are a central factor in the operations of an economy and represent significant economic as well as social functions.

Deficit Financing

There is extensive discussion in the United States about the virtues and vices of federal deficit financing. Deficit financing is another form of governmental finance in which government borrows money and uses that money for its own operations. It is a tax because, ultimately, the money and the interest on the debt, which is paid to those who loaned the government money, are paid by taxpayers. According to the *Pocket Economist* (Pennant-Rea & Emmott 1983), deficit financing is the act of allowing a budget deficit as a way of putting money into the economy and expanding the demand for goods and services. Governments may sometimes simply expand the amount of money in circulation, but, in the United States, the money is borrowed from lenders and paid back to them.

It should be noted that deficit financing is only an option for the federal government. Only sovereign, or autonomous, nations that control their own money supplies are able to add to the nation's economy through some of the mechanisms already discussed. Similarly, only sovereign nations—such as Germany and Mexico—can issue bonds to spur investment and participate in the kinds of borrowing and lending discussed in this section. Most state governments, by law, must operate on strictly balanced budgets. They must show that their revenue estimates will pay for their planned expenditures. If their revenue estimates fall short and less money is available than was anticipated when the budget was developed, they must reduce expenditures for the rest of the fiscal year so that it will end with a balanced budget.

Of course, some states are permitted to borrow—from retirement funds and other trust funds and from banks—but they must pay back the loans plus interest, just as they would pay for any other expenditure. Only the federal government may determine that it wants to borrow money and authorize itself to borrow and spend more through the issuance of bonds, treasury notes, and other financial instruments. State governments generally must spend only as much as they receive in taxes. If they need more money, they must borrow it from banks, just as families must.

Despite the criticism and expressions of concern, however, deficit financing is often a convenient and efficient way to improve a nation's economic situation. Like individual citizens, nations are able to do things through borrowing, which they could not do with cash. An individual might want to purchase a house and do so by borrowing money. Saving the money for the house, on the other hand, might require twenty years. Borrowing the money and paying off a mortgage may make it possible for the person to live in the house twenty years sooner. That is not terribly different than a national government borrowing money to undertake new projects without cutting back on other services and without waiting to save the money through tax revenues.

There is one essential difference between borrowing by a national government and individual borrowing: the individual must eventually pay back the money. Individuals and families ultimately die, while nations do not. One always hears, in discussions of deficit financing, that by borrowing money, we are mortgaging the quality of life of our children and grandchildren. That sounds reasonable, but, in reality, a nation's debt can go on forever. The children, grandchildren, great-great-grandchildren need not pay the debt back either. They can simply continue paying interest and borrowing more to pay off old debts, into infinity. The nation is not going anywhere and does not have the same constraints a family has.

This does not mean there are no consequences for nations that do not pay their debts. They may find it impossible to borrow, to buy the products of other nations, or even to sell their own goods on world markets. Nations that have become economically unsound have typically experienced widespread poverty, revolutions, and other severe problems. In addition, the interest payments on the debt are a major item in the national budget. Paying for the interest competes with all other demands for money, including social welfare programs. The national debt occupies a larger and larger share of the national budget and thus reduces the amounts of money available for appropriation for social needs.

It is important to note that deficit financing is far from a universally accepted idea. Many political figures campaign against it. There has been a national movement to introduce and adopt a new amendment to the U.S. Constitution which would require the government to operate with a balanced budget, the so-called balanced budget amendment (Burns, Peltason, & Cronin 1995). At times the movement has been strong and popular, although, at the time this is being written, it is not often reported in the media as a change that is being actively pursued. Nevertheless, President Clinton campaigned on a promise to reduce the federal deficit over a period of several years and has been proposing fiscal measures that would achieve that goal. Congress has also attempted to reduce the deficit through legislation, the most important of which has been the Graham-Rudman-Hollings bill, which focuses on balancing the budget.

In 1995, as part of the Republican Contract with America, additional efforts were made to eliminate the budget deficit over a period of years, efforts with which President Clinton continued to agree. However, the approach of Congress was to eliminate the deficit and cut taxes at the same time, largely through eliminating and reducing government programs. There was special emphasis on reducing social welfare programs. The President tended to oppose the depth of the social welfare reductions approved by Congress. The desire for a balanced budget became a major point of contention between the president and Congress in 1995 and 1996, resulting in deadlocks that closed down many federal agencies for periods of days and weeks. However, in 1997 Congress passed and Bill Clinton signed the Balanced Budget Act, which was to provide for a balanced budget. In fact, the last federal budgets of the twentieth century were balanced.

Some observers point out that deficit financing has further policy implications. When the government operates through borrowing, who receives the interest? Generally, the debt is to other Americans, often the most wealthy Americans, who own the Federal Reserve notes and other fiscal instruments through their own investments. Therefore, the interest goes to the wealthy. K. Phillips (1990) points out that during the presidency of Ronald Reagan the U.S. debt and deficit increased because taxes were reduced without a comparable reduction in spending. The borrowing which was necessary increased U.S. expenditures on interest paid on the debt, which went from $96 billion in 1982 to $216 billion in 1988. Because taxes were reduced at the same time, fewer dollars earned with that interest were repaid to the federal treasury as taxes. Phillips points out that the increase in the deficit combined with the decrease in taxes had a great deal to do with the U.S. redistribution of wealth which took place in the 1980s. During that time the wealthiest Americans had major increases in their incomes; the middle-income groups either stayed the same or experienced slight increases in wealth; while the lowest-income individuals, who have few investments and whose benefit programs were either reduced or not expanding, declined (Ginsberg 1995). Therefore, it is clear that deficit financing has an impact on individual taxpayers and the distribution of the burden of paying for government services.

THE BUDGET PROCESS

Economics and finance are such important components of social policy that they are central to much of the work done by the executive and legislative branches every year in the form of budgeting and budget preparation. The budget process continues throughout the year in the federal and state governments. (For a current, sound, and detailed discussion of the budget process, see Burns, Peltason, & Cronin 1995.) The budget process begins well before the end of the budget, or fiscal, year, which at this time is 1 October–30 September in the federal government and which varies among the state governments. The most common state fiscal year is 1 July–30 June, although some use the calendar year as the fiscal year.

In the federal executive branch the president proposes a budget to the Congress each year, which is based upon the estimates and requests of all the government agencies. The executive branch has an agency called the Office of Management and Budget (OMB), which studies all of the budget requests and makes a recommendation to the president for the new fiscal year. The president proposes the budget, which is a massive document, to Congress, where it is again studied by a number of groups, especially the Senate Finance Committee and the House of Representatives Ways and Means Committee. Congress also has an agency called the Congressional Budget Office, which serves as something of an auditor and planner on financial matters.

The Office of Management and Budget and the Congressional Budget Office both have large staffs of experts on every phase of government. They carefully study the agencies' budget requests and try to determine the impact of those requests as well as the impact of any recommended changes in them. How many fewer people might be served, for example, if the budget for food stamps were reduced? What level of health care will be available with the recommended appropriation for Medicaid? The policy experts in these two offices are familiar enough with the programs to make knowledgeable recommendations for budget or appropriations levels. Those who work within the programs find that influencing the staff of these two organizations may be more significant in producing results than anything else they might do in trying to improve their programs.

Ultimately, the president's executive budget, which specifies both income and expenditures, is acted upon by Congress after careful study by the two committees. There is intense negotiation, and at times conflict, between the executive and legislative branches about the budget. In fact, it is the budget that has caused most of the recent conflicts between the federal executive and legislative branches. The tax increases passed by Congress and signed by President Bush during his term of office were a source of conflict and of strong political maneuvering. In fact, the issue of taxes was probably the most widely discussed subject in the 1992 presidential campaign that followed. By 1993 President Clinton engaged in—and prevailed in—a major conflict with Congress over the economic program he was proposing for the coming fiscal year.

The president exercises some control over the budget with the veto power. However, the president must either accept and sign the budget or veto all of it. As discussed earlier, Congress passed a bill to provide the president with the "line item veto," which allowed Clinton, the only president to whom it applied, to pick and choose among the items in the budget, vetoing only some of them. However, the judiciary found the line item veto unconstitutional.

The federal budget also shows, at this time, deficit financing such as the amount that will be borrowed, the amount of interest expected to be paid, and the overall balance sheet of anticipated revenues, expenses, borrowing, and deficits.

Budgets are essentially plans. Less money may come to the treasury from taxes than is anticipated, or more money may be raised. Agencies may not choose to spend all of the money appropriated for them, or they may receive some additional money during the fiscal year to carry out a specific objective or to avoid reducing services to clients.

The state budget process is in some ways similar to but also strikingly different from the federal process. For example, states in general must always present and operate under a balanced budget. It is a violation of the law in most cases for the state to operate in a deficit position. And in most states, as mentioned, the governor has line item veto power and can eliminate or reduce a specific budget item without vetoing the whole appropriations bill.

As in the national government, on the state level there are professional staffs in both the executive and legislative branches whose members know about all the various state agencies, study their budget requests, and help develop the final budget legislation. In most states it is the governor who presents the executive budget, which is, as it is in the federal process, the most important working document in the fiscal planning process. In a few states a board of the key elected official develops and presents the budget on behalf of a kind of executive committee. Those are generally states with weak governors. Even in those states, however, the governor presents an executive budget, although it does not have the same importance as the executive budget has in states with strong governors. Even in the states with weak governors the governor has the line item veto power and exercises it often in creating the budget bill.

The bill that is finally passed is usually a combination of the executive budget and changes made to it by the legislative branch. Battles over the budget are so important that in many states, and at times in the federal government, the budget does not pass the legislative body and become law until the fiscal year ends. In those situations the state often passes a kind of bill called a "continuing resolution," which allows government to spend money at the same level as it did in the prior year for the functions specified in the now-expired budget. Failing to do so, which has happened from time to time, may mean that essential services are abandoned and that government employees are not paid for their services or required to work. Such situations usually last only a few days because they paralyze the government so that everyone works to resolve the problems and pass a budget.

An issue that often becomes critical in budget debates is the efficiency of government, or its avoidance of duplication of services. The Congressional Budget Office and many private groups, including lobbying groups, study the budgets of the state and federal governments and look for ways to eliminate waste and conserve funds. A popular book, *Government Racket* (Gross 1992), summarizes the problems of duplication and waste in a variety of federal government programs.

In American state and national government there is nothing quite so fascinating as the ways in which presidents, governors, Congress, and state legislatures deal with the budget. It is the budget that contains the real details of social policy, and it is the budget that reflects what government wants to do and will do in a multitude of specific programs and procedures.

CONCLUSION

The levels of and the ways in which government finances itself have great impact on the levels of human services programs that government is willing to sustain. Spending money on social welfare programs may have a very positive impact on the economy through the multiplier effect. Spending too much may cause inflation, which is often harmful to everyone because, no matter how little or how much money they have, it is worth less than it would have been had there been less or no inflation.

It is important to understand that economic policy and social policy are closely connected and that government can increase and decrease the money available to citizens through its own policy decisions. Budget and finance policies are the highest form of social policy in some ways. In fact, there is no such thing as a social policy that does not have some financial implications. Therefore, understanding social policy also requires an understanding of economic policy. What is and is not done in the social policy field is always related to some form of economic issues.

DISCUSSION QUESTIONS

1. Are social welfare programs more likely to have an impact through the "multiplier" or the "leverage" effect? Explain your answer.
2. This chapter suggests that the free market, classic economic theory of Adam Smith is fundamental in the U.S. economy. Try to list three examples, not already used in the chapter, of the ways in which free market economic principles are followed in the U.S. economy.
3. Describe some of the ways in which the U.S. economy appears to be a "mixed" economy. Identify elements from all three economic approaches discussed in this chapter.
4. John Maynard Keynes is considered a giant in economic theory because of the contributions he made to showing governments how they might control their economies. In your own words, describe what you believe are some of the practical consequences of Keynes's economic discoveries.

REFERENCES

Bullock, A., & Stallybrass, O. (1977). *The Harper dictionary of modern thought.* New York: Harper & Row.

Burns, J. M., Peltason, J. W., & Cronin, T. E. (1995). *Government by the people,* 16th ed. Englewood Cliffs, NJ: Prentice-Hall.

Cassidy, J. (1997, October 20, 27). The next thinker: The return of Karl Marx. *New Yorker,* 248–289.

Cassidy, J. (1998, November 30). Profile: Height of eloquence. *New Yorker,* 70–75.

Dolgoff, R., Feldstein, D., & Skolnik, L. (1993). *Understanding social welfare,* 3d ed. New York: Longman.

Galbraith, J. (1998). *The affluent society,* 40th anniversary edition. Novia Scotia: Mariner Books.

Gibbs, N. (1996, January 29). Knock 'em flat. *Time,* 22–27.

Ginsberg, L. (1987). Economic, political, and social context. In A. Ninahan et al. (Eds.), *Encyclopedia of social work,* 18th ed. Silver Spring, MD: NASW Press, xxxiii–xli.

Ginsberg, L. (1995). *Social work almanac,* 2d ed. Washington, DC: NASW Press.

Greenberg, E. S. (1989). *The American political system: A radical approach,* 5th ed. Glenview, IL: Scott, Foresman, Little.

Gross, M. L. (1992). *Government racket: Washington waste from A to Z.* New York: Bantam.

Hirsch, E. D. (1993). *The dictionary of cultural literacy: What every American needs to know.* Boston: Houghton Mifflin.

Moreau, R. (1993, April 12). The "Saigon virus": It's catching—business is booming in South Vietnam. *Newsweek,* 71 (15), 34–38.

Pennant-Rea, R., & Emmott, B. (1983). *The pocket economist.* Cambridge: Cambridge University Press.

Phillips, K. (1990). *The politics of rich and poor.* New York: Random House.

Popple, P. R., & Leighninger, L. (1993). *Social work, social welfare, and American society,* 2d ed. Boston: Allyn & Bacon.

Smith, A. (1910). *The wealth of nations.* New York: Knopf (Everyman's Library). Original edition published in 1776.

Snider, D. A. (1965). *Economic myth and reality.* Englewood Cliffs, NJ: Prentice-Hall.

Chapter Six

The Descriptive Component: Economic Assistance and Entitlements

A fundamental requirement for understanding social policy is understanding social programs. Throughout this book, programs—or, as they are sometimes called, provisions—are discussed as the outcomes of social policy. Problems are addressed through the development of policies, and programs are developed to implement the policies and resolve the problems.

In this book programs are discussed and described as examples of public policy and analysis and as benchmarks in the historical development of social welfare and social work. This chapter and the chapter that follows are designed to describe the basic categories of social welfare programs and certain facts about the programs to provide an understanding of the American social welfare system and the ways in which it operates.

Although social programs are an important part of overall American government and charitable activity, they are not as well known as one might expect among American citizens. It is critical, however, that human services workers, especially social workers, have a detailed and working understanding of social programs. In many ways social programs are the subject matter of social work and other human services professions, just as medicine is the subject matter of physicians and law the subject matter of attorneys. Social programs are what social and other human services workers use, in addition to their own professional skills for serving clients, to help people. A knowledge of social programs is indispensable for every kind of practice in every kind of situation, yet it must be understood that even the most experienced human services professionals cannot know the details of all the programs that are available to their clients at all times and in all places. Learning about programs and keeping up with their development is, for the human services worker, the equivalent of the physician maintaining current knowledge about medical advances.

FAMILIARITY WITH SOCIAL PROGRAMS

There are several reasons social programs are not as well known to the general public as other programs such as education and health care. First, information about social programs is not typically taught to students in elementary or secondary schools. In most cases students in higher education—unless they happen to be students of social work or social problems or policy courses in fields such as political science, psychology, and sociology—learn little about social programs. In college curricula there is usually no requirement for the study of such issues, although students may be exposed to them through elective courses or through the selection of specific social sciences as part of their basic undergraduate requirements.

For many social work students at the baccalaureate and graduate levels social work courses are the first in which they learn about such fundamental social services as Social Security, mental health, child welfare, and corrections.

Second, most Americans, especially younger Americans, do not have very much contact with social services systems. We all pay Social Security taxes and Medicare taxes. We may hear about or read about social services programs in the media, and we may even have relatives or friends who are recipients of social welfare programs and services. Yet, personal involvement with the social services is not a typical experience for healthy, relatively prosperous American young people and their families. Many people come to social agencies for the first time when they encounter a disabling personal or family crisis such as mental illness, unemployment, or severe physical illness and have no knowledge or skills for gaining access to the services that are available to them.

As other parts of this book demonstrate, the recipients of social welfare services are typically special groups, such as older people; young mothers who, because of lack of support from the fathers of their children, need financial assistance; children who cannot live with their own families and therefore become part of the foster care or adoption systems; aspiring adoptive parents; foster parents; people with a variety of physical and mental disabilities; and those who encounter difficulty with the law.

Even when they are all added together, the groups who receive social services constitute a relatively small proportion of the American society. More important, they are often isolated geographically and generationally from college students and many employed adults. At some point during their lives, most Americans have some contact with social programs—when they retire, when their parents are ill, when they become unemployed—but, so long as everything in their lives is satisfactory, most have little or no contact with social services programs or agencies.

Third, even political figures are reluctant to discuss social welfare programs in great detail during elections. Those who speak most about social welfare programs typically oppose them, using them as a surrogate enemy that stands for "government waste," poor economic policy, and a number of other negative indicators against which political campaigns may be launched. Consequently, a detailed knowledge of American social welfare programs is a requirement for most people who are newly exposed to the human services professions.

WHAT ARE THE PROGRAMS?

It is a practical impossibility to describe in detail all of the social welfare programs that operate in the United States. The programs are extensive and complex. Many who work in them full-time for decades do not know every detail of all of the programs in their own organizations.

A conscientious study of social welfare programs would include some comparative analysis of services in the United States with services in other nations. Adding the international dimension makes it even less likely that a human services curriculum would be able to describe comprehensively all of the relevant programs and services. Even if it were technically possible to do so, it would also be challenging because the programs are constantly changing through judicial, legislative, and executive actions, as chapters 4 and 5 suggest. But even if all the roadblocks to describing every program in detail were removed, doing so would probably prove to be so boring for most students that instructors and authors would not attempt such comprehensive descriptions.

Reference works such as the *Encyclopedia of Social Work*, 19th ed. (Edwards et al. 1995), *The Social Work Dictionary*, 3d ed. (Barker 1995), and

Social Work Almanac, 2d ed. (Ginsberg 1995) provide the kinds of descriptive information on individual programs which can help students understand enough to write about them or bring them to the attention or benefit of their clients. Information and referral services operate in most communities so that those who are in need of services can find out what the services are and how they operate.

It is necessary for beginning students as well as those at any level of professional practice to remember that there are several broad categories of services. The eligibility rules and the nature of the specific services available to specific individuals or families vary considerably.

Income Maintenance

Income maintenance services are those that help people with their basic financial requirements such as buying food, paying rent, paying for medical services, purchasing clothing, and meeting other fundamental needs. In the United States income maintenance is subdivided in a variety of ways. The basis for most income maintenance programs in the United States is the Social Security Act of 1935, the development of which is described in chapter 2.

A Non-Means-Tested Program. Income maintenance programs are divided into those that are "means tested" and those that are not. R. L. Barker (1995) says that a means test is one that evaluates a person's financial resources and uses the results to determine that person's eligibility for services. The largest and most important income maintenance program in Social Security is the Old Age Survivors and Disability Insurance, or OASDI, which is available to elderly, blind, and disabled people as well as to survivors of persons who were covered by Social Security but are now deceased. The amount of OASDI depends upon a variety of factors, including the length of time the person worked in employment for which Social Security taxes were paid, age, and income when he or she worked. In the case of families that are collecting benefits under the coverage of a deceased wage earner, the amount paid depends upon the factors already mentioned plus the number of children in the family who are eighteen or under.

OASDI is an example of a non-means-tested program. The means of the recipient are not a factor in determining benefits, just as they are not a factor in receiving benefits from a private insurance policy. That is, the wealth or poverty of the recipient is not a factor in determining eligibility or the amount of the benefit. A very wealthy person may receive a significant amount of money in monthly benefits based solely upon his or her earnings, age, and the number of years payments were made to Social Security. A very poor person may receive no more than the legal minimum, no matter how great his or her needs may be. The specific amounts of OASDI change each year to reflect inflation. In 1997 the maximum amount was $14,976 per year for an individual and $22,464 for a couple (Bernstein and Ma 1996). However, because benefits depend on one's earnings, the amounts vary. The average is much lower than the maximums.

Some Americans doubt that OASDI, which many call by the more popular name Social Security, will be available to them when they retire. Actually, the Social Security Trust Fund has enough money to cover retirees and people who become disabled or die for the next several decades. At many times since the act was passed in 1935, adjustments have been required in Social Security payments and in benefits. If the program encounters great problems in the future, it is likely that it will be revised rather than abandoned. Because many Americans depend on or will depend on the program, eliminating it would be a cause of major social and economic dislocations probably more costly to resolve than maintaining the existing system would be.

Of course, there are regulations governing OASDI that prevent recipients from collecting maximum benefits while continuing to work for relatively high earnings during their early retirement years. And recipients who have other income must pay taxes on a portion of the OASDI benefits. Ultimately, therefore, wealth has some impact on the benefits one may retain after taxes. Yet to calculate the specific benefits no means test is used.

Entitlement Programs

One of the complicated terms in social welfare is *entitlement*. According to Barker (1995, 121) an entitlement is "services, goods, or money due to an individual by virtue of a specific status." He goes on to define an entitlement program as a government-sponsored benefit that is due to people who are in a specific class. It is important to note that entitlements are provided as a right, not as charity. That is true not only of the benefits to which people contribute, such as OASDI, but also of assistance that is paid for with general government funds raised through taxes. A service is an entitlement because the laws establishing it say that people in a specific class are legally entitled to that service. Governments have no discretion over eligibility; if someone fits the defined status or class, he or she need only apply for the service to receive it. A good bit of thinking, especially conservative economic and political thinking, finds the concept of entitlements repellent. If one person is entitled to something, that means someone else is obligated to provide it, says Block (1986), among others. Others who are more supportive of welfare assistance, such as Peter Edelman (1997), believe that *entitlement* is a perfectly good term. It simply means, says Edelman, who resigned from the Clinton administration because of his disappointment with the president's signing the new welfare law, that the state is entitled to funds that will benefit citizens who are entitled to the help. However, it is unlikely that the term will be used frequently in the future to describe assistance programs; it has too many negative connotations for those who were instrumental in developing and putting the new welfare law into effect.

Income Maintenance and the 1996 Law.   In 1996 Congress passed the Personal Responsibility and Work Opportunity Reconciliation Act, which represented major changes in the ways income maintenance is handled in the United States (see additional discussions in earlier chapters). The fundamental change in the new welfare law, which is the most significant change since national public assistance came into existence with the Social Security Act of 1935, has been to end the national character of the welfare program and turn substantial portions of it over to the states.

In the 1930s four welfare programs were established, and each of them was a state program that used federal matching funds—the amount depending upon the per capita income of the citizens of the state. Those four programs were Aid to Dependent Children, Old Age Assistance, Aid to the Disabled, and Aid to the Blind. In 1975 the three "adult categories" were integrated into a new federal assistance program, Supplemental Security Income, which provides for a standard assistance payment to people who are aged, blind, or disabled and who are also poor.

Supplemental Security Income.   There are strict limits on the amount of assets someone may have and also draw SSI, as the program is popularly known. Those who have more than the maximum amount of assets, including cash and life insurance, must spend those assets before becoming eligible. The monthly SSI grant per individual in 1997 was $484. For an eligible couple, the amount was $726. These three categories—aged, blind, and disabled—remained part of SSI. Supplemental Security Income also covers some of the financial needs of children with disabilities, although their families may have relatively large assets. In the revised law, however, eligibility has been redetermined for many children with disabilities who were included in SSI before the change in the law. In 1997 some 95,000 children who had been receiving SSI lost those benefits. Many fell into a category of recipients eliminated when maladaptive behavior was eliminated as a reason for receiving the aid. (Pizzagati 1997). Although some states subsidize their residents' federal SSI payments (from a token of less than ten dollars in some states to several hundred dollars in others), the program relies primarily on federal financing.

In the original Personal Responsibility and Work Opportunity Reconciliation Act of 1996, SSI and Medicaid benefits for immigrants were strictly limited. Even legal aliens who had not yet attained citizenship and who may have been receiving SSI for years were to be cut off the program in 1997. However, the 1997 Balanced Budget Act (National Association of Social Workers 1997) rescinded those plans for legal immigrants who were living in the U.S. by August 22, 1996, the day the new welfare law was signed by the president. That change restored benefit eligibility to some 350,000 immigrants. However, later arrivals were not eligible for assistance, no matter what their legal status. The Balanced Budget Act also extended eligibility for assistance programs to seven years for legal immigrants who arrived after the new law passed. The assumption was that by the time that deadline had passed, the immigrants would have attained citizenship.

Aid to Families with Dependent Children (AFDC). The program for families and children, which was originally known as Aid to Dependent Children and renamed Aid to Families with Dependent Children in the 1960s, continued to be a federal-state-financed program. The state determined the amount of the grant, based on formulas for determining financing need—although few states paid what their own calculations determined would be the need level for a family with children. However, the program had a national character, and there were many rules and regulations that required all states to operate the program in similar ways. Standards for the amount of assets a family could own, for example, were set nationally. Rules on eligibility were clearly established. Mothers, married or single, widowed, or divorced, were eligible to receive assistance for themselves and their children if they met the poverty guidelines. Families of specific sizes were treated in the same way, no matter that their children might have been born while they were receiving aid. And families were eligible for help so long as they needed it until their youngest child was older than eighteen, even though they may have received help for many years. These features were controversial, and many American policy makers and critics said that AFDC, as it was operated, created dependency. There were strong efforts made to eliminate or revise it in major ways. President Clinton suggested, when he ran in 1992, that he would work toward the elimination of welfare as it then existed. Attacks on the AFDC program were also central to the Contract with America, discussed earlier, and to the thinking and writing of House of Representatives Speaker Newt Gingrich.

Temporary Assistance to Needy Families. Under the revised law, AFDC was eliminated and replaced with a program, TANF (pronounced TANIF, Temporary Assistance for Needy Families).

The major change in the program lies in the delegation of administration and standards to the states in the form of block grants, with many fewer restrictions and requirements than the former AFDC program. Now states can exercise great latitude concerning the way in which the program will be administered, how much assistance families will receive, and what some of the requirements will be. The federal formula for helping states pay for welfare assistance to low-income families continued with states with lower per capita income receiving a greater percentage than states with higher per capita income.

However, the federal government also set some strict guidelines for the TANF program. The primary change, as well as the most dramatic, was the end of AFDC as a program of entitlement for those who qualified for it for as long as they were eligible to receive it. Under TANF a lifetime limit of five years of assistance was placed on families. That is, even if they remained poor for ten years or twenty, they could receive assistance only for five.

The new federal law also gives the states the right to make the time limits shorter. Several states cut the length of time families could receive assistance to no more than two years for a lifetime. The five-year federal limit is a maximum, not an entitlement or right. States may also refuse to add to the assistance of families that have additional children while they are receiving benefits.

The federal rules also allow states to exempt up to 20 percent of their recipients from the five-year limit if they choose to do so (some states do and some states do not). States may also, of course, provide any kind and level of benefits they choose to disadvantaged families.

The revised federal law also expands work requirements for assistance recipients and demands that every state place a substantial portion of their recipients in work sites within two years after they begin receiving assistance. Each year, the specific requirement for the percentage of clients working is increased. By 2002, 50 percent of the clients must be employed. The work requirements had been implemented into the assistance programs over a long period of time, beginning in 1981 with the Ronald Reagan administration, which allowed for community work experience for clients under specified circumstances if a state chose to exercise the option.

The TANF program is outlined in appendix 2, which contains a description of its major features. Several of those features are additional restrictions on assistance to low-income families, especially one-parent families. For example, women who are teenage mothers cannot receive assistance on their own if they are living independently. They must reside with their parents or in another approved adult residential situation. They must also be studying for a high school diploma or GED or be participants in some other state-approved educational or training activity. But states may, if they choose, deny benefits to any teen parent. States are given a bonus for reducing their illegitimacy rate. There are also special funds set aside for states that encounter large amounts of unemployment.

Food Stamp Restrictions. The new law changed more than the family assistance program. It also instituted major restrictions on the provision of food stamps. Initially, some adult food stamp recipients without dependents were restricted to just three months of benefits every three years. Benefits for those adults in need of financial help were liberalized through changes in the law which were incorporated in the Balanced Budget Act (National Association of Social Workers 1997).

Child Support Enforcement. There is an important federal-state program designed to locate parents who should be but are not paying child support. It is called the Child Support Enforcement Program, and it is required to operate in every state. The failure of families to receive adequate child support is the most important reason for their eligibility (Committee on Ways and Means, U.S. House of Representatives 1993). Therefore, families are required to cooperate with the Child Support Enforcement Program if they receive TANF so that the state can attempt to find the absent parent and obtain support from that parent. The Child Support program is also available to non-TANF families. For a small fee—as little as one dollar in some states—the program will attempt to locate the absent parent through Social Security numbers and other data provided by the parent receiving assistance if the absent parent's whereabouts are unknown; arrange for a court to determine the absent parent's child support liability; and enforce the court order with deductions from the absent parent's wages, tax refunds, and benefit payments. The objective is to get financial support for the child as well as to force absent parents to meet their obligations, sometimes through punishment such as fines and imprisonment.

The policy associated with child support programs is that legal parents or guardians of children are expected to pay for their care. In addition to the public programs for securing support payments that result from court orders, there is also a variety of private resources, such as certain businesslike organizations or attorneys who specialize in obtaining child support—that help families who are having difficulty receiving the support to which they are entitled.

Some writers who opposed AFDC would probably not feel comfortable with or positive about the TANF program, either. George Gilder, in an article in *American Spectator* (1995), said that the AFDC system tended to make low-income women economically superior to low-income men and diminished the possibility that men who were not self-sufficient would become so. He says that the program drove men, especially African American men, into socially and economically subordinate positions. Spending money to place low-income women in jobs and away from their children, as the AFDC program eventually did and the TANF program does, is expensive and requires massive government expenditures. He would have preferred a program that supported marriage and built male competence. He even raised questions about child support enforcement, something that is usually supported by both liberals and conservatives and by welfare reformers of every orientation, because it takes assets and opportunities away from men and gives more to women. Although he thought family allowances were the best solution, as is discussed in chapter 8, his basic belief, like Murray's (1994), is that all government assistance programs should be eliminated because they cause dependence rather than cure it.

Abramovitz says in the 1997 supplement to the authoritative *Encyclopedia of Social Work* that the replacement of AFDC with TANF could cause harm to poor and working class people, especially women and children. In her analysis of the reasons for the changes, Abramovitz compares the two programs and suggests the need for political action to overcome the threats to families resulting from the more restrictive TANF.

Even before the new welfare program had been in effect long enough to be evaluated, there were significant changes under way in assistance services for low-income people. President Bill Clinton noted that the welfare rolls had their largest drop in the history of social welfare programs. He said that caseloads fell by 3.1 million people between January 1993, when he assumed office, and April 1997, before the bill became law in July 1997 (Associated Press 1997).

It is possible that the rolls decreased because new clients, believing they would not be eligible, did not replace the large numbers who left the program—as clients have done throughout the history of federally supported welfare assistance. The period during which the declines occurred was also one of great economic activity and job creation. President Clinton also noted that 12.5 million jobs had been created during his presidency. The availability of jobs often reduces the numbers of people who need and apply for financial assistance.

As the economic services associated with the Personal Responsibility and Work Opportunity Reconciliation Act began to be implemented, critiques in the media questioned the consequences of the massive changes the revised law made.

The possibility of requiring assistance recipients to work for their benefits began in 1981 under the federal budget Omnibus Budget Reconciliation Act. That act permitted the states to require clients to participate in community work experience programs. The author of this text, while serving as Commissioner of Human Services in West Virginia, led the implementation of those requirements in that state, an effort that received national and international coverage in publications such as the *Wall Street Journal* and *People* and on television networks in the United States and Great Britain. The idea was popular—put people to work for what they receive. In West Virginia we found that the clients were pleased with the opportunity to be employed. Most did not object to working for their benefits, and most preferred work to simply receiving assistance.

A number of studies on the implementation of work requirements help explain the complexities and costs of those efforts. Several are published by the Manpower Demonstration Research Corporation of New York, a major research organization dealing with welfare reform and work programs, which contracted with foundations and state governments to evaluate a variety of work initiatives. Another study is by O'Neill and O'Neill (1997), and yet another, edited by Garth Mangum and Stephen Mangum (1996), honors Sar A. Levitan, one of the major writers and scholars on work programs and other efforts to improve social policy for the disadvantaged.

Generally, studies of work programs, along with the experiences of Congress in attempting to implement its new legislation, show that such programs may have long-range advantages in that they make recipients of assistance independent and economically self-sufficient. In the short run, however, they cost government more than simply giving assistance because they require child care arrangements, training programs, supervision, job finding, tools, uniforms, workers' compensation coverage, and all of the other costs associated with working. Policy developers often overlook these additional costs, which are an important consideration in efforts to reduce dependency and increase participation in the work force.

Of course, all three of these income maintenance programs can work together. One family may have a Social Security recipient, for example, who may also be eligible for Supplemental Security Income because the Social Security payments are less than SSI would provide. In such a case the recipient would receive a combined payment of no more than the SSI payment level. The children in the family may also make them eligible for TANF in some states. The complexities of calculating the amounts of payments and the degrees of eligibility are great and often require specialized computer programs for definitive answers. The greater latitude given the states under TANF makes the calculation of income maintenance benefits even more complex.

An entitlement program for low-income people that is of growing importance is the Earned Income Tax Credit. Under the program, employed people with low earnings are able to receive the equivalent of cash income tax refund that may be significantly more than their overall tax payments. This is like the "negative income tax" proposed by the Friedmans (1980) as an alternative to assistance payments.

The programs that have been described are cash income maintenance programs. That is, clients receive cash assistance that they can use for necessities. In some few cases in which assistance clients demonstrate that they are incapable of properly caring for themselves or their children—because they spend their assistance funds without paying for their necessities—states may establish "vendor payments" in which the government directly pays landlords, utility companies, and other debtors so that a family's basic requirements are fulfilled by the assistance (Ginsberg 1983). States have more options under TANF, but they will be able to make "vendor" payments if they choose. The TANF program allows more restrictions on clients such as requiring teenage mothers to live with their parents or other responsible adults if they are to receive assistance.

Workers' Compensation Programs. Another of the important income maintenance programs in the United States is provided under the title of workers' (or, in some states, workmen's) compensation. Those programs compensate working people and their families for illnesses, injuries, or deaths that are connected with employment. Each state has a program, but each state program (and the levels of compensation it offers) is different. In general, the programs are funded by taxes or insurance premiums paid by employers. In some states the government collects the fees and pays the benefits. In some states companies purchase coverage from private insurance companies, which administer the benefits. In yet other states there is a combination of state-operated and insurance company-operated programs.

Workers' compensation is paid to those who sustain injuries in connection with their work or who become ill because of that work. The coverage, however, is not only for industrial accidents or illnesses. Employees who are injured in auto accidents while they are on duty, for example, may be entitled to benefits such as payment for their medical care and financial support while they are recovering. If they are killed in the accident, their families may receive financial support. Industrial illnesses caused by environmental problems in the workplace and other factors may make workers eligible for health care and income maintenance assistance.

Workers' compensation is not means tested. That is, eligibility is based upon the fact that the worker was injured or killed in connection with work. That, and not the financial needs of the worker, is the criterion.

Pensions and Insurance. Self-employed people and those employed by others may also be covered for income maintenance and retirement pensions through publicly or privately financed insurance

156

programs. In some cases individuals purchase their own coverage, and in others their employers pay all or part of the costs. Employees of government typically receive some kind of retirement benefits, and the same is true of most employees of large corporations and many other organizations. When the individuals retire, they receive pensions that may be combined with Social Security retirement. These pensions may be the basis for retirement and may, in many cases, be much larger than the Social Security benefits. Government assists with these programs through tax incentives. Private employers may deduct the costs from their taxes. Public employers operate the programs in part through appropriations. Employees usually contribute part of the costs, but they also receive tax incentives in that they may often exclude their payments from their taxable incomes and pay taxes on their contributions only when they retire and receive them. Retired people are typically in lower tax brackets than those who are working.

The federal government also provides for taxpayers to establish Individual Retirement Accounts through which some families are able to deduct contributions to a retirement plan from their personal income and thus pay lower income taxes. They may withdraw their contributions at age 59½ without penalty—but there is a penalty for earlier withdrawals, with exceptions. They must begin withdrawing funds by age 70½ to avoid penalties on their retirement accounts. A 1997 tax change increased the limits on the amounts families may earn and still tax deduct their contributions to IRAs. A new program, called the Roth Individual Retirement Account, allows for some tax deductible contributions to IRAs and withdrawals from them without paying taxes on the money withdrawn. Congress has also allowed IRA holders to withdraw their funds before retirement age if they use them for home purchases or their children's college expenses. Withdrawals for other purposes incur penalties, as mentioned above.

There are also insurance plans that provide income to people who become disabled. These plans, which may also be paid by the employee and the employer or by one or the other, provide payments to workers when they are ill or injured and unable to continue working.

As is discussed earlier in this chapter, all of these programs may work together and may have some impact on one another. For example, the amount of workers' compensation payments may be deducted from the Social Security disability payments. All or some of the private or public resources of individuals are considered in their income tax payments.

Health Care Financing

A major form of income maintenance is assistance with the financing of one's health care, especially when there are catastrophic, expensive medical needs. The two basic public health care programs in the United States are Medicaid and Medicare, which are authorized as parts of the Social Security Act. Medicaid is provided to pay the costs of care for low-income people or people who would be of low income if they had to pay their own medical care costs. It generally is available to those who receive TANF and SSI as well as other people who would be eligible for TANF or SSI if they paid their own medical bills. The levels of coverage and eligibility vary, however, from state to state. In most states Medicaid covers hospital care, physicians' services, some prescriptions, and nursing home care. The costs are paid by the federal and state governments, with the federal government providing half or more of the costs.

Medicare is an insurance program to which employed people and their employers contribute. It is provided to all people sixty-five years old or older, no matter how much, if anything, they have paid. It also covers some other categories of people, including, under some circumstances, those covered by Social Security disability. It provides coverage for hospital care and many other kinds of expenses. Recipients may also pay additional premiums under "Part B," which provides coverage for physician costs and other services. Although Medicare is a federal government program, it is often administered by private insurance companies under contracts between the government and the companies, an example of the blurring of the private and public sectors which will be discussed later in this chapter. In 1996 major changes in Medicare were an area of much discussion and contention between Congress and President Clinton.

The two programs work together in many cases. For example, many states purchase Part B coverage for their elderly Medicaid recipients so that Medicare pays for costs that might otherwise have to be covered by the state. People who are in need of health care may receive Medicare benefits for part of their costs and Medicaid benefits for the rest.

There are many rules, regulations, and procedures that are required in the Medicaid and Medicare programs. For example, providers of services may bill Medicare recipients for the difference between the amounts Medicare pays and what the provider usually charges. It is a violation of federal law, however, for a provider to bill a Medicaid recipient for those additional amounts. Special efforts are made by the federal and state governments to hold down the costs of these expensive programs, a major public policy concern. There are also special efforts to prevent fraud or abuse of these programs, which have been problems in many parts of the United States.

In addition to these programs there is also a federally financed program for crippled children, which is administered in each state. In most cases there is a means test to determine how much assistance will be provided, but the levels of need are often higher than they are for Medicaid. That is, families of modest but not necessarily poverty-level incomes may obtain help for children with disabling conditions or illnesses. In some states mentally ill as well as physically disabled children are covered.

Some health care financing is also available through local and state governments. Free hospital care for the indigent or payments for that care are sometimes provided.

Managed Care

Health care financing and its reform have been social policy issues of major consequence throughout the 1990s. The costs of health care have grown rapidly; many people do not have and cannot afford private health insurance; the cost of public programs such as Medicaid and Medicare have increased; and there are strong desires among many policy-making groups to reduce health care costs. President Clinton, following through on a plan developed by his wife, Hillary Rodham Clinton, proposed a major reform in health care planning and delivery in 1994. However, strong opposition to the plan, especially among health care providers such as hospitals and health insurance companies, along with some concerns that the changes would lead to significant departures in the ways patients received health care and chose their physicians, caused the plan to fail passage in Congress.

The complexity and seeming irrationality of the health care system in the United States are still of concern. Hospitals and other providers often supply health care services to people who are not insured or who have no funds to pay for their own care. The costs of the free care is typically passed on to those who pay for their care privately or through private insurance companies. Consequently, there are examples of very high costs for simple medicines and medical supplies. A single aspirin tablet may be billed to patients at a cost of several dollars, although consumers know they can buy large bottles of aspirin for just a few dollars.

The high charges reflect the cost of providing care to those who cannot pay themselves. It is an odd financial mechanism for the indigent, and it is also uneven because not all hospitals in all parts of the United States or even in all parts of any one state provide health care to those who are not able to pay for it themselves.

The solution that was most popular among many health care organizers and planners in the 1990s was "managed care." The intention was to require patients to have their care rationally managed, often through the screening of a primary care physician—a general or family practitioner—rather than allowing them to go directly to specialists whose care they might prefer. Primary care such as that provided by a general or family practitioner is usually less expensive than that provided by specialists, whose fees are generally higher and who might use more tests and even hospitalization for something a primary care physician might handle through a simple office visit. The managed care approach is characteristic of efforts such as health maintenance organizations (HMOs), in which increasing numbers of corporations and other entities are enrolling their employees rather than providing them with open-ended health insurance that allows them to use whatever health care services they choose. These prepaid health care programs may hold down the costs of employee care. They also allow employers to plan for and predict the amount of their expenditures for employee health coverage.

It is possible that managed care policies will become central to the efforts to reform health care payment services in the United States and that, at some point, most Americans will receive their health care benefits and coverage through a managed care organization such as a health maintenance organization.

When the Medicare and Medicaid programs were changed in 1995 in ways designed to hold down the increasing costs of those programs, one of the provisions was to encourage Medicare clients—primarily older adults—and state Medicare programs to use more extensively managed care, especially health maintenance organizations. There were also provisions to reduce the reimbursements for care to hospitals and other providers, such as nursing homes, although physicians were not expected to feel much impact on their own fees from these programs.

Employment and Training Programs

Assistance to the unemployed is another example of income maintenance services. These are services administered by state employment services agencies with funds that are usually totally provided by the federal government with revenues collected from payroll taxes paid by employers. These programs provide unemployment compensation for those who are without work for a period of time, without regard to the assets of the unemployed persons—although they must report and deduct income received from other employment. Unemployment of the wage earner or wage earners is a financial disaster for most families. It is also a problem that affects a large number of families every year. In the 1990s the unemployment rate in the United States was low. The average weekly unemployment benefit was $186 in 1996. The range in 1996 was $119 per week in Louisiana to $262 per week in Hawaii (Committee on Ways and Means, U.S. House of Representatives 1996).

Those who collect unemployment compensation must have lost their jobs for reasons other than their own misconduct or unwillingness to continue working. Employees who misbehave on the job or resign voluntarily are not eligible. Generally, unemployment compensation continues until the recipient finds work or for twenty-six weeks, whichever comes first. In times of severe economic problems the federal government may extend the period of eligibility beyond twenty-six weeks.

There is also a human services element associated with unemployment compensation services. The unemployment agency makes referrals to jobs and training programs, which is a way of helping people overcome their unemployment problems. Those who are assisted must be available for work in their general area of skill, must demonstrate that they are seeking work, and must report to the unemployment office periodically to receive their compensation.

There are also many kinds of training programs that are financed by government and industry or, most typically, by a combination of government and industry efforts. Programs such as the Job Training Partnership Act provide federal training funds to states, which in turn use those funds to train or retrain workers. Some of that training is in the form of apprenticeship programs, other parts are in more-formal courses, and other portions are in work experience activities, in which trainees learn basic job skills by working for public and private employers. Some work experience programs are associated with TANF, which requires most recipients to work or participate in work training if they are physically able to do so and do not have infant children. There are efforts to involve the private sector heavily in such programs. Part of that

161

involvement is in the training itself, and part is in the form of tax incentives. In some programs special federal tax benefits are provided to employers who hire assistance recipients.

General and Emergency Assistance

Federal programs are usually entitlements for people who meet specific needs requirements. Many of those who are desperately in need of help are not blind, disabled, or elderly, however, so they do not qualify for SSI; do not have children, so they do not qualify for TANF; and are not recently unemployed, so they do not qualify for unemployment compensation—they are just poor. Many such individuals are women who have recently become single because their male wage-earning partners have left them or have died. If they are younger than Social Security age, have no work history, and have no disabilities, they do not qualify for the basic programs.

Therefore, there are many local and state general assistance programs that help people who need assistance, without regard to their characteristics other than poverty. Those programs vary dramatically from place to place. That is because there are no national standards for such assistance. State or local governments may provide whatever kinds of help they choose. Some states have regular, monthly assistance programs. Other states provide help only once and then for only one month's needs.

Emergency assistance is similar to general assistance in its variability, except that the federal government provides some help to the states for families that are in need of it. Under the current law, the federal government's block grant funds for family assistance can be used, if the states choose, for temporary or emergency assistance. Specific emergency assistance programs may include temporary housing, food, medical care, and other in-kind assistance as well as limited cash assistance.

Emergency and general assistance may be provided by county or other local governments or by the same agencies that provide TANF. Frequently, one of the tasks of the worker in the TANF program is to help needy clients connect with some of these limited assistance programs to help them overcome their immediate needs.

In-Kind Programs

There is also a variety of entitlement or income maintenance programs that are paid "in kind." As the chapter on social welfare history describes, benefits have traditionally been provided in either cash or in-kind payments, with in-kind benefits providing greater control of the nature of the assistance received and the ways in which it is used. The largest of the in-kind benefits in the United States is the food stamp program, which provides coupons on a monthly basis to individuals and families who cannot meet their basic food needs on their incomes. Again, the amount of food stamps depends upon the size of the family, its income, family assets, and other factors. Although the food stamp program is administered by a different federal agency than TANF and Social Security—by the U.S. Department of Agriculture—at the state and local levels, food stamps are generally provided through the same agencies that provided TANF. As is mentioned in chapter 2, the Personal Responsibility and Work Opportunity Reconciliation Act of 1996 made some detailed restrictions in the food stamp program for adults who had no dependents. The plans are detailed in appendix 2. However, those plans were modified in 1997. Those 1997 modifications liberalized the food stamp program so that adults in need of food assistance may receive it. The original legislation provided for them to receive food stamps for only three months out of every three years. Another rule which denied food stamps to legal immigrants for five years was changed so that those who were living in the United States when the new law was signed by President Clinton in August 1997 remained eligible to receive help. Under the original legislation, they were to be cut off assistance through food stamps.

Another important nutrition program is called WIC, which is the Special Supplemental Food Program for Women, Infants, and Children. The program is national and is typically administered through health departments at the local level. It provides nutrition education, health services, and food checks to buy milk, eggs, cheese, juice, cereal, and infant formula for pregnant and breastfeeding women and young children.

There are also many other income maintenance assistance programs provided on an in-kind basis, including low-cost public housing; subsidized housing in privately owned apartments; and assistance with utility payments, especially in the winter, through the Low Income Energy Assistance Program, which is discussed in chapter 7. Nutrition needs are also addressed through emergency food rations and food banks directed by charitable or government antipoverty organizations and often supplied by food manufacturers. There are also programs that assist with clothing, emergency shelter for the homeless and dispossessed, and a great variety of other kinds of direct help, based upon local communities' interests and abilities to assist people in need.

Many of the in-kind programs and services are provided by voluntary charities rather than by governments. Churches, neighborhood centers, and civic clubs often organize in-kind services projects such as clothing and food distribution programs for those in their communities who need help.

These income maintenance services are discussed first because they are so fundamental to the needs of those who receive social welfare assistance. There are many kinds of human need, but if basic financial needs are not met, the others cannot be effectively addressed.

Assets-Based Programs

An emerging idea in social welfare assistance is the assets-based approach, developed by Michael Sherraden (1991). Sherraden, who is a professor at Washington University's George Warren Brown School of Social Work in St. Louis, believes that low-income people can be helped through providing them with assets or savings which they can use for major purchases, home ownership, and education. Current programs focus on immediate spending for immediate needs. Assets approaches would give people long-term objectives and possibilities.

One of Sherraden's later ideas was for the development of Children's Savings Accounts (Curley and Sherraden 1998), which would start children at birth with $1,000 and which could be augmented by contributions that could be fully tax refundable. The funds would receive interests or would be invested in securities. Over the years, children could develop assets that could help them with their adult years—and help break family poverty cycles. There is interest in Congress in such approaches, and the new welfare law of 1996 gives states the opportunity to try out such ideas.

The assets-based approach fits well with a popular and central concept of social work practice{<m}>strengths-based approaches (Chapin 1995). R. K. Chapin is one of several theorists who have written about strengths approaches to serving clients (Chapin 1995). Social workers have long found it useful to focus on client strengths rather than problems and, of course, assets-based services help build client strengths.

LOCATION AND OPERATION OF SERVICES

Another way to describe services is in terms of the level of government or the location in which they are provided. Generally, government

164

or public services are provided at the federal, state, and local—which includes counties, regions, cities, and towns—levels. As indicated, some services are largely local, while others are national or statewide in scope. There is great variability within the United States in the kinds and levels of services provided.

In the United States many services are provided through joint financing by the federal and state governments. The services, however, are usually delivered at the local level—in counties, cities, or regions. Very few services are provided directly from the federal government. Social Security, Supplemental Security Income, some services to Native Americans, and veterans' benefits are the primary exceptions.

It is a truism of American government and the federal system, discussed in chapter 4, that services are largely financed by the federal government, partly financed by state governments, and delivered at local levels, although often by divisions of state government. Services may on occasion be financed by county or city governments with locally collected taxes. That is especially true of certain services that are relatively new in the social services system, such as domestic violence shelters, rape crisis programs, and self-help groups as well as others that have not had the long history of mental health, corrections, mental retardation, and vocational rehabilitation services, which have long been established with financing from federal and state sources.

Another distinction made in describing the structure of services is whether the auspices of the services are religious or secular. Many of the social services provided to people in the United States are developed, administered, and financed by Roman Catholic, Protestant, Jewish, and other religious bodies. These services may include child care, counseling, financial assistance, health services, or any number of other aids to people who are in need. A variety of nonsectarian, or secular, organizations also provide human services. These include civic clubs such as Kiwanis, Lions, Rotary, and Civitan.

In addition, other nonreligious private, voluntary, charitable groups organize and deliver human services. Groups of people with special interests, such as parents of children with mental retardation, and advocacy groups, such as the Alliance for the Mentally Ill, which is composed largely of relatives of persons with mental illness, are also examples of nongovernmental, nonsectarian services.

There are also a large number of well-known organizations devoted to the resolution of specific personal or health problems, such as the

March of Dimes, Cystic Fibrosis Foundation, the American Lung Association, Easter Seals, the National Association for Mental Health, and numerous others.

A detailed description of all the services and auspices under which services are provided is, of course, impossible because of the dynamic nature of social services. Services develop, go out of existence, combine with other services, change patterns, become affiliated with government agencies, and otherwise modify themselves or are modified periodically by others.

FINANCING

To pursue another theme that pervades this book, understanding the financing of human services is crucial to understanding the services themselves. Although this chapter has so far suggested that there is a clear distinction between governmental and nongovernmental, or between public and private organizations, that distinction is more traditional or historical than it is real. As chapter 2 discusses, for much of human history there was no governmental involvement in human services. In the United States it was not until the 1930s that the federal government became involved in the organization and delivery of services to residents.

One of the least known but most important developments in the human services is the blurring of the lines between governmental and nongovernmental programs. Although the distinctions once were absolute, there are now many programs in which federal and other government funds are used to support nongovernmental services. These examples usually involve contracts or grants in which a government agency employs a voluntary program to carry out certain governmental functions or to achieve some of the objectives of a governmental program. Although that is more likely to be the case in personal social services—services other than those that are designed to assist people in maintaining their incomes, as described in chapter 7—that pattern can also be true in financial assistance programs. In some states, for example, the distribution of assistance checks and food stamps is handled by banks, finance companies, private check-cashing companies, or other financially oriented institutions. Governments pay the organizations a fee for carrying out those responsibilities, believing they save money and increase efficiency by doing so. Some refer to this trend as the "privatization" of services (Barker 1995).

Some of the newer experiments in the food stamp program involve the use of electronically encoded cards that look and function like debit cards of the kind issued by corporations such as Mastercard or Visa. Instead of receiving a book of food stamps, the client receives a credit to his or her account each month. That account information is maintained in a central place. When the client purchases groceries with his or her food debit card, the amount of credit is reduced by the amount spent on the groceries. The cards are usually produced and maintained by a private corporation, as are the records and the special machines used in the food stores, under contract with the governmental agency responsible for food stamps.

ANTIPOVERTY PROGRAMS

Several efforts first developed under the Economic Opportunity Act of 1964 continue to help clients with basic needs. Although these are not typically income maintenance organizations or programs, they often assist low-income people in obtaining help that is not covered by major programs such as SSI or TANF. They may provide weatherization services to help low-income people keep their dwellings warm during the winter months; maintain food and clothing emergency supplies for people who need them; and operate advocacy and information programs for people who need economic assistance of one kind or another.

PLANNING AND FUND-RAISING AGENCIES

There are also a number of agencies that are organized to serve other agencies. The United Way organizations, which are found in most communities, are perhaps the best example. They raise funds in a coordinated way to provide help to voluntary agencies in their communities. These fund-raising organizations have the support of local governments and business communities for a variety of reasons. First, they are usually able to raise money for less administrative cost than the dozens of agencies they represent would incur if they conducted their own campaigns. One single, efficient campaign is conducted each year on behalf of large numbers of individual voluntary member agencies. The agencies request amounts each year, and the United Way determines the amount it will attempt to raise for each. In turn, each agency agrees that it will not embark on public campaigns for funds but will instead contribute to the overall United Way effort.

United Way agencies also contribute to the rational financing of voluntary agencies by setting budgets that appear to be reasonable for the community. They try to ensure that the most important community needs are served and that the role of emotion in determining who receives what is minimized. For example, certain disabling conditions that largely affect children may have strong appeals in the community, even though the number of children affected is small. The "health" organizations established to deal with specific conditions may raise more money than their problems warrant in the community. When organizations are part of United Way fund-raising efforts, such problems are reduced. United Way board members put health problems in perspective so more-appropriate funding levels are provided. Combined campaigns reduce the amount of work time that might be devoted to raising funds for worthwhile causes by concentrating the whole effort on one campaign rather than on dozens of smaller efforts.

Typically, the United Way raises voluntary funds for most of the longest established local and national charities such as the YMCA and YWCA; Boy Scouts, Girl Scouts, and Campfire; family service agencies; and many others. Most of the services it supports are not income maintenance oriented, although a few, such as the Salvation Army, help individuals and families meet some of their fundamental needs through the provision of food, clothing, and lodging. As mentioned earlier, the United Ways function as policy-making organizations in their communities.

Although they remain popular and important in communities, United Way organizations faced some serious problems in 1992, when it was reported that the chief executive officer of United Way America, the national coordinating body for all local United Ways, was paid an unreasonably high salary and was also spending the organization's money lavishly on his personal expenses. Several local United Way organizations withheld money from the national body and also scrutinized their own administrative expenditures to see if similar abuses might be occurring. An excellent and detailed book on the United Way was written by E. L. Brilliant (1990).

Coordinating and planning councils also operate in many communities in ways designed to help those communities rationally and efficiently provide services without duplicating assistance to the same clients or groups of clients. Such organizations have a long social policy history oriented to the objective of avoiding the duplication of services. Readers will recall that avoiding duplication and the possible waste of limited resources have been preoccupations in social services for as long as those services have existed.

In the classic example of the centralized planning council, records are maintained on all of those who seek and receive services. Then, before an organization helps someone, it checks to determine whether or not the person has already received or is continuing to receive help. In some communities computer-stored records are used to investigate such possibilities.

However, because government provides most of the financial assistance that is available and government agencies are required to maintain and consult specific records on all those they help, the need for a community central registry has declined. Planning and coordinating councils are now more likely to devote their efforts to studying and trying to find the means for dealing with human need. Such groups may discover that there are special housing needs for abused spouses and may work to find a solution for them. Or they may find that the real need is for information on services and establishing an information and referral service to those who call. Or they may discover that, although there are ample services, those who need them most are confused by the application procedures or not received enthusiastically when they apply for help. Thus, the planning council may focus its efforts on providing "advocacy" services—on making sure someone is available to help applicants obtain what they need.

Some central planning efforts are focused on coordinating services rather than providing new services. In some cases central locations are developed so that an individual who needs help may apply for a variety of services in the same building or, ideally, with one application, which is then duplicated and distributed to all the programs and services with potential resources available to the client. Some central planning bodies provide "case managers" to clients—people who coordinate the services that the client is receiving or ought to be receiving.

CONCLUSION

It is clear that publicly funded and administered human services are a complicated and extensive part of American community life. Understanding everything there is to know about these services is impossible, yet those involved with social work and related fields must be aware of the broad structures and categories that describe and govern the human services. Perhaps more important, one must be able to understand and analyze social policy in one's locality to better understand how to gain access to those services for clients.

This chapter has covered many of the public and voluntary, cash and in-kind, income maintenance programs found in the United States. These are, in many ways, the keys to social policy in the United States, Although human needs are numerous and varied, financial need is often a key ingredient of other kinds of needs, whether for mental health assistance, child protection, or health care. Financial assistance and income maintenance programs are thus fundamental to all social programs.

DISCUSSION QUESTIONS

1. List and define three income maintenance programs that fall in the category of entitlements and three that do not.
2. What are some of the differences between means-tested and non-means-tested programs? Why do you believe both of these kinds of programs have been developed and maintained as part of the U.S. human services system?
3. What are the advantages of cash and in-kind programs? What are some of the reasons, in your opinion, that social policy leans toward most programs being organized around cash rather than in-kind assistance?
4. This chapter describes a large number of income maintenance programs for many different groups of people. Do you think there are any gaps in the provision of assistance to Americans? If so, who are the people affected? Why would they be left out of the benefits available to people in need?
5. Carry out some practical exercises. Visit your local Social Security office and obtain instructions for inquiring about your Social Security account by mail or on-line by computer. You will receive an up-to-date report about your earnings and contributions while in the program and your potential for retirement benefits. While there, obtain pamphlets and brochures about Social Security.

REFERENCES

Abramovitz, M. (1997). Temporary assistance to needy families. Edwards et al. (Eds.) *The encyclopedia of social work,* 19th ed. Supplement, 1997, 311–330. Washington, DC: NASW Press.

Associated Press. (1997, July 6) President praises welfare overhaul. *Columbia, SC State*, A7.

Barker, R. L. (1995). *The social work dictionary*, 3d ed. Washington, DC: NASW Press.

Bernstein, P., & Ma, C. (1996). *The practical guide to practically everything: 1997 edition*. New York: Random House.

Block , W. (1986). Private property, ethics, and wealth creation. Berger, P. L. (1986) *The capitalist revolution: Fifty propositions about prosperity, equality, and liberty*, 107–128. New York: Basic Books.

Brilliant, E. L. (1990). *The United Way: Dilemmas of organized charity*. New York: Columbia University Press.

Chapin, R. K. (1995, July). Social policy development: The strengths perspective. *Social Work*, 506–514

Committee on Ways and Means, U.S. House of Representatives. (1992). *Overview of entitlement programs: 1991 green book*. Washington, DC: U.S. Government Printing Office.

Committee on Ways and Means, U.S. House of Representatives. (1993). *Overview of entitlement programs: 1993 green book*. Washington, DC: U.S. Government Printing Office.

Committee on Ways and Means, U.S. House of Representatives. (1996). *1996 green book: Background material and data on programs within the jurisdiction of the Committee on Ways and Means*. Washington, DC: U.S. Government Printing Office.

Curley, J. & Sherraden, M. (1998). *Policy report: The history and status of children's allowances: Policy background for children's savings accounts*. St. Louis, MO: Center for Social Development, Washington University in St. Louis.

Edelman, P. (1997, March). The worst thing Bill Clinton has done. *The Atlantic Monthly*, 43–58.

Edwards, R. L. et al. (Eds.), *Encyclopedia of social work*, 19th ed. 1849–1855. Washington, DC: NASW Press.

Friedman, M., & Friedman, R. (1980). *Free to choose: A personal statement*. New York: Avon.

Gilder, G. (1995, June). End welfare reform as we know it. *American Spectator*, 28 (6), 24–32.

Ginsberg, L. (1983). *The practice of social work in public welfare*. New York: Free Press.

Ginsberg, L. (1995). *Social work almanac*, 2d ed. Washington, DC: NASW Press.

Katz, J. L. (1995, September 23). Senate overhaul plan provides road map for compromise. *Congressional Quarterly*, 2908–2911.

Kopp, M. A. (1995, July 24). The family sufficiency act of 1995. *Washington Social Legislation Bulletin*. Washington, DC: Child Welfare League of America, 34 (14).

Mangum, G., & Mangum, S. (Eds.) (1996). *Of heart and mind: Social policy essays in memory of Sar A. Levitan*. Kalamazoo, MI: Upjohn Institute.

Murray, C. (1994). *Losing ground: American social policy, 1950–1980, 10th anniversary edition.* New York: Basic Books.

National Association of Social Workers. (1997, October). Budget law for '98 alters social programs. *NASW News,* 9.

O'Neill, D. M., & O'Neill, J. E. (1997). *Lessons for welfare reform: An analysis of the AFDC caseload and past welfare to work programs.* Kalamazoo, MI: Upjohn Institute.

Pizzagati, K. (1997, September). Children lose SSI benefits under new welfare law. *Children's Monitor,* 1997 Supplement, 4.

Sherraden, M. (1991). *Assets and the poor: A new American welfare policy.* Armonk, NY: M. E. Sharpe.

Those who want current, detailed information on these programs may find what they need within current government documents, especially those published by the Social Security Administration. The series of House Ways and Means Committee "green books," three of which are cited above, provides one of the best compendiums of data on all entitlement programs. In addition, the annual "Statistical Abstracts," published by the Bureau of the Census, is a good source of information.

For additional information on the programs described in this chapter, see the above sources; R. L. Edwards et al. (Eds.) (1995). *Encyclopedia of Social Work,* 19th ed.; and L. Ginsberg et al. (Eds.) (1990). *1990 Supplement.* Silver Spring, MD: NASW Press.

Chapter Seven

The Descriptive Component Continued: Special Care for Special Groups

Chapter 6 described the economic assistance services that are the foundation of social programs in the United States. This chapter describes the other side of social services—the personal social services, which R. L. Barker (1995, 279) says are designed "to enhance the relationships between people and between people and their environments and to provide opportunities for social fulfillment. . . . [They] include counseling and guidance, development of mutual help and self-help groups, family planning, and services for older people and for children." Barker says that personal social services are those that do not provide money, health care, education, or housing.

Personal services are crucial, and developing and administering them is the focus of most professional human services jobs. They require high levels of professional skill because services are individualized to meet the requirements of a multitude of clients. The economic assistance programs described in the last chapter, for example, can make a dramatic difference in the lives of clients, but one has to know just what programs are available, how they can best be applied to a particular case, and what the limits are. Once policies and programs are established, however, people with less professional human services education, and even computers, are able to make basic decisions about them and run them. In today's human services programs it is the personal social services for which most students are educated and in which most human services professionals are employed.

The care of people with special needs is a distinctive area of social policy in the United States. Although the poor have traditionally been viewed as the primary category of those with needs and the major subject of social policy, the vulnerable and disadvantaged include many sub-categories of individuals such as widows, orphans and other dependent children, the elderly, people with mental and physical disabilities, those suffering from illnesses, people found guilty of breaking the law, and others. The establishment of the human services profession is part of that history of developing services for people with special needs.

INSTITUTIONAL CARE

Institutional care has long been a factor in the social services for people who cannot care for themselves, as chapter 2 describes. According to C. A. Alexander (1995), in the eighteenth century a number of institutions were established for people with specific needs. A privately financed home for mothers and children was established in New Orleans by the Ursuline sisters, for example, primarily to care for survivors of Indian massacres and a smallpox epidemic. A public mental hospital was established in Virginia in 1773. A public orphanage was founded in Charleston, South Carolina, in 1790. Schools, often residential, for the deaf and blind were founded in many parts of the United States, as were schools for persons who were mentally disabled and for juvenile delinquents. Prisons, had, of course, existed from the beginning of the nation, but in that earlier time they were not considered part of the social welfare system. Institutional care remains one of the primary means of serving people in the twentieth century.

CARE FOR CHILDREN

Children have traditionally been the focus of many of the resources provided for personal social services. Although it may be difficult for current readers to imagine, children were not always treated specially by society, as if they were any different from adults. Although they are obviously smaller, weaker, and less skillful, generally, than adults, children were not always considered a population group with special needs and requiring special care; that concept is relatively new, a development from late in the last century.

Children constitute a large population group everywhere in the world. In the United States it is estimated that more than 20 percent of the population will be under fourteen years old in the year 2000. In the world as a whole, however, people in that age group will constitute 31 percent (Committee on Ways and Means, U.S. House of Representatives, 1996). More than one third of the members of the National Association of Social Workers (NASW) are involved in serving children and their families (Ginsberg 1995).

CHILD LABOR REGULATIONS

Even prohibitions against children working with the same kinds of circumstances as adults are relatively new developments. Not only was there no social policy prohibiting child labor in earlier U.S. history; in some ways it was encouraged. P. J. Day (1997, 146) noted that child labor was "viewed as beneficial to both child and society, teaching the sanctity of work and the evils of idleness." Although there were concerns earlier, policies to end child labor were not in effect until the twentieth century. In certain industries, such as mining, children were prized because they could reach places that larger workers could not reach, and since they were not responsible for supporting families, they could be paid lower salaries than adults. If they were injured or killed in industrial accidents, the impact, it was felt, would not be as great as if a principal family wage earner, such as a father or mother, had been injured or killed.

Many of the states have had laws against child labor for much of their history. Yet there was no federal prohibition against it until the early twentieth century; in 1916 the U.S. Congress passed a law called the Child Labor Act to forbid interstate commerce in goods that were manufactured by children. The bill was declared unconstitutional by the Supreme Court, however, in 1918 (Alexander 1995). The states enacted strict laws prohibiting child labor and the employment of children in dangerous occupations and requiring school attendance.

Child labor is reemerging as an American social problem. In a 1993 article in *Fortune* magazine, B. Dumaine cites current examples throughout the United States which suggest that employers are hiring children for long hours and to do dangerous work in fast food restaurants, garment factories, and grocery stores and in door-to-door night sales of such things as candy. Children are also working with their parents as migrant workers in agriculture. Clearly, the provisions that now exist to prevent the use of child labor are in need of revision or better enforcement.

The Children's Bureau and Policy Concerns for Children

Congress established the Children's Bureau in 1912 (Alexander 1995) to work toward the protection of the rights of children and to promote children's well-being. Despite the Supreme Court invalidation of the Child Labor Act, the Children's Bureau was given directives to prohibit federal contractors from using child labor (Jansson 1997), another example of executive branch policy making which worked even though the legislative and executive branches were unable to implement the same policy.

The Children's Bureau, one of the oldest of the federal agencies that deals with human services, has throughout its long history monitored the problems of children in the United States and advocated better treatment of young people. Its creation followed the precedent-setting 1909 White House Conference on Children, the first to be held (Alexander 1995); these were continued for the rest of the century in some form although the national, high-profile conferences were dropped during the presidency of Ronald Reagan. That first conference was initiated under the sponsorship of another Republican president, one of the most innovative of all American history and an activist, Theodore Roosevelt. These conferences pushed for programs that eventually led to the Social Security Act and many other reforms.

Current children's services are many. In fact, most of the money spent for human services in the United States is devoted to improving the well-being of children. The largest and most expensive of these efforts is, of course, public education. Substantial amounts are also spent on the economic assistance included in the TANF and OASDI programs, among others.

Child Welfare Services

The major programs providing help to children, apart from financial assistance and education, are called child welfare services, which fall into several different categories. In every category, however, it is fundamental to child welfare policy that the focus is on the well-being of the child. The best interests of the child, always and without question, are supposed to be the fundamental concern of those who administer child welfare policies, including agency personnel and the courts. The goal is that the best interests of the child be served, even when his or her interests may conflict with the wishes of parents, relatives, and other interested parties. And very often the child's best interests are the same as those of the child's caregivers. One of the social policy themes that permeates child welfare is that children ought to be able to remain with their families—biological, adoptive, or any other kind—whenever possible. But a related policy theme is that children should be removed from abusive family situations when a satisfactory resolution and reunification cannot be expected, so the child may be placed with another family on a permanent basis. Obviously, delaying proper care for children too long is equivalent to denying children their childhoods. Waiting too long can mean waiting until near adulthood, when having a satisfactory childhood is no longer a possibility.

Child Protective Services

The most important of the categories of child welfare is *child protective services,* which is a collection of services provided to children who are in danger of neglect or abuse by their parents or others who are caring for them. In every state there are child protective services provided to children whose need comes to the attention of the child protective agency. Children who require protective services fall into a number of categories, such as those who are victims of physical abuse, sexual abuse, medical neglect, emotional and psychological maltreatment, and neglect. In 1995 there were nearly 2.7 million children reported to authorities as abused or neglected (Petit & Curtis 1997). Over one million of those reports were confirmed. That is, the cases were investigated and found to be real cases of abuse or neglect that required some of the interventions in the family that are discussed later in the chapter. The data on the nature of child maltreatment are sketchy, but most studies show that over half the children who require protective services have been neglected rather than abused. In many cases, however, children suffer from a combination of maltreatments, which is one of the reasons it is often difficult to isolate neglect from abuse. In general, younger children are the ones most often neglected, and older children the ones most often abused (National Center on Child Abuse and Neglect 1993). The differences are not as important as they might initially seem because both abuse and neglect endanger the lives and well-being of children.

Fundamental to the concept of child protective services is that children are vulnerable and, therefore, in need of special protection by society. That idea emanates from the twentieth-century redefinition of children as a special category of people, just as the laws against child labor emerged from a new cultural ideal that children should not work, especially in dangerous occupations. Although child welfare and child protection are state and local government functions, substantial amounts of federal funds are provided to the states to help them with that work.

Informing the Authorities about Child Abuse and Neglect

In recent years there have been large increases in reports of child maltreatment. According to the Child Welfare League of America (Petit & Curtis 1997), reports of child abuse and neglect per 1,000 American children grew from 33 per 1,000 in 1986 to 42 per 1,000 in 1995. The same report, which is based on studies conducted by the federal government and a survey taken by the National Committee to Prevent Child Abuse, says that the highest number of reports was 112.4 per 1,000 children in Idaho, and the lowest was 7.9 per 1,000 in Pennsylvania. The median or midpoint was 43.6 per 1,000 in North Dakota. The highest number of substantiated reports was in Alaska, with 37.9 children per 1,000; the lowest was 2.3 per 1,000 in Pennsylvania; and the median, 12.6 per 1,000 in South Dakota. Although these increases in child abuse reports are attributed by some observers to stricter requirements for reporting, most experts agree that there have been genuine increases in the incidence of child maltreatment. Miringoff (1995), for example, says that the problem of child abuse has grown more extensive almost every year since 1970. Public knowledge of the problem has also expanded, and the media regularly report on child maltreatment cases. Greater public awareness has led to more reporting of suspected abuse and neglect. The legal requirements in almost every state now compel those who have contact with children—such as nurses, physicians, teachers, child care workers, social workers, psychologists, and almost all other professionals—to report promptly to the state child protective services agency any suspicions about possible neglect and abuse. Failing to do so, in most states, is a crime, and a professional who fails to report a suspected case could be fined or imprisoned. In all states any person can make such a report and cannot be charged with making a false report, even if his or her suspicions are unfounded, unless the reports are deliberately made despite the fact that they are false and the person making the report knows that it is not true. The social policy is that government seeks the widest possible range of reports, which can be culled and rejected when appropriate.

When a report is made, the child protective services agency—which is often a division of the same social services organization that provides TANF and food stamps—is required to investigate the report, often within a day. The investigation attempts to uncover whether the complaint is legitimate or unfounded. In some situations reports are made mistakenly because the observer thinks a child is being abused or neglected when, in reality, a family has merely punished and not abused a child. Or perhaps the child suffers from an illness or has sustained an injury that appears to be the result of maltreatment but is not. Sometimes the child protective services system has been used by an angry relative, former spouse, or a neighbor as a means to retaliate against parents for some reason. No matter what the suspicions of the child protective agency or worker, however, in most states a complaint must be investigated.

When a report is confirmed and neglect or abuse is verified, the protective services agency and its worker may exercise one or more of several options for dealing with the problem. Parenthetically, the popular media often suggest that child protective matters are investigated and addressed by law enforcement agencies; in truth, almost all such investigations are handled by the child protective services agency staff. Police departments are more likely to report the problem to child protective agencies rather than investigate them. Much of the involvement of law enforcement officers is in visits to homes under circumstances that may appear to be dangerous. In those cases, when the worker has reason to believe that there might be an assault by a parent or caregiver, the police may be asked to come along to protect the worker. It is true that most forms of abuse and some forms of neglect are crimes. Occasionally a child's caregiver may be arrested and tried for such a crime, yet those cases are only a small fraction of the many handled every year. Even child sexual abuse and abuse that leads to serious physical injury are not always handled within the criminal justice system. Child welfare matters of almost every kind are treated as confidential everywhere in the United States. Court proceedings are secret, reports by child welfare workers may not be divulged, and the names of the children and their families are kept out of the press.

The options that may be used in indicated cases of maltreatment, which are spelled out in some detail in the agencies' policy manuals, include the following:

1. Counseling with the household, in which the worker talks with household members about the nature of the problem and helps them plan to avoid future incidents of maltreatment.

2. Emergency removal of the child or children. If the children in the household appear to be in imminent danger, they may be removed to an emergency shelter, which may be a group home, an institution, or another household that receives children for temporary, emergency protection.

3. Foster care. One of the solutions often used is foster care, which is temporary care in another home. The foster parents may be relatives of the child or strangers who are recruited and paid by the protective services agency.

4. Long-term or permanent substitute care. It is the philosophy and strategy of child welfare services programs to place children in as few different substitute care arrangements as possible. Child welfare workers believe that the well-being of children is compromised when they move from one foster home to another. Therefore, their preference is for longer-term care with a single family so that, if a child is removed from his or her household, there is placement in only one other home until, and if, the child may be returned. If the child cannot be returned, there is often an effort made to make the foster home placement permanent or to arrange for the child's adoption. These approaches follow the mandates of federal and state policies that carry out the provisions of the 1980 Federal Adoption Assistance and Child Welfare Act, which emphasizes *permanency planning* for children, so that they are not lost in the system (DiNitto 1995).

5. Referral to specialized services. When it appears to be potentially useful, members of the household are referred to counseling and mental health services to help them overcome their problems associated with caring for the child or children. In some cases, especially neglect cases, caregivers may be referred to financial assistance agencies so that they can better meet the material and health needs of the child through programs such as TANF, food stamps, Medicaid, and public housing.

6. In cases in which it is doubtful that the family can improve, the agency may take steps to call upon the courts to terminate legally the rights of the caregivers to be guardians of the child so that the child can be placed in a more permanent foster care arrangement or be adopted.

Another critical social policy is that children should not languish in temporary care—that they should either be returned to their households or placed permanently with foster or adoptive families. Families are permitted, by social policy found in the state statutes, to have a period during which they may try to improve the care of their children, often through the services offered to them. When they are unable or unwilling to improve, the children may be removed. As suggested, these policies are long-standing, but they are underscored in the 1980 Adoption Assistance and Child Welfare Act; for an excellent and detailed discussion of that legislation, see Jansson (1997).

The whole area of protective services, including removal of children from their homes, has become controversial in recent years. There is a national organization, Victims of Child Abuse Laws, or VOCAL, which says it has members in every state and some other nations who are battling public agencies because, VOCAL claims, they are targeting parents who discipline their children but are not abusers, yet have been charged as such (Zupan 1993). Media reports about discontented parents who believe the protective services system has harmed them are common. These protests have become more frequent as the number of reports and other activities by the system to combat child abuse and neglect have grown.

Substitute Child Care

The discussions above deal with foster care, which is one of the three main forms of substitute care of children; the others are adoption and group care. Much of the foster care provided in the United States is by relatives rather than strangers. The official foster care population in the nation is well under 1 percent of the child population (Fender & Shaw 1990). Although foster care is an important program and one that many social policy specialists believe requires additional attention and reform, it does not affect a large number of children.

A former foster child, Kevin Sieg, wrote about his experiences in Newsweek (1998). He described his life in foster care, which resulted from his mother's serious mental illness—he had never met his father. He said he began his life as an orphan in 1987, when the state removed him from his biological mother and explained that orphans are not necessarily people whose parents have died but that the term also includes people who have been separated from their parents for other reasons.

He describes some of his conflicts with his various foster parents and the abrupt end of his care because he had "aged out" at 18. Now a student at the University of Akron, Sieg's story is one o the most moving about the realities of foster care for some children. He says he survived the system but that many other foster children are not so lucky.

Public and governmental concern about children spending their lives in less than desirable foster care led to new federal legislation with the Adoption and Safe Families Act of 1997 (Public Law 105-89). The legislation encourages states to terminate parental rights as early as practicable, when the possibilities of reuniting families with children seem remote. States are provided opportunities to receive financial help as an incentive to more rapidly remove children from foster care and place them with adoptive families. There is also emphasis on "special needs" adoptions, which involve children with disabilities, minority children, and older children. In addition, the new law provides help with criminal records checks on potential foster and adoptive parents. This is part of the effort to achieve permanent homes for children who would not otherwise have them.

Adoption.   Some one million American children under 18 live with their adoptive fathers and mothers. Adoption, the permanent, legal placement of a child in a substitute family, is also a complicated area of social policy. The circumstances under which adoptions can be made is not the same in all states; some require that adoptions be handled through licensed public or private child welfare agencies; others allow families to arrange adoptions independently between themselves, but only with a prior study by a licensed agency, which conducts an investigation and makes a report to the court that is hearing the case. In other states, adoptions may be handled privately, often through attorneys or medical practitioners who know about the availability of an infant (usually because a young, unmarried woman plans to release the child for adoption after it is born) or an older child.

In 1986 there were over 104,000 adoptions in the United States. Half of all these adoptions were by relatives (U.S. Bureau of the Census 1991). In many states adoption by relatives is not handled through agencies at all, even though adoption by strangers might be. In many cases those relatives are stepfathers or stepmothers who merely formalize their parent-child relationships. In other cases children are adopted by their grandparents or by aunts and uncles. Many times these family members already are the child's primary caregivers and have been for a long time.

Social policies to protect children in adoption situations are abundant. Those that require preadoption interventions by agencies are examples. In those cases human services professionals study the potential adoptive home and interview the parents to ensure that the child's best interest will be served. In addition, many states have policies that forbid an adoption to become final less than a few days after the birth. Other states require that adoptions become final only after a trial period of several months, with visits by human services professionals during those months to ensure that the families remain suitable. According to the Child Welfare League of America (Petit & Curtis 1997), there were 66 million adopted children in the United States in 1992. There were 125,248 new adoptions of children under eighteen in that year, only 6 percent more than the 118,539 who were adopted in 1987.

Group Care for Children.   One of the substitute care arrangements used for children who cannot live with their caregiver families is group care, which is provided in a number of forms by many different groups. The traditional group care service for children was the orphanage, which generally cared for children whose parents had died. In modern American society there are few true orphans, largely because of the extension of the adult life span. For decades there has been no need for orphanages in the traditional sense of the concept.

One of the issues in the Contract with America of 1994 (Gillespie & Shellhas 1994) was major reforms in the care of children who could not satisfactorily live with their biological families. Proposals were made to replace foster care with orphanages. *Orphanages* was probably a general term for group care of various kinds. However, once it was understood how much more expensive group care is than foster care or even adoption, the subject was quickly dropped. Adoption assistance is endorsed in the Contract with America, and adoption assistance has been, for a long time, one of the major strategies of professionals in human services. Government assists adoptive families financially so they can adopt the child.

There have been, however, consistent needs for some group care to serve children who cannot live with their families or in substitute families. Therefore, over the years many of the orphanages that did not go out of existence when there were no more orphans to serve changed their function to that of providing care for children who were not able to live at home. These facilities, which house varying numbers of boys and girls, are typically used for children who cannot live with relatives or in foster homes. Many such children are placed in group care because, for instance, they are one of a group of siblings who do not want to be separated from one another; because they are older and, therefore, more difficult to place in foster homes; or because they have behavioral or emotional problems that make it difficult for them to be placed in private homes.

Group care homes have various kinds of organizational structures. Some have their own schools, for example, while others send their children to public schools. Some are religiously affiliated, following the tradition of the orphanages from which they came, while others are operated by nonsectarian community boards. Others may belong to governments and are operated by counties, cities, or states. Most carry out fund raising to pay for any costs that are not otherwise covered. Many of the children in group care facilities, however, are supported by state child welfare agencies, which provide a fixed monthly stipend to the facility for caring for the children. In some states the facilities are paid the audited cost of caring for the children. In others the state provides a flat amount, often the same as is paid to the foster parents who maintain children in their homes. The balance of the cost of caring for the children, which is often more than the direct costs of foster parents, is obtained from donations, endowments, or the sponsoring organization such as a church or civic group.

Modern group care is expensive for several reasons. Group care facilities require paid employees twenty-four hours per day along with the operation and maintenance of buildings, which is also expensive. Those who study caring for people who cannot care for themselves have begun to believe that in almost every case large institutional or group care is not the first choice. Not only is it expensive, but it is typically less desirable in human terms—more familylike care is preferable.

There are many interesting policy issues associated with group care, many of them dealing with money, which, as noted, is a central feature of social policy. For example, many children in group care also attend the local public schools, even though their official residences may be in other communities. Where does the state per-child education allocation go—to the district that is the official residence or the district in which the group facility is located? For another example, what are the legitimate costs that public agencies ought to pay for children, beyond food and shelter? Should the public pay for their school pictures, Scout dues, prom dresses, class rings, and football game tickets, just as parents typically do for their children? In many cases these issues are resolved informally, with voluntary contributions. Some agencies cover certain of these costs as a matter of policy.

Small group homes also are operated for children who need group care. These may house as few as two or three children. Care is provided by houseparents, whose profession is the operation of the small group home. In some cases therapeutic or specialized foster care homes are developed to house children with severe emotional or physical problems. In those cases the adult caregivers earn their living by serving as substitute parents; that is their sole employment. Small group homes are used in particular with children who have physical or mental disabilities or histories of juvenile delinquency. They often arrange for care and treatment by social workers and psychologists as well as routine medical services.

Although there is discussion later in this chapter of the special services for people with physical, mental, and behavioral disabilities, the general pattern in child welfare is to treat children as children. A juvenile delinquent is not a special species of humanity but is, the child welfare policies of the nation assert, a child with special behavioral problems. That is, a child is first a child; special characteristics or problems are considered secondary issues.

The movement in child welfare has gone from protection of individual children from abuse or neglect to preserving families. It is now federal law that states which accept federal money for children's services (and all do) have programs that work intensively toward the preservation of families. The idea is that families are the best location for children and that families can best nurture children. However, some families need help in freeing themselves from abusive or neglectful behavior or in preventing such behavior. The family preservation programs such as Homebuilders provide vulnerable families with services from professionals, usually master's level social workers. Those workers spend several hours each week with the family, providing both "hard" and "soft" services. Hard services are concrete kinds of help, such as food, cash assistance, food stamps, health care, housing, clothing, and other tangible aid. The soft services are primarily education and counseling for families that have trouble appropriately and effectively raising their children. Workers who visit their families carry out activities ranging from helping them repair their cars or clean their houses to assisting in resolving conflicts between parents and between parents and children.

Evaluation of these intensive family preservation programs indicate that they are high successful. In the most successful programs, almost all of the families stay together and none of the children have to be placed in foster care. And even in the less successful programs, rates of maintaining families and keeping children in their own homes may be as high as 70 percent. Although the costs of intensive family preservation are great, because of the small caseloads carried by workers, the long-term cost may be less expensive than providing children with substitute foster care, mental health services, or care in group homes and other facilities. If it is also better for the children, which most child experts now believe it is, family preservation services may also prevent future problems such as unemployment, incarceration, or desertion by people who were not reared satisfactorily. For some, family preservation is a controversial matter. They are concerned that the emphasis on family preservation—keeping the child with the biological parents—may work against the health and well-being of the child. (This discussion of family preservation is taken from the book *The Family at Risk* by Marianne Berry [1997].)

Child Day Care

For several complex social, political, and economic reasons child day care for preschool-age children has taken on new importance in American social policy. Increasing numbers of children require care outside their homes during the day. The policies requiring TANF recipient families to work or train for work (the original philosophy of the program was to provide assistance to families so that mothers, especially, would be free from working and could remain in the home and care for their children) has also accelerated the need for day care.

Social policy recognizes two general kinds of day care: care in centers and family day care. The first is familiar to most Americans; the second is also widely used. Parents, often mothers who have their own preschool age children, care for others' children during the day. Many families have used such arrangements for years. The United States has long been an industrial nation with a large labor force, which has always included large numbers of women, many of whom have needed day care or after-school care for their young children. (Current debates about equal employment opportunity for women have more to do with the quality and level of women's work than with whether or not women should work. Historically, women have been employed in manufacturing and service industries, among other work.) Family day care has been and commonly continues to be called "babysitting." In some cases the family day care providers are relatives of the children they are taking care of. Some states and localities have training programs for family day care providers, while others do not.

When children are in day care so that their parents may participate in compulsory employment or employment training programs, the cost of the care is normally borne by the agency that requires the employment or training. Therefore, a sizable portion of day care in the United States is paid for by human services agencies.

Nutritional Assistance to Child Care Facilities

In addition to financial payments and training for centers and family day care providers, under some arrangements and in some states food or cash to purchase food is provided to day care programs, including family day care centers. Food or money for food is provided through the U.S. Department of Agriculture to group child care facilities. The policy is to make nutritional assistance available to the children and to facilitate group care and day care services without adding financial burdens to the institutions or families. Of course, the primary purpose of Department of Agriculture programs is to maintain the food production capacities of the nation and to ensure that the farming industry is sustained. Purchasing and redistributing surplus food is a byproduct of those policies. Payments are provided under the same agency, the Food and Nutrition Service, which operates the food stamp program.

Licensing Policies

One of the major elements of social policy is the control of facilities for children. It is the policy of all the states to license facilities that care for children as well as the aged and other groups. Each state's licensing laws and procedures are different, but the essential features of all cover specific elements of the facilities' operations. These include:

1. Fire and other safety controls. Facilities must comply with fire prevention strategies, have extinguishers available, store hazardous materials properly, be constructed in ways that will allow people to exit burning areas safely, organize regular fire drills,

and avoid dangerous structural features and materials that may cause injury or death. Such arrangements are, of course, especially important when institutions house vulnerable groups such as children, people with disabilities, and older people.

2. Public health inspections to ensure properly maintained food preparation areas, environmental safety, general good health practices, and general cleanliness.

3. Programs that can help residents with their problems or basic needs. These parts of the licensing process usually involve human services professionals who try to ensure that there are sufficient numbers of qualified staff and that facilities operate programs that can educate, develop, and treat or maintain the morale of residents. A facility that has no program beyond eating, sleeping, and watching television—which many do not—may find its license threatened.

Operating a facility without a license is a violation of the law, so facilities treat the licensing requirements seriously. In some states, however, facilities that are operated by religious bodies are not subject to the licensing requirement. The belief is that the children's home or facility for the aged is a "church" and, as such, is not subject to state regulations. Of course, that is not a constitutional issue. A facility that provides care for people, no matter what its sponsorship, is not automatically constitutionally exempt from state regulation—just as the profit-making business enterprises of a nonprofit organization are subject to taxes, even though the nonprofit organization itself may not be. An anomaly of social policy in some states is that religiously affiliated human services facilities are legally exempted from licensing laws. Many of those facilities are of high quality and would have no difficulty in meeting licensing requirements; others may operate in ways that are detrimental to their residents.

For a more detailed study of child welfare services, see Kadushin and Martin (1988), one of the most complete and reliable texts on the subject.

YOUTHFUL OFFENDERS

Children who have had difficulty with the law pose a special set of social policy issues. Child welfare specialists tend to include *juvenile offenders* with children who face other problems and to view them as people who are in need of treatment or supervision rather than punishment. In U.S. tradition a child who violates the law is not treated as a criminal; in fact, the assumption is that a child is not capable of knowing that he or she is violating the law—that the concept of crime is one that children do not fully comprehend. There are, of course, exceptions. Children who commit what would be serious crimes if they were adults, such as rape, armed robbery, and murder, are in some states treated as adults and may be punished as adults, including capital punishment. Most legally established juvenile offenses would be considered crimes if they were committed by adults. Because of the age of the perpetrator, however, the acts are not considered criminal. Cases are heard in special courts. Policies prohibit releasing the names or photographs of the children who are involved. Sentences for offenses are not viewed as punishment but rather as a means of controlling children's behavior, rehabilitating children, and treating them so that they learn not to commit future crimes.

A recent example of the complexity of policies dealing with conduct by young people that would be considered criminal if it were by adults is the case of Gina Grant, who had been accepted for admission to Harvard University as an undergraduate student in 1995. However, Harvard discovered that as a fourteen-year-old she had killed her mother in Lexington, S.C., but had not stated that on her application. The state juvenile justice system and the juvenile court in South Carolina treated her as a juvenile, gave her only a minimum juvenile sentence, and maintained the record of her mother's killing as a confidential matter. However, authorities released information on the case to the press, and there was extensive coverage of it. Her denial of admission to Harvard after she had been admitted followed an anonymously provided packet of information to Harvard on the killing and newspaper clippings about it.

There were extensive complications to the killing. Apparently the girl's mother had a long history of alcoholism and made threatening as well as physically aggressive and insulting statements and gestures to the child virtually daily.

Expert attorneys, mental health experts, and family members considered this a classic case in which a child should not be held responsible, as if she were an adult, for her mother's death. They suggested that the publicity about the case, which was actually prohibited by law—a law the county sheriff broke—should not have happened.

The girl was subsequently admitted to several other distinguished universities. She had been an honor student in South Carolina before the killing and in Massachusetts, where she lived with relatives, afterwards. One attorney who works closely with many juvenile offenders, Paul Mones of California, was quoted as saying that "most of these children who have killed their parents have been treated violently and told they're worthless by their parents. And in the eyes of society they've proved that their parents were right" (Mayer 1995, 51). Mones also said that he had encountered large numbers of comparable cases and that most of them were alike. He said that many of the children involved are honor students in school and that they don't tell anyone about the abuse they have suffered.

Status offenders are young people who commit acts that may be forbidden for children but are not offenses when they are committed by adults. Status offenses include such acts as consuming alcohol, engaging in sex, and staying on the streets past a specified curfew.

For many years juvenile delinquents (young people whose acts would be considered criminal if the perpetrators had been adults) and status offenders were treated in the same way by the juvenile courts. Many status offenders were—and in some states continue to be—held in juvenile correctional facilities. In recent years, since the 1970s, there has been a trend, spawned in large part by a federal policy that rewards states that distinguish between the two groups, to separate the treatment of juvenile delinquents and status offenders. It is now unusual for children who have committed status offenses to be held in correctional facilities.

Although there is a decreasing emphasis on institutional care for juveniles who have been in trouble with the law, just as there is for other children and people with disabilities in institutions, national data reflect an increase in the numbers of children who are being held in facilities. Small group homes and foster care are used for youthful offenders, just as they are for children who cannot live with their biological or legally constituted families. Some of these facilities are private rather than public, and, as can be seen in other forms of care discussed in this chapter, there has been a shift from the public to the private.

Yet the total number of children in custody has increased. Clearly, the issues of juvenile misconduct and violence are serious. In 1992 juveniles were taken to courts for almost 1.5 million offenses. Of those, 842,000 were property offenses, such as theft or vandalism; 301,000 were offenses against persons such as assault and murder; 255, 000 were public order offenses, such as public drunkenness and public disorder; and 72,000 were drug offenses. More than 80 percent of the youthful offenders were male. Nearly two-thirds were white, and almost all the rest were black. The definition of juvenile varies from state to state. Many young people defined as juvenile offenders are under thirteen. And for some serious offenses such as murder, even young juveniles can be treated as adults in some states, although the decision on their treatment is typically made by a judge, who evaluates the maturity of the young person (Maguire & Pastore 1995).

INSTITUTIONALIZATION TRENDS

The shift from public to private facilities for those who need institutional care can be seen in most areas of services. Care for the infirm and aged, dependent children, youthful offenders, persons who are mentally disabled, and persons with mental illness has moved from public to private resources. Some observers of social policy, as noted, refer to the shift as the privatization of services. For example, in 1970 there were 189,956 residents with mental retardation in 190 state facilities. By 1993 there were 73, 856 people in 1,765 facilities. Clearly, those cared for by states have decreased in number, and state institutions are smaller facilities.

Public policy has swung in the private direction for a variety of reasons. Private care is often viewed as potentially more humane and, in some ways, less costly than public care. The care can be provided by contracts with care providers, which can be canceled or allowed to expire. When government builds facilities and staffs them with permanent employees, it takes on fiscal obligations that continue indefinitely and often expensively.

SERVICES FOR PEOPLE WITH MENTAL ILLNESS

One of the more complex areas of social services for people who need help is the care of the mentally ill. As chapter 2 points out, institutions for the mentally ill were an innovation and reform in the nineteenth century. Before the development of the asylum movement, the mentally ill might be incarcerated along with prisoners who had violated the law. They could be chained and even executed. The segregation of the mentally ill and the provision of humane treatment to them in asylums was a major reform pursued by Dorothea Dix and other advocates. The history of care for the mentally ill in America has been described in a fascinating, classic work by A. Deutsch (1949).

191

In later years, the mental hospital-asylum reform movement became its own problem, because such institutions were found to fall short of high-quality, humane care for the large population of Americans with mental illness.

The Discrediting of Mental Hospitals

In the twentieth century another famous reformer, Clifford Beers, became an important figure in mental health. His book, *A Mind That Found Itself,* written in 1908, following his own recovery from mental illness, spoke about inhumane treatment by the staff within punitive asylums—the very organizations that were originally designed to improve the treatment of the mentally ill and make it more humane (Beers 1953; Quam 1995). Beers helped organize state, national, and international organizations concerned with mental illness, which evolved into such groups as the National Association for Mental Health.

The social policy for much of the twentieth century had been to place mentally ill people in mental institutions, where they could be safely treated for their conditions. Yet as Beers and others reported, the institutions presented new kinds of mistreatment of that vulnerable population. In the 1960s other students of mental illness and mental health studied and wrote about the poor, often punitive treatment to which the mentally ill were subjected. One of perhaps the two most important works was *Asylums* (Goffman 1961), which described, on the basis of a participant observation, the social structure of a major mental hospital. The portrait's truth was persuasive. It demonstrated that treatment for patients in such institutions was unlikely to be a high priority. The second work, *The Myth of Mental Illness* (1961), is by a psychiatrist, Thomas Szasz; in it he effectively questions the nation that there is actually something that can be called mental illness in the same sense that a physical condition is illness. This book, and several that followed, challenged the mental health system in the United States, especially the system of committing people to institutions without their consent.

A development in the 1960s and the years that followed was a series of court cases that challenged the involuntary commitment aspect of the mentally ill laws which had for so long been the basis of social policy covering the mentally ill. One of the most important, *Wyatt v. Stickney* (1972), was a federal Alabama case that held that a person could not be confined in a mental hospital against his or her will unless treatment was provided to that person. It became clear that the mental health policies, as they had operated, could no longer continue because many mental hospitals had neither the programs nor the personnel to provide the treatment required. The states also discovered that supplying treatment to their mental patients was much more expensive than the essentially custodial care that had been provided for much of the history of the asylum movement. Therefore, many states began discharging patients who, prior to the court cases and the community mental health legislation, might have spent the balance of their lives in mental hospitals. The new requirement was that the mental health system and the mental hospitals become treatment centers designed to help and not simply restrain or isolate the mentally disabled.

Meanwhile, treatment had become more of a possibility with the development, beginning in the 1950s, of sophisticated drugs that could be used with severely mentally ill people in place of mechanical restraints, locked cells, and other artifacts of past methods. It became increasingly possible, because of these new drugs, for more people with mental illnesses to live in the community and carry on near normal lives.

Not all mentally ill people, even though they may not need hospital care, can live unsupervised in their communities. Therefore, there have been small group facilities established for the mentally ill, often operated by private individuals who house several patients who might otherwise be in hospitals; these facilities are not terribly different in structure from the small group homes described for children who cannot live in their own homes. In many cases the adult residents pay for their care with payments from Supplemental Security Income or Social Security Disability, for which they are eligible because of their disabilities. This is another form of the movement toward private rather than public care for vulnerable people.

Although some observers continue to believe that mental illness is simply a metaphor for socially unacceptable behavior (Szasz 1961), there appears to be strong societal acceptance of the idea that mental illness is, in fact, an illness and that it is treatable; psychoactive drugs have increasingly provided means for treating the kinds of behavior defined as mental illness.

Other observers have been bitter critics of the social policy to remove mental patients from hospitals, a process that is called *deinstitutionalization*. E. F. Torrey (1988) is one who insists that the removal of such individuals is directly related to the problem of homelessness. It is one of the ironies of current U.S. policy that many persons who would have once been held in mental hospitals because they have symptoms of mental illness are now residing in homeless shelters, which are typically not as attractive or humane as today's mental hospitals. Mental hospitals, especially after they were required to provide treatment to their patients, became so expensive that it was in the interest of the state governments to reduce their populations. Therefore, some observers believe that the whole shift from hospital to community services is an effort to save money more than an effort to preserve the rights and enhance the well-being of the mentally ill.

D. Mechanic's 1989 book is devoted solely to the whole issue of mental health and social policy. His book and other literature on the same subject are of increasing importance because it is clear than mental health is currently less a problem of medicine and treatment than it is a problem of social policy—for instance, policy about such fundamentals as deinstitutionalization.

Another important book is Elliot Liebow's (1993) *Tell Them Who I Am.* Liebow, an anthropologist, worked closely with homeless women in shelters and centers near Washington, D.C. Such shelters have in some ways replaced mental hospitals in housing people with mental problems. Although he does not specifically identify the women he met as mentally ill, Liebow notes that those who do not need mental health services are not likely to receive or be able to effectively use them. He writes, "Even if one can overcome the initial problem of locating such persons and persuading them that they need what the program offers, there remains the even more difficult problem of getting those persons to remain in one place long enough to receive continued treatments over time" (41–42).

Not all groups react the same to the use of mental health services. Many experts emphasize the importance of cultural sensitivity in dealing with minority group clients. Bertha Holliday, director of the American Psychological Association's office of ethnic-minority affairs, says that therapy is not embedded in African American culture. Some African Americans can't afford it or don't have insurance, and others fear the stigma. While some use clergy for therapy, others consult psychics and astrologers. The suicide rate for young African American males is high, reflecting an increase in this decade and one element of the seriousness of mental health problems in the African American community. Dr. Linda James Myers of Ohio State University says that drug and alcohol use in the community is in part a reflection of people's efforts to medicate themselves for depression. African Americans are also concerned about showing weakness when they live in rough neighborhoods. There is something of a taboo about therapy in such areas, an additional reason for the resistance to it (Leland, Samuels, Rosenberg, & Springer 1997).

Many social work clients are members of minority groups, including African Americans. One of the strategies for dealing with a number of personal and family problems such as child and spouse maltreatment, delinquency, and crime is referral to mental health services. However, if minority clients are unwilling to or unable to use those services, the strategy is clearly not likely to be worthwhile. Mental health services providers, who include many members of minority groups, need to find alternative ways for dealing with mental illness among their clients, especially those who are culturally resistant to what they presently offer.

Community Mental Health Centers

Perhaps the major current policy response to the issues of mental health and mental illness has been a series of statutes establishing and financing a network of community mental health centers. That development was initially a product of President John F. Kennedy's New Frontier program. The statutes on community mental health were passed in 1963, 1975, and 1980. Those Community Mental Health Acts established local services for the mentally ill and were part of the virtual revolution in the care and treatment of the mentally ill which began in the 1960s. D. Chambers (1993), in his social policy analysis text, provides a detailed discussion of the community mental health legislation and policies.

By the 1990s community mental health centers dotted the United States to the point that virtually every citizen was covered by a program. The programs are generally less accessible to those in rural areas than those who live in cities, but the services are still available, to some extent.

Community mental health programs provide for mental health counseling, prescription drugs, "club houses" for people to spend their days in, hospitalization in community hospitals for people who require it for short periods of time, employment referral and training, and community education about mental health problems. Today's community mental health centers typically provide screening for those who appear to need mental hospitalization. The effort is to prevent commitment to an institution and to serve the patient in the community instead.

Who Are People with Mental Illness?

Although this section has discussed people with mental illness as if they were a single group of people, that is not the case. They include those who are diagnosed with existing mental illness, those with behav-

195

ior problems, those who abuse or are addicted to substances such as alcohol and other drugs, as well as older people who suffer from dementia and children with mentally disabling conditions. Some mentally ill people are defined as dually diagnosed; that is, they may be addicted to alcohol or other drugs and also diagnosed as mentally ill, or they may experience mental illness as well as a developmental disability such as epilepsy.

One of the key policy sources in defining mental illness and its treatment is the *Diagnostic and Statistical Manual of Mental Disorders* (4th ed.) of the American Psychiatric Association (1994). The manual specifies and codes mental illnesses. It is the basis for billing insurance companies and government agencies for mental health services as well as for separating those who are mentally ill from those who are not. Although it was not designed to serve as a policy manual, it has, in effect, become one.

People with Disabilities

People with disabilities have been a long-standing concern of social policy, even before the development of programs such as Social Security. Those who are blind, deaf, and orthopedically handicapped are provided protection and services through a variety of statutes and programs such as Social Security, Supplement Security Income, and Medicaid. Their right to accessible public facilities is guaranteed by the Americans with Disabilities Act, which was passed by Congress in 1990, during the presidency of George Bush.

Another population group whose care has evolved over the years is people with developmental disabilities, a category that generally includes people with mental retardation, autism, cerebral palsy, and epilepsy. Historically, each of those groups has been handled in ways that are comparable to those used with the mentally ill. In the past they have been restrained, isolated, punished, and killed. There have also been major changes in the care of the developmentally disabled toward deinstitutionalization and a shift from public to private care, as in the case of the mentally ill and juvenile offenders. Over the past several years there has been a remarkable reduction in the number of persons with mental retardation housed in state facilities. There have, however, been almost comparable changes in private facilities. In 1977 there were 89,120 in private facilities, but by 1993 that figure had jumped to 229,279 in 58,790 facilities (U.S. Bureau of the Census 1995). Clearly the movement has been from state institutions, which were typically large, to smaller community institutions.

A series of statutes and court decisions has also begun more aggressively to protect the rights of people with disabilities, including those with physical handicaps, to live lives as close to normal as possible. The policies of the nation now require schools to enroll and serve students with disabilities in public schools and higher education programs (sometimes in special classrooms for all or part of the day), require transportation companies to provide service to those who need special help, and require that public buildings be accessible to all.

Persons with developmental disabilities may also be provided with a variety of community services such as day centers, recreation programs, special education activities, and various other programs to enhance their lives and well-being.

People with disabilities, including the mentally and developmentally disabled, are eligible, as the preceding chapter makes clear, for Supplemental Security Income if they are of low income. Those who have worked prior to becoming disabled—who tend to be mentally or physically disabled, since developmental disabilities begin, in many cases, at birth—may receive OASDI.

Recipients of SSI are usually eligible for food stamps and for social services provided by state human services agencies as well. These may include chore services and homemaker services to help clients and their families handle their everyday living situations more effectively, as well as transportation assistance. They are also normally eligible for Medicaid to help pay the costs of their health care.

Offenders against the Law

A relatively new area for human services professionals, including social workers, is work with criminal offenders. Again, for much of human history, law violators were simply punished for their behavior. The assumption was that people were conscious of their own misbehavior and chose to commit any illegal acts. Therefore, punishment was the appropriate response. As time has passed, however, social policies have changed. Perhaps the most important of the changes has been the assumption that physical punishment is not the appropriate response to all misconduct. In fact, the Bill of Rights to the U.S. Constitution forbids cruel and unusual punishment. Incarceration and isolation from the larger community are acceptable, partly as the kind of punishment that can be imposed on those who violate the law and partly to protect the public from law violators. Capital punishment—the death penalty—is also permitted in many states.

Policy alternatives to imprisonment, such as probation, and early re-leases, such as parole, have required human services workers to super-vise and otherwise monitor offenders while they are serving their probationary periods. Even prior to sentencing, many courts rely upon professional workers to study convicted offenders and assess the best sentences for them in terms of community justice and the possibility of preventing them from committing future offenses. Incarceration in pris-ons, although not as expensive as mental hospitalization, is still a costly alternative. When it is possible, social policy suggests the need for com-munity care of offenders so they may be employed and so they are able to pay their own living costs. That trend is another example of the shift-ing of responsibility from the government to other resources. Although the trend is not as pronounced in adult corrections as it is in some of the other fields discussed in this chapter, some states are experimenting with contracting with private vendors to run all or a part of their cor-rections systems.

Current social policies have led to the employment of human ser-vices professionals not only in probation and parole programs but also within institutions themselves. A number of social problems are now en-countered within correctional institutions which were not commonly found in the past. These new phenomena include the following:

1. Many more people are sentenced to prisons or are serving pro-bation or parole sentences than in the past. Both the absolute numbers and the rates of incarceration have increased, largely because the federal and state governments are increasingly using sentences to deal with crime. In 1990 there was a total of 740,000 federal and state prisoners. By 1994 there were more than a million—1,012,463 (Beck & Gilliard 1995). The rate of incarceration per 100,000 people has also increased. In 1990 there were 297 people under sentences per 100,000 people. That number had grown by 1994 to 387 per 100,000 (Beck & Gilliard 1995); most of the growth is from drug crimes. The numbers have led to serious overcrowding and all of the prob-lems associated with it (Gilliard 1993).
2. Many more women are entering prisons and serving sentences, although the large majority of prisoners are men. In 1985 there were 21,345 female federal and state prisoners; in 1990, 40,564; and by 1994, 59,878 (Beck & Gilliard 1995). However, the rate

for male prisoners is 746 per 100,000 and for women, only 45 per 100,000 (Beck & Gilliard 1995). Many of those women are mothers, and they require human services workers or others to help them arrange for and maintain care for their children. Other women enter prison pregnant. Many penitentiaries have nurseries to care for newborn children, although when they become older most of the children are placed with family members in the community.

3. Large numbers of prisoners have problems with illegal drugs, although fewer are in prison because of drug offenses. A 1991 study of prisoners in state institutions found that some two-thirds had, at some time, been drug users on a regular basis (Beck et al. 1992). Thirty-two percent had used cocaine on a regular basis, compared to 22 percent in 1986. However, there was a small decline from 56 to 50 percent in the percentage who used drugs in the month before the offense in 1991, compared to 1986. There was a comparable drop, from 36 to 31 percent, in those who were using drugs at the time of the offense. The problems of drug users, as well as the problems of drug use within prisons, often require the intervention of human services workers.

4. Long prison sentences, which have often been associated with public policies designed to reduce drug use and abuse, have created an elderly prison population. It is not unusual for state and federal prisons to house inmates in their senior years, which creates a need for the kinds of health and human services other elderly people require (Harbert & Ginsberg 1990).

5. It is clear to many observers that law violators often suffer from mental disabilities, especially mental retardation and mental illness. Many also have learning disabilities. Such inmates often benefit from the services of human services workers who can help prisoners overcome or cope more effectively with their problems.

6. There are disproportionately large numbers of minority people among prisoners. In 1993 almost half of all prisoners were African American. The African American male incarceration rate is shockingly high—2,920 per 100,000 population in 1993 compared to 398 per 100,000 for white men. Hispanic men have a very high rate, too—994 per 100,000. African American and

Hispanic women also have high incarceration rates, about twice as high as whites for Hispanics and seven times as high for African Americans (Beck & Gilliard 1995).

CRIME VICTIMS

According to L. D. Bastian (1992), people over age twelve living in the United States in 1991 were victims of 34.7 million crimes. That figure actually represented a decrease of 16.2 percent from 1981. Of those crimes, 15.8 million were household crimes, 12.5 million were personal thefts, and 6.4 million were violent crimes.

Another developing social policy is that victims of crime ought to be compensated and helped. Most states now have crime victim programs, which include restitution plans for offenders to compensate their victims (Roberts 1995). Victims also receive counseling and similar services to help them overcome the consequences of the crimes against them, including the trauma they experienced.

PROGRAMS FOR OLDER ADULTS

Another special group that has traditionally been the target of social policy is the elderly. Older adults are probably the most diverse population in the United States. That is, the aging process affects different people in different ways. Health and economic status, mobility, and appearance all vary dramatically from person to person, within and among age groups. Some seventy-year-olds are healthier than some forty-year-olds; some sixty-year-olds need to retire, while some eighty-year-olds continue full-time employment. Given those variations in circumstances, it is not surprising that there are difficulties in developing social policies that make sense for the total population of older people.

Many of the programs for the elderly are contained in the Social Security Act, which is discussed in other sections of this book. The social services needed by and available to older people come from various sources, but largely from the Older Americans Act, which was passed in 1965 (DiNitto 1995). That legislation provides funds to the states for the establishment and operation of various programs for older people. Those programs include low-cost meals; home-delivered food; the operation of local "senior centers," which sponsor educational, recreational, and health programs; transportation services; telephone reassurance (in which older people who live alone receive daily telephone calls to determine whether or not they are all right); and many other activities and forms of assistance chosen and designed, in part, by the older people themselves. By policy the funds are allocated and administered through state commissions on aging and local-area agencies on aging. Conscious efforts are made to ensure that the programs meet the needs and interests of the elderly.

Some programs for older adults have been characterized by patronization and treatment of senior citizens as if they were senile. In his popular 1995 novel, *The Rainmaker,* John Grisham describes a law student's visit to a senior citizen center. The young man's impressions are familiar to those who have visited similar centers in the U.S. In his novel Grisham calls the center "the Cypress Gardens Senior Citizens Building," although he notes that there are no flowers or greenery around. The staff director deals with the aging clients by alternately shoving people into their seats when they stand and hugging and patting them. She leads song, helps serve food, chastises those who want alternatives to the served meal, introduces programs, and generally directs the activities of the older people as if they were children. In many cases, senior adults are so lacking in positive activities and positive social opportunities that they tolerate, without complaint, the authoritarian direction of their "leaders."

In 1995 *Consumer Reports* magazine conducted a study of nursing homes. In their study, they report that 40 percent of nursing homes have violated the Federal Health Care Financing Administration standards of patient care. Some 16,000 nursing homes, about 86 percent, are certified by that organization.

The magazine describes the quality of care of thousands of nursing homes as poor or questionable at best and says that serious health conditions such as bedsores, assaults on patients' dignity, and the use of physical restraints were present in many of them. They also found that food served in the nursing homes was frequently unsanitary. They said too that some homes hide their inspection reports and, because they have strong political influence, are allowed to stay open, even when state governments find them in violation of standards.

A reporter for the magazine visited fifty-three nursing homes and twenty-seven "assisted living or board and care" facilities ostensibly to find a home for her mother. She found that the statistics conveyed the facts about such homes. One posted its negative survey too high for anyone to read. They also posted it horizontally when it was printed vertically. Another posted its surveys of conditions, but the posted survey was three years old.

The *Consumer Reports* study implies that many homes get by with inadequate and even inhumane care by staying heavily involved with public policy and by making contributions to political candidates who help them overcome criticisms or negative action.

Consumer Reports gave scores to the national home chains, ranking them from best to worst, so that consumers could make decisions about the best facilities for themselves.

Low-income elderly people are eligible for SSI, as are the mentally and physically disabled. They may also receive the social services that disabled people may obtain through state human services agencies. An important distinction between social services and income maintenance is that the latter is an entitlement, while the former is not. Agencies may provide their social services on a discretionary basis because they have only limited funds and are not required to spend them equally on all clients, which is the case for economic assistance entitlement programs.

OTHER SERVICES

Many other policies establish agencies and programs for the benefit of Americans. It is beyond the scope of this book to catalog all of them, and, as has been suggested, they change so frequently that it is not productive to try to develop an exhaustive listing.

Some of the more important programs that are part of the social policy of the United States and are designed to improve the well-being of individuals in the nonfinancial assistance realm include:

1. Community Action Programs, which are outgrowths of the War on Poverty or Economic Opportunity Act of 1964, discussed in chapter 2.
2. Vocational Rehabilitation, which finances programs in each state, largely with federal funds, to train or retrain people for employment. Many of the beneficiaries have physical or mental disabilities.
3. Family service agencies, which provide family counseling, some adoption services, consumer credit counseling, and counseling

services for employees under contract with employers, among other services that vary with each local family service agency.

4. Informal education and recreation agencies such as Boys and Girls Clubs, Jewish Community Centers, YMCAs and YWCAs, Boy Scouts, Girl Scouts, Campfire, Big Brothers and Big Sisters, and a variety of comparable organizations that are local.

5. There are also many self-help organizations, including the Alliance for the Mentally Ill, Alcoholics Anonymous, programs for parents of children with disabilities, and similar organizations for people facing other problems.

6. Employee Assistance Programs, which operate in government agencies and corporations to help employees with personal problems such as alcohol and drug abuse, marital difficulties, and other forms of counseling and assistance.

7. Veterans' services, which are provided to veterans of various war eras. They include health and mental health care; pensions, especially for those injured during wars; education grants; and various other benefits, some of which are means tested.

In addition to the government and nonprofit agencies that have been discussed in this chapter, there is also an array of proprietary, businesslike organizations that provide human services. These include private practice counseling services and hospitals for those who are facing personal problems.

CONCLUSION

This chapter has provided information on the current operations of many of the most important human services, especially those that are targeted for special groups of people with special needs. The services delineated are not, by and large, entitlements, as are those described in the preceding chapter. They are, however, widely available to those who need them. They represent what some call the personal social services in that they help people with their personal, functional problems rather than their economic needs. They constitute a critical part of U.S. social policy and represent the nation's specific efforts to address tangible human problems with appropriate policies and programs.

DISCUSSION QUESTIONS

1. Contrast the services provided to persons with mental illness with those provided to older adults.
2. What are some of the ways in which the services described in this chapter are different from the entitlements discussed in the last chapter?
3. Discuss some of the factors that have caused offenders against the law and the correctional system to become a concern of social policy.
4. Analyze some of the reasons for the shift from institutional or group care of children, mentally ill people, and offenders to community or family care.

REFERENCES

Alexander, C. A. (1995). Distinctive dates in social welfare history. In R. L. Edwards et al. (Eds.) *Encyclopedia of social work,* 19th ed. Washington, DC: NASW Press, 2631–2647.

American Psychiatric Association. (1994). *Diagnostic and statistical manual of mental disorders—DSM IV.* Washington, DC: American Psychiatric Association.

Barker, R. L. (1995). *The social work dictionary,* 3d ed. Silver Spring, MD: NASW Press.

Bastian, L. D. (1992, October). *Bureau of Justice Statistics: Criminal victimization, 1991.* Washington, DC: U.S. Department of Justice.

Beck, A., et al. (1992, May). *Bureau of Justice Statistics: Survey of state prison inmates, 1991.* Washington, DC: U.S. Department of Justice.

Beck, A. J., & Gilliard, D. K. (1995). *Bureau of Justice Statistics bulletin: Prisoners in 1994.* Washington, DC: U.S. Department of Justice.

Beers, C. W. (1953). *A mind that found itself.* Garden City, NY: Doubleday.

Berry, M. (1997). *The family at risk: Issues and trends in family preservation services.* Columbia: University of South Carolina Press.

Chambers, D. (1993). *Social policy and social programs: A method for the practical public policy analyst,* 2d ed. New York: Macmillan.

Chester, B. (1995). Victims of torture and trauma. In R. L. Edwards et al. (Eds.), *Encyclopedia of social work,* 19th ed. 2445–2452. Washington, DC: NASW Press.

Committee on Ways and Means, U.S. House of Representatives. (1996). *1996 green book: Background material and data on programs within the jurisdiction of the Committee on Ways and Means.* Washington, DC: U.S. Government Printing Office.

Day, P. J. (1997). *A new history of social welfare,* 2d ed. Englewood Cliffs, NJ: Prentice Hall.

DiNitto, D. M. (1995). *Social welfare: Politics and public policy,* 4th ed. Englewood Cliffs, NJ: Prentice-Hall.

204

Deutsch, A. (1949). *The mentally ill in America: A history of their care and treatment from colonial times,* 2d ed. New York: Columbia University Press.

Dumaine, B. (1993, April 5). Legal child labor comes back. *Fortune,* 127 (7), 86–95.

Fender, L., & Shaw, D. (1990). *The state of the states' children.* Washington, DC: National Governors' Association.

Gillespie, E., & Shellhas, P. (1994). *Contract with America.* New York: Random House.

Gilliard, D. K. (1993). *Bureau of Justice statistics bulletin: Prisoners in 1992.* Washington, DC: U.S. Department of Justice.

Ginsberg, L. (1995). *Social welfare almanac,* 2d ed. Washington, DC: NASW Press.

Goffman, E. (1961). *Asylums.* New York: Anchor.

Grisham, J. (1995). *The rainmaker.* New York: Doubleday.

Greenfield, L. A., & Minor-Harper, S. (1991, March). *Bureau of justice statistic special report: Women in prison.* Washington, DC: U.S. Department of Justice.

Harbert, A., & Ginsberg, L. (1990). *Human services for older adults: Concepts and skills,* 2d ed. Columbia: University of South Carolina Press.

Jansson, B. S. (1997). *The reluctant welfare state: A history of American social welfare policies,* 3d ed. Pacific Grove, CA: Brooks-Cole.

Jansson, B. S. (1999). *Becoming an effective policy advocate: From policy practice to social justice,* 3d ed. Pacific Grove, CA: Brooks-Cole.

Kadushin, A., & Martin, J. A. (1988). *Child welfare services,* 4th ed. New York: Macmillan.

Leland, J. Samuels, A., Rosenberg, D., & Springen, K. (1997, July 14). 'Don't show weakness': Black Americans still shy away from psychotherapy. *Newsweek,* 60.

Liebow, E. (1993). *Tell them who I am.* New York: Free Press.

Maguire, K., & Pastore, A. L. (Eds.). (1995). *Bureau of justice statistics sourcebook: Criminal justice statistics—1994.* Albany, NY: Hindeland Criminal Justice Research Center.

Mayer, J. (1995, June 5). The justice file: Rejecting Gina. *New Yorker,* 43–51.

Mechanic, D. (1989). *Mental health and social policy,* 3d ed. Englewood Cliffs, NJ: Prentice-Hall.

Miringoff, M. L. (1995). *1995 Index of Social Health: Monitoring the social well-being of the nation.* Tarrytown, NY: Fordham Institute for Innovation in Social Policy.

National Center on Child Abuse and Neglect (1993). *National child abuse and neglect data system, working paper 2: 1991 summary data component.* Gaithersburg, MD: National Center on Child Abuse and Neglect.

Nursing homes: When a loved one needs care. (1995, August) *Consumer Reports,* 518–527.

Petit, M. R., & Curtis, P. A. (1997). *Child abuse and neglect: A look at the states. 1997 CWLA stat book.* Washington, DC: CWLA Press.

Quam, J. K. (1995). Beers, Clifford Whittingham (1976–1943). In R. L. Edwards et al. (Eds.), *Encyclopedia of social work,* 19th ed., 2573. Washington, DC: NASW Press.

Roberts, A. R. (1995). Victim services and victim/witness assistance programs. In R. L. Edwards et al. (Eds.), *Encyclopedia of social work,* 19th ed., 2440–2444, Washington, DC: NASW Press.

Sieg, K. (1998, October 26). My turn: Gorwing up a foster kid. *Newsweek,* 20.

Szasz, T. S. (1961). *The myth of mental illness.* New York: Harper & Row.

Torrey, E. F. (1988). *Nowhere to go.* New York: Harper & Row.

U.S. Bureau of the Census. (1990). *Statistical abstract of the United States: 1990,* 110th ed. Washington, DC: U.S. Government Printing Office.

U.S. Bureau of the Census. (1991). *Statistical abstract of the United States: 1991,* 111th ed. Washington, DC: U.S. Government Printing Office.

U.S. Bureau of the Census. (1995). *Statistical abstract of the United States: 1995.* 115th ed. Washington, DC: U.S. Government Printing Office.

U.S. House of Representatives, Select Committee on Children, Youth, and Families. (1989). *No place to call home: Discarded children in America.* Washington, DC: U.S. Government Printing Office.

Wyatt v. Stickney. (1972). 493 F. Supp. 521, 522.

Zupan, F. H. (1993, March 31). Critics organize against "heavy-handed" DSS. *State* (Columbia, SC), 3B.

Chapter Eight

Analyzing Social Policies and Models for Policy Analysis

Fundamental to understanding and working with social policy is the ability to apply policy analyses. In human services education, especially social work education, the emphasis in social policy curriculum is on learning to analyze policies effectively and accurately. One cannot deal with policies as a practitioner or even intelligently apply social policy without a clear, systematic understanding of what the policies are and how they operate.

Part of the competence of a professional is systematic knowledge of one's roles and the reasons for one's work. In the human services the simple following of rules and regulations, which implement social policy, minimizes the professional role of the professional. One should know why the policy is being applied, the social values the policy reflects, the alternative ways in which the policy might be applied, alternative policies, the sources of funding and the financing alternatives, and the effectiveness of the policy. A well-prepared professional will want to be sure that he or she fully comprehends the policy and ways that it might be improved. Human services professionals should think and act beyond their daily tasks to the larger concepts of social change and human services delivery planning.

The Curriculum Policy Statements that govern accredited baccalaureate and master's social welfare policy and services curricula, for example, state that "students must be taught to analyze current social policy within the context of historical and contemporary factors that shape policy" (Edwards et al. 1995). Such an emphasis on policy analysis can be traced to Boehm's 1959 study of and recommendations for the social work curriculum. Volume 12 of the landmark thirteen-volume study of what social work education should teach and what social workers should know was written by Irving Weissman (1959), who was then a professor at Tulane University School of Social Work in New Orleans. Its title, *Social Welfare Policy and Services in Social Work Education,* standardized the name of that curriculum area. The concepts were actually developed by an eighteen-person panel of social work educators, organization leaders, and federal officials (Weissman 1959). They based their ideas on their own thinking and experience as well as on an examination of course outlines from many of the schools that were teaching social work at the time.

As an analytic framework, the study presented a three-part model for understanding and evaluating social policy, a model that remains useful for current policy analyses and appears to be implied in all of the current models that are suggested for social work. The model presented by Weissman and his colleagues said that there were three elements necessary for understanding social welfare policy and service:

Problem
Policy
Provision

Their theory was that policies developed from the understanding and definition of social problems. *Problems,* Weissman wrote, were those situations that could not "be worked out with available resources institutionalized in society" (1959, 32). Chapter 3 discusses in greater detail the social problems orientation, which deals with the definitions of how a phenomenon becomes a social problem.

Policy, Weissman and his colleagues believed, "refers to the process of social decision-making by which a course of social action is determined, formulated and promoted . . . as well as the product of that process" (1959, 32–33). In other words, once a problem is identified and agreed upon as a problem, society determines policies that are designed to deal with the resolution of the problem.

The way in which the policy is implemented is defined as *provision,* which deals with making resources available to meet social problems or implement policies (Weissman 1959). Clearly, one of the first systematic models for understanding social work and social welfare was Weissman's three-part model. It is interesting and perhaps historically significant that three-part analytical models were well regarded in social work. In fact, the most fundamental conceptualization of the social casework, or direct practice, approach that was originally developed by Mary Richmond and later defined more specifically by G. Hamilton (1940) had three phases—study, diagnosis, and treatment. That conceptualization was widely used at the time of the *Social Work Curriculum Study* (Boehm 1959) and was likely to have influenced the model chosen by those who developed the concept for social welfare policy and services. In more recent years, as this chapter will demonstrate, much more detailed and longer lists of elements have been developed for policy analysis. Similar expanded conceptualizations of direct practice are also now used (Meyer 1987).

The fundamental reasons for the emphasis on policy analysis in social work education are discussed in chapter 1. To serve people effectively, social work believes that it, in the corporate sense of the whole profession, and its individual practitioners must influence social policies—that policies are a major tool for helping those in need. Most of the current textbooks on social policy place their greatest emphasis on policy analysis.

ELEMENTS OF UNDERSTANDING

R. L. Barker (1995, 285) says policy analysis consists of "systematic evaluations of a policy and the process by which it was formulated. Those who conduct such analyses consider whether the process and result were rational, clear, explicit, equitable, legal, politically feasible, compatible with social values, cost-effective, and superior to all the alternatives, in the short term and in the long term."

Effectively analyzing policies presupposes various kinds of knowledge. One cannot analyze social policy by simply understanding and applying a policy analysis framework. Instead, one must have some knowledge of the public policy-making process, politics, public opinion, public finance, the structure and function of the social welfare system, and economics. That is why policy analysis is only one of the components of understanding social policy, as it is discussed in this book. One needs the background information provided by the other components of understanding social policy as well as the learnings associated with other areas of the curriculum, especially research and human behavior and the social environment.

A person from another planet, for example, might develop an analysis of a social policy and a strategy for changing it which might objectively appear reasonable but might be horrendously inappropriate and unattainable. For example, when I was a state human services commissioner in the 1970s, my staff told me about a budget crisis in the line item for providing services to adults. They suggested that we make some simple modifications of the "chore services" program, which paid people to provide cooking, cleaning, and personal care for adults with disabilities in their own homes. The staff suggested that we simply tell those chore services providers who were relatives of chore services recipients that we would no longer pay them for their help. It seemed reasonable that relatives ought to take care of one another without the state paying them. Because it seemed to be a worthwhile policy that ought to be well understood by all parties, including legislators, we decided to announce it to the chore services providers and recipients.

When we implemented the policy we learned more about the issue than we had known. First, we discovered that half the chore service providers were relatives. In other words, half of the people who were receiving the services were being helped by their relatives. Second, we learned that the providers had chosen, or had been persuaded, to supply care for their disabled grandparents or aunts or uncles or cousins in lieu of working in the regular economy. If they were not paid, they would have to quit providing services to their relatives. The families wanted their disabled family members to remain at home, which they could do only with financial help. The state had an interest in maintaining the arrangements as well, because care in the clients' own homes was much less costly than nursing home or institutional care. Other relatives, legislators, the press, and other groups pointed to the impropriety and wastefulness of the policy change. A reasonable-sounding policy proved totally unreasonable, and we quickly abandoned it.

Candidates for political office have had similar difficulties with Social Security, which appears to many to be a dispensable source of funds which can be cut to reduce deficits without hurting anyone too badly. Republican candidate Senator Barry Goldwater proposed converting Social Security to a private program when he ran against President Lyndon Johnson in 1964. It was a major factor in his decisive loss. President Reagan made similar suggestions early in his presidency but quickly abandoned the position, although he made some changes in benefits for college-age survivors of recipients. They were essentially eliminated from receiving Social Security payments. He was also able to implement a tightening of eligibility requirements for persons with physical and mental disabilities. Those targets were young people and people with disabilities, who are not as effective advocates as the elderly. President Bill Clinton's administration spoke of taking action to waive the annual cost of living adjustment for Social Security beneficiaries and of increasing the income taxes on the benefits they received. Those moves would have their major impact on elderly people. After strong protests, some of them by members of Congress, the proposals were abandoned.

Social Security is a costly program, and the Social Security Trust Fund, which holds the payments employees and employers make, has generally contained large amounts of money. Members of Congress, advocacy groups for the aging, and others protested strongly against any reductions, and the Clinton proposals were abandoned. Social Security is difficult to reduce for several reasons, as any clear analysis would demonstrate. First, its principal advocates are older people, who are effective in influencing elected officials because they can articulate the issues that affect them and are also more likely to vote than other population groups. Older people and their organizations also strongly protect Social Security because, over the past decades, it resolved one of the most critical problems in the United States—the poverty of older adults. Although they are not all wealthy now, before Social Security was improved and stabilized in the 1970s and 1980s, the elderly were the poorest group in the nation. After the reforms that was no longer true. The levels of benefits were increased, and the annual cost-of-living adjustments kept those benefits from being eroded by inflation. Furthermore, older people often feel financially vulnerable because most of the means available to younger groups to prevent future poverty—such as seeking better-paying work or setting up pension plans for their retirement—are not available to them. They feel trapped because they are subject to public policy decisions that are beyond their own control. A critical analysis makes it clear to most elected officials that threatening Social Security will often literally be self-defeating.

Part of the problem with analyzing policies such as Social Security and social services such as chore services is knowing all of the sources of information available to various groups of people. New presidents, for example, have since the 1960s been from the executive branches of the federal or state governments. Presidents Carter, Reagan, and Clinton had most recently been governors. Presidents Nixon, Ford, and Bush had mostly recently been vice presidents, although all three also had prior experience in Congress. Those who hear most from constituents about problems with income and concerns about Social Security are members of Congress. That is because, as discussed in chapter 4, members of Congress devote major portions of their time and effort to "constituent services"—to hearing from and trying to resolve problems for their constituents. Executive branch officials such as presidents and governors do not devote much of their time to constituent services. They work instead with members of Congress or the state legislature on legislative programs. Therefore, they do not always know the extent of concerns about individual problems such as poverty among the elderly. In many cases representatives of the legislative branch, whether the U.S. Congress or a state legislature, will have much better information on constituent reactions to specific proposals than will executive branch leaders.

The Role of Human Services Workers in Policy Analysis

Human services workers need the ability to analyze policies for a variety of reasons. To carry out their professional responsibilities to be aware of and influence policy, they must be skillful in understanding and analyzing skills to implement policies effectively. Skill in social policy analysis is a necessary part of the ability of social policy practitioners, some of whose roles are discussed in chapter 9.

Intentional and Unintentional Consequences

Perhaps the primary overall objective of policy analysis is to develop policies that have the results, or consequences, they are designed for and to avoid results that are not intended. Unintended consequences are the nightmares of policy makers, who may set out to solve a problem such as developing a new catastrophic health insurance program with Medicare, as Congress did in 1988. The costs were to be financed largely from additional taxes on upper-income elderly people. Advocates for the new program appeared to approve of it partly because many older people thought they would be receiving new coverage for nursing home care. When they discovered that their taxes increased and that there was no nursing home care included, the elderly rebelled and demanded that the program be repealed, which Congress did in 1989 (Ginsberg 1990).

Unintended consequences are always a social policy concern that is just below the surface of policy making. If the federal government provides health insurance coverage for all citizens, which had been proposed by the Clinton administration, would the policy increase the use of health care so greatly that the costs for everyone would rise prohibitively? If Temporary Assistance for Needy Families benefits are increased to a more generous level, will assistance compete with low-wage employment and, in turn, reduce the labor force and the amount of tax revenues? If TANF benefits are reduced, will children suffer? When involuntary commitment procedures for public mental hospitals were made more restrictive, was an unintended consequence for creation of the problem of homelessness? Those who work with social policies always want to achieve specific objectives. They also try to analyze their policies so that they will know about and perhaps be able to avoid unintended consequences.

A variety of conservative social policy analysts from fields such as sociology and economics have also advocated major changes in social welfare and concluded that existing social welfare policies caused more problems than they cured. Prominent among these analysts is Charles Murray, whose book *Losing Ground* (1994) was highly influential in the passage of the 1996 welfare reform legislation which, in substance, eliminated Aid to Families with Dependent Children and replaced it with Temporary Assistance for Needy Families. Murray's thesis was that the AFDC program and federally financed welfare assistance in general caused poverty and dependency. By allowing low-income people to receive welfare assistance without working, the nation created a new welfare culture. People who had been too proud to accept the assistance in the past began to view it as rational and foolish to deny themselves assistance. Young women, married or not, Murray said, could receive help simply by having a child. Many chose not to marry and had children in order to receive assistance from government that would allow them to live independently, have families, and set up their own households.

Murray (1994) points out that it made little difference that some states provided more support for children and parents than others because the food stamp program's benefit levels were based on the size of assistance grants. In states that paid larger amounts of assistance, families received less in food stamps. In states that provided low levels of assistance, families received more in food stamps. Therefore, he believed that there was a fairly consistent pattern and level of assistance in all states and that this assistance caused dependency rather than curing it.

Some newspaper columnists, policy makers, and voters agreed with Murray or had reached similar conclusions even before he wrote his book. Milton and Rose Friedman (1980) said that the then-current welfare system as well as the whole Social Security program were examples of poor public policy that ought to be changed. They proposed doing away with Social Security and providing families with a negative income tax that would, through the tax system, provide help to families who needed it without the large bureaucracy associated with public welfare. George Gilder (1981) and other writers questioned the whole concept of entitlements. Gilder was a proponent of family allowances, and he believed that the eligibility and entitlement systems of American family assistance were improper and counterproductive.

Herrnstein and Murray, in their book *The Bell Curve* (1994), suggested that the nation could be moving toward a "custodial state." Their concern was that large numbers of people would become dependent on government because they could not cope with the complexities of modern American society. The authors concluded that a more gentle and less complicated society would be necessary to help people of low intelligence (the major theme of their book) to survive in American life. They suggested that even the rules of criminal justice and law violation were so complicated that people with less-than-average intelligence would have difficulty staying out of trouble without even being concerned about their ability to support themselves financially.

Newt Gingrich (1995), the former Speaker of the House of Representatives, also was persuaded that major changes were needed in the public assistance system, and he described in his book those that he thought necessary. Although Gingrich faced his own difficulties later, culminating in a congressional investigation that required him to pay a fine of $300,000 for misusing contributed funds and mingling foundation monies with campaign support, his influence was great, as mentioned earlier, on the major welfare revisions that occurred in 1996.

All of these analysts also believed that federal welfare assistance was inappropriate and that assistance should be provided by the lowest level of government and the political entity closest to the citizenry. They believed that private charities, foremost, and local governments could provide any necessary assistance. They also believed that states should be able to set up any kind of welfare assistance program they chose but that federal involvement in such efforts was incorrect. In this they were much like the earliest thinkers about federal relations with citizens.

These analysts of public assistance programs focused on the unintended consequences of such programs. Their views, more than any others, prevailed in the most recent changes in American assistance programs. Their assertion that the entitlement programs were the root causes of dependency were counterintuitive but struck chords with many who found the existing entitlement programs offensive and inappropriate for American government. This author's book, mentioned earlier, *Conservative Social Welfare Policy* (1998), provides detailed discussions of the prevalence of conservative opinions and influence on current social welfare policy in the United States.

Financing

Another overriding issue in analyzing social policy is financing. How much is actually allocated to implementing a policy? How will a carefully developed, idealistic policy be financed, or will it be financed at all? Understanding policy also means understanding the financing of policy. In the public policy component it is important to look not only at the content of legislation or court decisions and administrative orders but also at the financing that goes with them. Everything costs money, even if it is a charitable effort directed by volunteers. Such fundamentals of program operation as postage, telephone costs, and transportation are always required. If all the funds are donated, that is the answer to how the program is financed. But financing is always a factor and is probably the first series of questions one must answer when analyzing policies. Whatever one is examining—the human services that are to result from the policy, the relationship between the extent of the funding and the actual impact it will make, or the priorities of the agency or government that develops the policies—money is at the heart of any analysis. The same point is made in chapter 5 in the discussion of the credibility of economics in a free enterprise society.

An example of money driving policy comes from *The Chronicle of Higher Education* (1993), which reported in its "Marginalia" column that employees of Pennsylvania State University were forbidden to drink soft drink products that compete with Pepsi-Cola because the university had a contract with the parent corporation, Pepsico, which required employees, when they publicly consumed soft drinks, to drink only Pepsi.

FRAMEWORKS FOR ANALYSIS

There are many social work and social science frameworks or models for analyzing social policies. None is universally accepted or used in social work. Most include similar elements, although the emphases differ from model to model. H. A. Burch (1991), D. Chambers (1992), A. W. Dobelstein (1996), D. Gil (1976), N. Gilbert, H. Specht, and P. Terrell (1992), W. J. Heffernan (1992), D. Iatridis (1995), C. S. Prigmore and C. R. Atherton (1997), P. H. Rossi and H. E. Freeman (1989), D. Stoesz and H. J. Karger (1992), and J. E. Tropman (1987) are among the authors who have developed policy analysis approaches. All of these frameworks vary, and all are much more complex than the "problem, policy, provision" model proposed by Weissman in 1959.

The models differ in length. Some contain just a few elements, as the specific illustrations in this chapter demonstrate, while others include a larger number of elements. Some focus more heavily on philosophical and value issues while others place more emphasis on finances. Some place more emphasis on quantification than others. All, however, if systematically and carefully applied, should give the analyst a better understanding of the policy that is being analyzed than would be possible without a systematic model.

Most of the models follow, to some extent, the general features of the scientific method as E. D. Hirsch, J. F. Kett, and J. Trifel (1993) describe it: (1) careful observation; (2) deduction of natural laws (in the case of the social sciences and human services, reviewing what knowledge has been developed and what questions have already been answered through, for example, a review of the existing literature); (3) formation of hypotheses or generalizations (in the case of social policy of specific policy solutions designed to deal with the issues being addressed); and (4) experimental or observational testing of the validity of the hypotheses, or policy solutions. The problem, policy, provision triad (Weissman 1959) is in some ways an abbreviated version of the scientific method.

J. E. Tropman (1987) suggests that there are five phases to the policy cycle:

1. Problem definition
2. Proposal development
3. Decision phase
4. Planning and program design
5. Programming and evaluation

Within each of the phases Tropman (1987) details a number of methods or techniques, several of which are technical methods such as needs assessment, Delphi, flow charting, and lobbying. (Many of these are more applicable to the policy practice component and are discussed in more detail in chapter 9).

In one way or another the policy analysis models described in this chapter deal with the phases specified by Tropman. The models tend to incorporate the approaches of other models, even though they do so in different frameworks and with different language. Einbinder (1995) has added to basic concepts of policy analysis.

Who Wins, Who Loses

Policy analysis usually involves specific examinations; for example, one of the classic policy analysis questions is "Who benefits, and who loses?" This is similar to a classic political science policy analysis question: "Who gets what, when, and how?" (Lasswell 1958). There is a general, usually correct assumption that every social policy helps some individuals and groups and also costs some individuals and groups. Often these costs can be translated into money. President Clinton, for example, early in his term of office, laid out that proposition clearly (*Los Angeles Times* 1993); he said that there were sacrifices needed to render the American economy healthy and that the sacrifices would be greater among those who had benefited most during the Reagan and Bush administrations. Those were the wealthiest Americans, whose proportion of American income increased dramatically during those years (Ginsberg 1992), as opposed to the least wealthy and lower-middle-income groups, whose incomes declined or remained steady. His policy would, he suggested, help all wage earners by reducing the budget deficit and the interest on national debt while it would disproportionately hurt the highest wage earners. Seldom are matters so clearly stated.

There is another example from my experiences in state government. During one exceptionally cold winter the administration learned that many people were being forced to choose between heating and eating. They could not afford both adequate food purchases and the utilities or heating fuel to stay warm. Energy costs had increased dramatically because of conflicts in the Middle East. Illness and death seemed the potential consequences for many residents. We thus tried to develop a policy that would require the utility companies to provide low-income people with lower cost service. Utility rates, however, were set in our state—and in all states—by regulatory commissions that allow the electric and gas companies to charge on the basis of their costs. If they gave reduced costs to low-income families, those reductions would be passed on as increases to higher-income families. In effect, we would be imposing a tax on some for the benefit of others.

Fortunately, the federal government developed and has maintained a program for home heating assistance called the Low Income Energy Assistance Program. The funds are appropriated from the regular tax revenue of the government and given to the states on the basis of their weather; states with the coldest climates and the longest winters receive more funds per low-income person than warmer states. Less directly, that program is still one in which people pay taxes that are redistributed to low-income people to help them with their utility costs. The mechanism was not as direct as it would be if the companies would lower the costs to lower-income people, but the principle is the same: *In any policy decision some people benefit, while others pay.* The utility companies also provided means for their customers to make voluntary contributions that would be applied to the utility bills of low-income customers. Those efforts have yielded some assistance for low-income people, but not as much as a government appropriation provides.

Cost-Benefit Analysis

Another technique often used in policy analysis is cost benefit, or, as it is sometimes called, cost-effectiveness, analysis. Does the cost of the policy, one asks, provide commensurate benefits? One example of applying that concept is in determining eligibility for assistance programs such as Temporary Assistance for Needy Families and food stamps. Those who study aid programs know that most of those who are certified as eligible are, in fact, eligible. There are a few fraudulent claims that can be prosecuted through the law enforcement systems. There are also several cases in which people are slightly, almost technically, ineligible because they neglected to report some earnings or a gift or because the value of their property increased and they did not report it. The cost of eliminating *all* of the ineligible applicants—down to the last fraction of a percent—is now viewed as beneficial enough to justify the cost. Eliminating all ineligible clients costs a great deal more than eliminating almost all of them, especially all who only slightly exceed the eligibility guidelines. Another way to express it is to say that such an intense effort is not likely to be cost-effective, because it costs more than it is worth.

Another example of cost-benefit analysis was offered in 1995 by *Consumer Reports,* which analyzed the potential consequences of reducing expenditures on nutrition programs through making them block grants

218

to the states rather than federal entitlements. The programs, including food stamps and WIC, are discussed in chapter 6.

Consumer Reports (June 1995) quotes President Richard Nixon about the importance of adequate nutrition for children and workers and then cites a report by the General Accounting Office which said that "every $1 spent on WIC produced Medicaid savings of between $2 and $4." The article goes on to say that adequate diets for pregnant women and children can prevent the expenditure of much more money to deal with severe health problems in later years. The magazine suggests that the increased malnutrition problems and long-term social and economic costs should be considered in the whole discussion of reducing federal expenditures.

EXAMPLES OF POLICY ANALYSIS MODELS

As suggested, there are many examples of policy analysis outlines and models. Most require the analyst to answer a series of questions about the policy. The result of answering those questions is an analysis of the policy. The following sections describe some currently used policy analysis models.

It is worthwhile to note that any usable policy analysis framework will include several dimensions. One is the nature of the decision-making process associated with the policy, changes in it, or its replacement. Who are the contending parties? Who has the power to make the decisions? What values are inherent in all sides of the issue? And who is affected, positively or negatively, by the policy? If one takes one of the most controversial social policy issues of the 1980s and 1990s, abortion, the issues may be clearly seen. The debate over abortion is, fundamentally, over two value questions: When does life begin, at birth or at the moment a sperm and an ovum unite? And are there justifiable social limits on the rights of a woman over her body and its functions? Those with opposite value positions are arrayed against each other on the issue. The "pro-choice" position is favored by those who believe women have authority over their own bodies and bodily functions as well as by those who want women to be as free as men to make their own plans and live their own lives. On the other side are some who believe abortion is a form of murder (because they believe life begins at conception, not at birth); some aspiring adoptive parents, who believe abortion has reduced the number of children available for adoption; and a variety of

219

others. Analyzing the issue of abortion, and any other issue, requires some effort to investigate the decisions that led to its implementation or to its rejection.

Finances are also always a subject of discussion in any policy analysis model. How much will the policy cost? How will the funds be raised to pay for it? And what else might have to be eliminated to make the policy affordable?

What are the alternative approaches to solving the problem or implementing programs that could be solutions? If government wants to make it possible for more parents, especially mothers, to work outside their homes, should government set up a national day care program? Should government give money to parents to purchase day care from centers or in-home providers? Or should government provide vouchers to parents than can be used only for day care? What, the next question becomes, are other alternatives, and what are the strengths and weaknesses of the alternatives? For example, if government gave money to families, some might simply keep the money and use it as a substitute for employment outside the home. Or they might use the money to pay a relative (like the chore services providers described earlier), who would then care for children rather than working outside the home themselves—and stay free of trouble—with their new money. A cash approach has many more possibilities than other approaches. Yet cash payments may not be viewed as being in the best interests of the families, children, or society. Setting up a network of day care facilities could assist in educating children, screening them for health problems, and gaining access to their parents for educational and other activities. In fact, Head Start is in part a day care program that achieves some of those other advantages.

Those are the kinds of debates in which social policy experts engage. When they do so they also consider the experiences of others in addressing similar problems. They search the literature for comparable examples, communicate with comparable governments to learn how they might have addressed the problems, and otherwise attempt to propose the best alternatives with full knowledge of what has and has not worked in other locales or at other times.

Another pertinent question is how the program will be implemented. Some methods are through mailing applications, word of mouth, or a formal public education and outreach effort or by adding resources and the new program to an existing organization.

How will we learn what the policy is achieving? Some form of program evaluation, designed to determine the program's impact, is generally part of any proposal for a program. The evaluative information is used to improve the program or as a basis for canceling the program in the future.

The Hobart Burch Framework

A useful model of policy analysis is explicated in Hobart Burch's 1991 book, *The Why's of Social Policy: Perspective on Policy Preferences,* which he wrote with the assistance of Donna G. Michaels. His model follows a thorough analysis of social welfare and social policy issues, which are the basis for his book. The four steps of analysis he proposes are:

1. Identify the issue.
2. Analyze what exists.
3. Determine what should be.
4. Decide what is possible.

(Burch 1991, 211)

Burch points out that if there is no concern about an issue, there is, in effect, no issue. He suggests moving from there to existing resources and services to the ideal state of what should be. Then he suggests that the analyst decide what is possible—what can actually be done, considering all of the constraints on public support and money. Developing lists of alternative solutions helps the process of choosing the possible solutions to the issue or problem.

The Donald L. Chamber Models

Donald L. Chambers (1993) presents a policy and program analysis system in his book *Social Policy and Social Programs.* He defines the elements of his analysis process as "operating characteristics," which he believes are essential to the operation of any social policy or social program. They are:

1. Goals and objectives
2. Forms of benefits or services delivered
3. Entitlement (eligibility) rules
4. Administrative or organizational structure for service delivery

221

5. Financing method
6. Interactions among the foregoing

(Chambers 1993, 77)

Like Gilbert and Terrell, whose model is discussed below, he attributes much of his framework—all but goals and objectives and financing—to Eveline Burns, who used the other elements of the model in *The American Social Security System* (1949), which was an early policy analysis textbook widely used in social work education.

Chambers's book explicates his "operating characteristics" in detail and defines the subtypes or concepts associated with each as well as the criteria for evaluating and appraising them. He also provides an example of applying his model to specific policies—the U.S. community health centers legislation. His book is thorough and detailed, and many find it useful for analyzing social policies.

The Andrew W. Dobelstein Model

Andrew W. Dobelstein (1996) developed a model for policy analysis and the essential elements of it. He says those elements are

1. Identifying, understanding, or clarifying the problem
2. Identifying the location for policy decisions
3. Specifying possible solutions (alternatives)
4. Estimating or predicting the impact (outcomes) of those solutions on different populations

(Dobelstein 1996).

He also presents three models of policy analysis—a behavioral or rational model developed by Herbert Simon (1964), a criteria-based model developed by James Gallagher and Ron Haskins (1984), and an incremental model developed by Charles Lindblom (1964). Dobelstein explains all three models and applies them to examples in his book. Simon's and Lindblom's models are in Gore and Dyson's *The Making of Decisions* (1964).

The Bruce Jansson Approach

Jansson's primary thrust in social policy is to educate people to practice the discipline, an orientation that is discussed in a later chapter. He also, however, includes extensive discussion of analytic skills in his book

Social Welfare Policy: From Theory to Practice, 2d ed. (1994) and presents a straightforward model that includes three steps:

1. Analyzing the presenting problem
2. Finding a policy remedy that will effectively address the problem
3. Convincing other persons to accept the recommendations

When he explains his three steps, Jansson includes the kinds of issues cited by others who present analytic models, such as developing and presenting data to explain the problem and solutions to it, examining alternative policy solutions, and making choices.

Although Jansson's emphasis is on practice skills, he offers some important insights into elements of social policy which are often overlooked, especially the nonrational components of the subject (Jansson 1994). Some human services workers are puzzled when they encounter opposition to or strong support for policies that do not appear to be in the interests of those on either side. Jansson devotes a part of his 1994 book to understanding some of the nonrational factors that have an impact on policy; the roles played by emotion, sentiments, prejudices, and power in the development of policy are important in any effective analysis.

The Gilbert and Terrell Model

Neil Gilbert and Paul Terrell were at the University of California, Berkeley, School of Social Welfare when they developed their policy analysis concepts in *Dimensions of Social Welfare Policy.* Actually, the 1992 volume is the third edition of a book that was published in two earlier editions by Gilbert and Harry Specht, who is deceased. The model is one of the most widely accepted in social welfare policy analysis. One of the authors' major theses is that there are three approaches to analyzing policy: studying the process of formulating the policy; studying the product, or what is actually done; and studying performance—that is, evaluating the outcomes of implementing the policy. A fourth edition was published by Gilbert and Terrell in 1997.

Their book is primarily an explication of their model, which focuses on the process of policy development or formulation. They present and develop a basic four-part model, with four questions:

1. What are the bases of social allocation?
2. What are the types of social provisions to be allocated?

3. What are the strategies for the delivery of these provisions?
4. What are the methods of financing these provisions?

(Gilbert, Specht, & Terrell 1992, 43)

They attribute their model in part to Eveline Burns, who was one of the architects of Social Security and who, for many years before her death, was a leading writer and thinker about policy development. Burns's four questions were narrower because they focused on issues of Social Security, including a variety of financing assistance programs. The authors explain that they wanted to develop an analytic framework that could cover the larger spectrum of the entire social welfare field (1992). Their four-part framework , which they describe as their dimensions of social welfare policy, also ties their four dimensions to three "axes," which are the range of alternatives that are possible, the values that are part of the alternatives, and the theories behind the alternatives.

Gilbert, Specht, and Terrell (1992) describe their first dimension, the bases of social allocation, as the "who" of social welfare—the same who as in the "who wins" issue described earlier. They also describe the various alternatives, values, and theories that could apply to this who. This "basis" is much more complicated than it seems. For every possible group to be served there are alternative approaches. As pointed out, one of the persistent conflicts in social welfare history and social policy theory is over how one might best help financially disadvantaged individuals. One group of approaches would provide assistance directly to those individuals, with revenues collected in the form of taxes from the nondisadvantaged. Another group of approaches would suggest providing money, tax relief, or other advantages to the affluent, who would, in turn, attempt to earn more by expanding or creating new businesses. Actually, these two approaches are both always being used in the United States to some extent. TANF is an example of helping disadvantaged individuals directly. Tax reductions and depreciation allowances for businesses are the opposite approaches. The first, as will be recalled, is popularly known as "trickle-up" theory, based on the idea that the disadvantaged will receive their help and spend it so that it will ultimately reach all levels of the economy, including the top, where businesses will use their new earnings to begin new enterprises or expand their existing ones. The second is called "trickle-down" theory, in which top earners use their wealth to expand, thus creating jobs, and ultimately the added wealth trickles down through all levels of the economy.

This example represents all three of the axes that Gilbert, Specht, and Terrell describe. Two alternative approaches exist for examining the serving of the disadvantaged. First, there is the issue of *values,* such as are revealed by such statements as "People deserve to be helped directly when they are in need" and "People should not be helped directly, but growing employment in a growing economy will provide for them." Second, there are *theories* about how money is distributed in an economy. In fact, both of these approaches, these ways of looking at the problem, have worked and continue to work in different ways at different times, just as both the trickle-up and trickle-down theories have been correct at times. The differences are probably in degrees rather than absolutes and in what the values of proponents and opponents are.

Gilbert, Specht, and Terrell make a valuable contribution to social policy analysis by defining their axes because they show that, almost always, there are many alternative ways of achieving a social policy objective; because they explain that social policy is not simply a technical concern but one that is affected by values and beliefs; and because they show that theoretical considerations and theories are also part of the process of social policy analysis.

The second element of the framework, the types of social provisions to be allocated, deals with what is actually done. The various ways in which child care could be provided is an example of the types of social provisions that could be applied when serving the who, or parents, in that case. Social provisions are the "what" element of the "who wins" questions. Who wins?. . .What is the issue? The what can be financial assistance, day care, mental health counseling, nutrition assistance, housing, family planning, health care, and almost anything else that can be assumed under the social policy rubric. The three axes of alternatives, values, and theories are also applied in analyzing a policy or issue.

Gilbert, Specht, and Terrell's third element, the strategies for delivering the provisions, is the "how" of social policy analysis. The strategies, however, are not programmatic but, rather, administrative in nature. An example might be the ways in which financial assistance has been delivered to low-income people with disabilities. Chapter 2 shows that in early history, that group was, in many cases, served by counties through institutional care. When the provision of assistance evolved from assistance in kind, such as housing and food, to assistance in cash and from "indoor" to "outdoor" relief, the delivery strategy changed too. In the original version of the Social Security Act the economically disadvantaged disabled received assistance through a matching program of federal and state funds which was administered by the states, as chapter 5 describes. Each state had a different payment level, based upon its appropriations. In 1972 the Supplemental Security Income system was established; it provided the national standards and set provisions for its administration by the U.S. Social Security Administration. So the delivery system has changed from local to state to federal government.

Medical insurance for the low-income population with disabilities, however, has not been handled in the same way. Had the disadvantaged disabled been incorporated into Medicare, which is principally for people sixty-five and older, they would have received medical insurance in the same way and through the same federal agency as Social Security beneficiaries. Yet they were not. Instead, the states are essentially required to cover SSI recipients through their Medicaid programs, which are financed with state and federal funds and administered by the states. To help them meet their nutritional needs, food stamps are available to almost all SSI recipients. The food stamp program is another delivery system. The stamps are provided at no cost to the states by the U.S. Department of Agriculture. The states, in turn, provide the stamps to the individuals and families who are eligible for them.

Housing for the disadvantaged disabled population is delivered in a variety of other ways, many of them with some federal financing but, in most cases, with local administration. As can be seen from the example, the delivery systems are varied, even for meeting the basic economic, food, housing, and health needs of a special population. For each delivery mechanism it is necessary to discuss the three axes of alternatives, values, and theories.

The fourth dimension is the financing of the services, or provisions, which is also affected by the three axes. Some of the variations in financing have been discussed already. One might recall that Social Security's social insurance and Medicare are financed by employee and employer contributions, which are held in trust funds. Those who benefit tend to believe that they are fully entitled to what they receive—that they paid for it. Other programs, especially those designed for people who cannot pay for their own, are financed through general tax revenues.

How programs are financed is often the most interesting of the policy analysis discussions. In recent years there have been many artful examples of financing good works by taxing perceived evils. Some suggest that health care for people who are cigarette smokers ought to be financed by cigarette taxes, for example, so that those who cause their problems also pay for treating them. In North Dakota, nonprofit organizations are permitted to support their own human services, or to finance those of other organizations, by sponsoring gambling. The net revenues from the gambling are then used to support the services (Conrad 1990). In other cases "luxury taxes" on expensive items such as automobiles, boats, furs, and the like are dedicated to paying for services to the disadvantaged. In other situations services are paid for through full or partial fees for those services. Community mental health centers, family service programs, day care centers, leisure time and recreational programs, and many others are financed in whole or in part by fees that the recipients of the services pay. Whatever the arrangements, however, it is always important to examine the nature of the financing that is used or planned for the services. Finances are a crucial part of any social policy analysis, if not the most crucial part.

The foregoing brief examples show how alternatives, values, and theories are important in decisions about the financing of social provisions. There are many alternative ways to finance services, and the alternatives chosen are products of the values as well as the theories of those who make the decisions.

Special attention has been given to the Gilbert, Specht, and Terrell (1992) approach because it takes into account so many of the relevant elements that ought to be considered when analyzing policies. It provides a comprehensive approach to analyzing any kind of social policy. It is also a popular model that is widely used in baccalaureate and master's social work education.

Gilbert and Terrell (1998) wrote a fourth edition of this book, after the death of Dean Harry Specht. Their new edition suggests that the basic concepts of social welfare policy and policy analysis have not changed. However, the new book focuses on the context of social welfare policy, especially with regard to the 1996 dramatic changes in welfare laws, which are also discussed in several sections of this book. The new law is found in appendix 2.

The Prigmore and Atherton Model

Charles S. Prigmore and Charles Atherton of the University of Alabama presented a useful analysis model in the second edition of their 1986 text *Social Welfare Policy: Analysis and Formulation*. In 1997 they revised their model, which suggests a number of "factors" that can be used to consider a proposed policy or to evaluate one that already exists.

A. Political and Value considerations

1. Is the policy compatible with contemporary administrative themes or style? That is, is the agency head, mayor, governor, or president likely to support it?

    Consciously or unconsciously, most administrators become identified with certain long-term themes as well as distinct policy styles. They are more likely to be receptive to policy and program proposals that are compatible with those themes, since they are likely to be the things that got them elected or made them popular. Increasingly, however, administrators are becoming more conscious of public relations than they used to be, and one must be prepared for them to abandon principle for public opinion. One must recognize this without too much cynicism. Looked at one way, administrators, as public servants, *ought* to be sensitive to public opinion and shift with it when it appears to have legitimacy.

2. Is the policy appealing to the appropriate legislative body? That is, is the agency board, city council, state legislature, or Congress likely to follow the policy in decisions or legislation?

    Legislators generally are less concerned with overall themes or styles but tend to be more sensitive to their perceptions of current public opinion than administrators are. Only the most well-entrenched politician can afford to ignore the frequent shifts in public opinion.

    Agency boards, which are often self-perpetuating, are different from elected legislative bodies since *usually* they are not as subject to public scrutiny as are publicly elected legislative bodies. The conventional wisdom is that voluntary and nonprofit agencies are more flexible. In reality, a self-perpetuating board may be the hardest group in which to induce change because it is not accountable to the election process.

3. Does the policy satisfy relevant interest groups (professional associations, citizen lobbies, business associations, and civic groups)?

228

It seems simpler to combine all interest group politics in one factor for teaching purposes, but in reality there may be great diversity of interests that get masked in so doing. On a given policy, there may be a number of relevant interest groups to be considered.

B. Practical considerations

1. Is there any good research or practical trial that suggests that the policy is both "doable" and effective?

Practical trials (e.g., pilot programs or a local program that does on a small scale what you might like to do on a larger scale) are probably more useful exemplars than some of the more esoteric research reports which may involve more artificial conditions. Your case may be strengthened if you can find a demonstration project that supports a new policy proposal.

2. Is the policy efficient? Or if the cost is high, can the case be made that the outcomes justify the cost?

Efficiency includes cost-effectiveness. It is now generally recognized that we do not live in a world of unlimited resources, and welfare is only one of a number of interests competing for money. While social workers may believe that, say, a shelter for battered children is badly needed, city government may think that it is more important to build a new fire station. Voluntary contributors may think that more good can be done for more people by providing a new library. It is important, therefore, when evaluating existing programs and proposing new ones, to consider how much a service costs and how well it works.

Cost effectiveness is not the only value that matters. For example, it probably is not cost-effective to recommend annual mammograms for all women over fifty. It is cheaper (from a strictly monetary point of view) just to treat the diagnosed cases of breast cancer. The higher cost of annual mammograms, however, is justified by the savings in both the quality and span of life. The conscientious policy analyst should recommend a cost-effective policy only when it will yield the same as or better results than the existing policy.

If a better policy costs more, the policy activist will probably be better off spending her or his time in justifying the expense rather than in either denying or concealing the cost by deceptive rhetoric.

It is also important to realize that there may be some services and programs that one would like to offer in an ideal world but that would be judged by the public as simply too costly under any circumstances.

3. What consequences can be reasonably anticipated if an organization or government adopts a new policy?

Policy analysis and formulation is more of a craft or art than any form of "science." Not all outcomes of a policy change can be anticipated. This is, in part, because policy deals with what have been described as ill-structured problems rather than puzzles. Puzzles usually have only one right answer. Ill-structured problems involve choices between better answers or worse ones and thus clearly involve trade-offs. For example, if a city considers rent controls as a way to keep rents affordable, it may keep rental costs down for the existing tenants. On the other hand, there may be a lessened incentive for investors to build additional housing if they cannot recover their increasing costs and make a profit. The result can be a shortage of available low-cost housing as population pressure increases.

Policy Analysis and Research Methodology

Einbinder (1995) says that policy analysis uses fundamental social science research methodologies, many of which she says are not taught to social work students at the baccalaureate or graduate levels. To those discussed here, she adds multiple regression, a statistical technique; case studies; and meta-analysis, which she describes as a "quantitative method of summarizing the results of existing outcome research" (1852). She also says that micro-simulation techniques may be useful in determining the consequences of a policy. She suggests that statistics and a sound understanding of economics are important tools for policy analysts.

Iatridis (1994) writes about policy analysis and offers a model based upon the word *science,* which consists of seven steps. S—The sociopolitical environment. What is the societal context of the problem, the ideological and social justice implications? C—Causes. What caused the problem and what information does literature provide about causation? I—Intervention approaches. What other needs are unmet? E—Establish and rank recommendations. What are the recommendations for change, the pros and cons, and their possible impact on needs? N—Narrative. The step involves listing and explaining programs and plans that can be converted into action along with the resources needed and any criteria to be used for evaluating success. C—Characteristics. What are the cost, prerequisites, problems, training requirements, and monitoring steps needed in the implementation of the policy? E—Evaluation, determining whether or not or to what extent the goals and objectives have been reached.

Diana M. DiNitto on Policy Analysis

Diana M. DiNitto, the author of another popular text in social welfare policy, *Social Welfare: Politics and Public Policy* (1995), discusses social policy analysis under the rubric of program evaluation. She focuses on the impact of social policies, on learning about the consequences of policies. In her discussion of the process of evaluation she makes the important distinction between understanding what social policy "outputs" (what the provisions are) and "impacts" (what the effects of policy are on the target population and the larger society). Although DiNitto focuses on government policies and provisions, the principles of program evaluation which she suggests also apply to nongovernmental organizational policies and provisions.

As her model for program evaluation, DiNitto incorporates a model proposed by P. H. Rossi and H. E. Freeman (1989). They suggest that an evaluation deal with several questions:

1. Is the problem correctly conceptualized?
2. What is the extent of the problem, and where is the target population?
3. Does the program design fit with the objectives?
4. Is there an underlying coherent rationale?
5. Are there efforts to maximize the chances of success of the provision?
6. What are the real or projected costs?
7. What is the benefit, as related to the costs?
8. Does the service reach the population targeted?
9. Is the program being delivered as it was designed?
10. Is the program reaching its goals?
11. Is something other than the program causing the positive results?

12. How much does it cost, and how much does it benefit the recipients?
13. Is this program the most efficient alternative?

Although this model is called program evaluation, it actually provides an outline that is similar to Gilbert, Specht, and Terrell's as a framework for policy analysis. It asks the questions of who, what, and how and deals with financing arrangements. It also deals with cost-benefit issues and unintended consequences when it asks if the results might not be the product of other forces. The question is an important one because sometimes social problems are resolved even if no programs are developed to assist them. It has been suggested, for example, that the Great Depression of the 1930s was resolved by the economic growth resulting from World War II, not from the New Deal social programs set in place by the federal government.

There are many other examples and a whole school of thought that suggest that the best approaches to solving human problems are to leave those problems and their victims alone while concentrating instead on economic improvement because that is the ultimate, lasting solution to human need of all kinds. Such points of view, which have varying degrees of support at different times, must be considered in any realistic policy analysis. That approach is part of the free enterprise economic philosophy espoused by some free enterprise advocates as well as by some supporters of radical changes in U.S. government. Both are discussed in earlier chapters.

The McInnis-Dittrich Model

McInnis-Dittrich (1994) offers another model of policy analysis. She uses the letters of the word *analysis* as the eight elements in her model:

1. Approach—a brief description of the methods used in the current or proposed policy.
2. Need—what need does the policy attempt to address?
3. Assessment—what are the program's or policy's strengths and weaknesses?
4. Logic—does the proposed or current policy logically address the connection between the need and a means of solving the problem?
5. Your reaction—from your professional experience does the policy seem effective?

232

6. Support—what is the financial support for the program?
7. Innovation—what provisions have been made for changing the program if necessary?
8. Social justice—does the program address the important issue of social justice as expressed by society and the social work professions?

(McInnis & Dittrich 1994, 133)

A second approach to analyzing social policy has been developed by D. Iatridis (1994). He analyzes social policy from an international perspective and also discusses some of the capitalist and socialist contrasts in the development and consequences of social policy.

ISSUES ANALYSIS

In addition to models of policy analysis there are books published annually on current social problems and on more comprehensive issues in social policy. There are books on child care, health services, crime and delinquency, race relations, and any number of other topics. These do not provide a general framework but, instead, analyze a specific issue in a detailed manner. One current and well-written example is Stoesz and Karger's *Reconstructing the American Welfare State* (1992), in which the authors propose a totally new way of organizing and delivering American social services.

Another author on policy analysis, Sanford F. Schram (1995), suggests that policy analysis has focused more heavily on the management of poverty than on finding means for eradicating it. On specific subjects such works provide detailed and helpful analyses of current issues or problems.

POLICY ANALYSIS MODELS—A SUMMARY

Only some of the policy analysis models that have been developed and published are included here. There are many others, and more are being created. They are important because it is necessary for social workers to be able to analyze social policies realistically and effectively. Because social policies are the heart of the practice of the human services professions, understanding what those policies are and developing the capacity to think about and suggest alternatives to them is a requirement for human services professionals.

Any one of the models presented here will help such professionals develop a sophisticated understanding of a given policy. Mastering one or more of them will help professionals achieve an even more sophisticated understanding. Then, when encountering a new policy, program, or problem, the professional will be able to examine it and think through its merits, possibilities, and deficits.

Policy analysis methods are critical to the well-informed professional because policies are the essential building blocks for resolving human needs and solving social problems. Without the capacity to critique policies or proposals for policies objectively and systematically, human services professionals may be encouraged to pursue approaches to problems that may not achieve the desired goals, may cost too much, or may conflict with strongly held public values. There are times when complex human problems such as substance abuse are under discussion. Invariably, simplistic policies will be proposed—lock up all of the users, give life sentences to all "pushers," legalize illegal drugs, expand treatment facilities. The sophisticated human services professional is able to evaluate all of these as well as think through alternatives that may be more comprehensive and more effective. The professional who wants to influence policy decision makers must be able to dispassionately convince them of the value of a specific policy. Doing so requires the capacity to analyze and communicate about policies in persuasive ways.

CONCLUSION

This chapter has presented information on the policy analysis process. It has suggested some of the elements that may be included in policy analysis. The analytical component is only one of the six necessary for a thorough understanding of social policy.

Social policy analysis is a dynamic tool that can be applied and reapplied to any social problem, policy, or provision. As such, it may be the most useful of the skills that one may learn from this book or from the study of social policy.

DISCUSSION QUESTIONS

1. Select a current social problem, policy, or program and analyze it with one of the models presented in this chapter. Answer all of the questions listed in the model to the extent possible with the infor-

mation available on the item to be analyzed. If you want more detailed information on the model, consult the source, which is listed in the references.

2. Some social policy specialists suggest that if one were to learn only one of the components of social policy, it should be policy analysis. Do you agree or disagree? Justify your answer.

3. Discuss the roles that alternatives, values, and theories play in the analysis of social policy. What are some examples of each, relative to a specific problem, policy, or program?

4. I. Weissman (1959) proposed a three-part model for understanding policy. Do you agree or disagree with the assumption that the current models of policy analysis, such as those discussed in this chapter, are really just expanded versions of Weissman's model? Justify your answer.

REFERENCES

Barker, R. L. (1995). *The social work dictionary*, 3d ed. Washington, DC: NASW Press.

Boehm, W. (1959). *Social work curriculum study*. New York: Council on Social Work Education.

Burch, H. A., with Michaels, D. G. (1991). *The why's of social policy: Perspective on policy preferences*. Westport, CT: Praeger.

Burns, E. (1949). *The American Social Security System*.

Chambers, D. L. (1993). *Social policy and social programs: A method for the practical public policy analyst*, 2d ed. New York: Macmillan.

Chronicle of Higher Education. (1993, March 10). Marginalia. 39 (27), A4.

Conrad, K. L. (1990). Charitable gambling in North Dakota. In L. Ginsberg et al. (Eds.), *Encyclopedia of Social Work*, 18th ed., 1990 supp., 94–96. Silver Spring, MD: NASW Press.

Consumer Reports. (1995, June). Nutrition reform: How much will it cost if kids go hungry? 380.

DiNitto, D. M. (1995). *Social welfare: Politics and public policy*, 4th ed. Englewood Cliffs, NJ: Prentice-Hall.

Dobelstein, A. W. (1996). *Social welfare: Policy and analysis*, 2d ed. Chicago: Nelson-Hall.

Edwards, R. L. et al. (Eds.) (1995). *Encyclopedia of social work*, 19th ed. 1849–1855. Washington, DC: NASW Press.

Einbinder, S. D. (1995). Policy analysis. In R. L. Edwards et al. (Eds.), *Encyclopedia of social work*, 19th ed. 1849–1855. Washington, DC: NASW Press.

Friedman, M., & Friedman, R. (1980). *Free to choose: A personal statement*. New York: Avon.

Gallagher, J., & Haskins, R. (1984). *Policy analysis.* New York: Ablex.

Gil, D. (1976). A general framework for social policy analysis. In J. Tropman, M. Dlhuy, & W. Vasey (Eds.), *Strategic perspectives on social policy.* Elmsford, NY: Pergamon Press.

Gilbert, N., & Terrell, P. (1997). *Dimensions of social welfare policy,* 4th ed. Boston: Allyn & Bacon.

Gilbert, N., Specht, H., & Terrell, P. (1992). *Dimensions of social welfare policy,* 3d ed. Englewood Cliffs, NJ: Prentice-Hall.

Gilder, G. (1981). *Wealth and poverty.* New York: Free Press.

Gingrich, N. (1995). *To renew America.* New York: HarperCollins.

Ginsberg, L. (1990). Introduction. In A. Minahan et al. (Eds.), *Encyclopedia of Social Work,* 18th ed., 1990 supp., 1–11. Silver Spring, MD: NASW Press.

Ginsberg, L. (1998). *Conservative social welfare policy: Description and analysis.* Chicago: Nelson-Hall.

Gore, W. J., & Dyson, J. W. (Eds.), *The making of decisions: A reader in administrative behavior.* New York: Free Press.

Green, C. (1993, February 9). Increase in benefits to stay put. *State* (Columbia, SC), 1A.

Hamilton, G. (1940). *Theory and practice of social work.* New York: Columbia University Press.

Hefferman, W. J. (1992). *Social welfare policy: A research and action strategy.* New York: Longman.

Herrnstein & Murray. (1994). *The Bell Curve.* Glencoe, IL: Free Press.

Hirsch, E. D. Jr., Kett, J. F., & Tretil, J. (1993). *The dictionary of cultural literacy: What every American needs to know,* 2d ed. Boston: Houghton Mifflin.

Iatridis, D. (1994). *Social policy: Institutional context of social development and human services.* Belmont, CA: Wadsworth.

Jansson, B. S. (1994). *Social welfare policy: From theory to practice,* 2d ed. Belmont, CA: Wadsworth.

Karger, H. J., & Stoesz, D. (1998). *American social welfare policy: A pluralist approach,* 3d ed. New York: Longman.

Lasswell, H. D. (1958). *Politics: Who gets what, when, how.* New York: Meridian.

Lindblom, C. (1964). The science of muddling through. In W. J. Gore & J. W. Dyson, *The making of decisions.* New York: Free Press.

Los Angeles Times. (1993, February 7). Economic sales pitch under way. *State* (Columbia, SC), 3A.

McInnis-Dittrich, K. (1994). *Integrating social welfare policy and social work practice.* Belmont, CA: Wadsworth.

Meyer, C. H. (1987). Direct practice in social work: Overview. In A. Minahan et al. (Eds.), *Encyclopedia of social work,* 18th ed., 409–422. Silver Spring, MD: NASW Press.

Murray, C. (1994). *Losing ground: American social policy, 1950–1980, 10th anniversary edition.* New York: Basic Books.

Pierce, D. (1984). *Policy for the social work practitioner.* New York: Longman.

Pinderhughes, E. (1995). Direct practice overview. In R. L. Edwards et al. (Eds.), *Encyclopedia of social work,* 19th ed., 740–751. Washington, DC: NASW Press.

Prigmore, C. S., & Atherton, C. R. (1986). *Social welfare policy: Analysis and formulation,* 2d ed. Lexington, MA: Heath.

Prigmore, C. S., & Atherton, C. R. (1997). Personal communication.

Rossi, P. H., & Freeman, H. E. (1989). *Evaluation: A systematic approach,* 4th ed. Newbury Park, CA: Sage.

Schram, S. F. (1995). *Words of welfare: The poverty of social science and the social science of poverty.* Minneapolis: University of Minnesota Press.

Simon, H. (1964). A behavioral model of rational choice. In W. J. Gore & J. W. Dyson, *The making of decisions.* New York: Free Press.

Stoesz, D., & Karger, H. J. (1992). Foreword by Midgley, J. O. *Reconstructing the American welfare state.* Lanham, MD: Rowman & Littlefield.

Tropman, J. E. (1987). Policy analysis: Methods and techniques. In A. Minahan et al. (Eds.), *Encyclopedia of social work,* 18th ed., 268–283. Silver Spring, MD: NASW Press.

Weissman, I. (1959). *Social welfare policy and services in social work education.* New York: Council on Social Work Education.

Chapter Nine

Practicing Social Policy

Thus far this book has focused on the ways in which human services workers can best understand social policy. The five components described here for comprehending social policy—the ways in which it is developed, its impact, and its outcomes in the forms of social provisions or programs—are historical, social problems, public policy, descriptive, and analytical. Yet there is a sixth component that is of growing importance in the human services field. That component is the practice of social policy—the actual involvement in making and implementing social policy.

For many human services workers as well as for those who write and teach about social policy, the discipline is something that one does rather than something that one simply studies. In 1991 N. Wyers wrote about "policy-practice" in social work. He called policy practice a "nebulous concept" (242) but said it was essentially the combining of the practice of social work with social policy.

Although the literature on the human services workers as practitioner of social policy is relatively new, in fact, human services workers have been policy practitioners for the whole history of modern welfare. A. J. Kahn (1993) is one of several social policy scholars who argue for the importance of preparing social workers for work in the practice of social policy.

One of the most recent sources on the practice of social policy was written by D. Iatridis (1995), who contributed the *Encyclopedia of Social Work*'s first article on the subject in its 19th edition.

THE TASKS OF SOCIAL POLICY

Practicing social policy includes a number of tasks, the first of which is the development, or simply the writing, of social policies. The prepa-

238

ration of statements of policy which can be turned into rules and regulations and, ultimately, social provisions or programs is the primary job
of many human services workers. Creating a policy that can be studied
and acted upon by a legislative or executive branch of government is a
complex task. The language must be specific, and the rules and regulations must be concrete.

A task that is related to the preparation of policies is the analysis of
policy alternatives, which is discussed in chapter 8. Understanding and
allowing for the consequences of policies, both intended and unintended ones, calculating the costs of the policies, estimating the numbers of people who will be affected by the policy, and examining other
analytical elements are part of the job of the policy writer.

In many cases the policy specialist develops policy statements, or
other documents, that are then used by executive branch agents or legislative bodies to create official social policies. For example, if a state government wanted to develop a policy for dealing with the homeless, one
of the first steps toward solving it, after the identification of the problem,
would be the preparation of some kind of policy statement, or plan. Perhaps the plan would include provisions for housing and feeding homeless people. Perhaps it would provide for cash assistance to the homeless
so they could purchase their own food and shelter. Perhaps the policy
would even be punitive, demanding imprisonment of those who did not
have permanent residences. In any case, revenue sources would have to
be identified, and a budget would have to be prepared to deal with the
problem of homelessness.

In most cases a policy of that magnitude would be undertaken by a
legislative body, such as a state legislature, for passage as a law or statute.
In some cases, however, an executive branch agency might be able to
promulgate a policy to deal with homelessness as part of its general powers. In still other cases a court might order the executive branch of government to provide assistance to the homeless. The policy for doing so
would be prepared by personnel in the executive branch.

PERSONNEL INVOLVED IN POLICY DEVELOPMENT

Although human services workers may often lead the way in developing social policies, they are not the only participants in the
process. In many cases, attorneys (especially those with experience in
drafting legislation), accountants, and other kinds of professionals col-

239

laborate on policy development. It often takes the knowledge and skills of several different disciplines to develop policies that are of major consequence.

There are thousands of human services workers throughout the United States who are engaged full-time in the development of policy. Some work for executive branch agencies. They spend their time preparing policy statements and plans to be proposed to higher level executive branch officials, such as governors, or to state legislative committees that have requested policy ideas for solving designated human problems.

Many of the human services workers who deal with such policies are not full-time policy specialists. They may also play roles as administrators of programs. The staff members of an adult social services office in a state department of social services, for example, might be assigned the job of preparing the policy on homelessness described earlier.

Preparing Legislation

As suggested, many executive branch human services workers develop legislative proposals to carry out specific social policies. They often do so at the request of legislative bodies such as committees on human services or social welfare. For example, a member of a legislative body, such as a state representative or senator, might wish to pass a policy into law which would resolve the problem of homelessness in his or her state. That legislator would very likely ask the state department of social services or a comparable organization to prepare a piece of legislation to accomplish that goal. A human services worker with policy responsibilities in that department would likely be assigned the task of drafting the legislation. Lawmakers often have access to human services workers who are employees of legislative bodies to carry out the same kinds of responsibilities.

Drafting a bill that can become a law is a complicated and technical task. Human services workers are generally well acquainted with elements of bill drafting. One of the most important technical tasks is identifying the portions of the existing state code, or laws, which need to be modified to include the new legislation. That might mean creating a new section of the law, or it might simply mean an amendment is needed for an existing law.

In addition, a specific budget note, or fiscal note, usually must accompany the legislation. Preparing such information often requires expert knowledge. Most often attorneys must handle the legal aspects of a new piece of legislation, and accountants or other financial specialists must deal with the fiscal information. The experts in human services often prepare the substantive parts of the legislation; that is, they define the program—the ways in which it will be operated, the ways it will be paid for—and otherwise write the portions of the legislation which describe its administration and implementation. Many human services workers also become experts on the legal and financial aspects of the law, either through their education or because of long experience in dealing with social programs.

In many places in the United States, legislatures employ human services workers full-time to work on social policy. Their task is to prepare legislation on social policy issues and to evaluate existing social policies, keep track of social problem indicators, and otherwise serve as experts on social policy for the legislative body. Social workers, teachers, counselors, and many other human services professionals are full-time employees of legislative bodies who regularly carry out these kinds of responsibilities.

TOOLS FOR POLICY PRACTITIONERS

One of the primary tools of the policy practitioner is the development of factual information about the nature and extent of social problems. To be effective in understanding problems and in developing solutions for them, policy planners must conduct research or be aware of and use the research conducted by others on specific social problems and solutions.

Legislative bodies, executive branch officials, and other decision makers in the policy-making process want to know the facts about problems and solutions before they make decisions. Therefore, policy practitioners are regular students of public documents, government statistical reports, and other sources of facts about human beings and issues affecting their lives. Major employers in the practice of social policy are "think tanks" and other policy study groups and institutions. Some of the most prominent are the Brookings Institution, the Institute for Policy Studies, the American Heritage Foundation, the American Enterprise Institute, the Center for Budget and Policy Priorities, and the National Center for Policy Analysis. There are hundreds of these around the nation, many of which receive funds from foundations and most of which are tax-exempt because they are engaged in study rather than in lobbying or politics. These groups are often important sources of information about social policies; executive and legislative branches call upon them for their data and their ideas.

Influencing Legislation

Another significant task in the practice of social policy is influencing legislation or, as it is often called in the United States, lobbying (which is also discussed in chapter 4). The job of the lobbyist is to work for the passage of legislation that is favorable to the organization that person is representing. Most of the national social welfare organizations have legislative representatives, many of them in Washington, whose job is to influence the U.S. Congress, and others in the states whose role is to influence state legislation. Such familiar organizations as the National Association of Social Workers, the American Public Human Services Association, the Child Welfare League of America, and similar groups have Washington representatives or legislative specialists who are, in fact, lobbyists. J. Figueira-McDonough (1993) points out that several social work scholars have proposed that all social workers be educated in lobbying and has also written about ways in which lobbying itself might be taught in social work curricula. In fact, many social workers and other human services workers are employed as lobbyists for voluntary and governmental organizations.

Some Observations about Lobbying

As discussed in chapter 4, lobbying is a normal, perhaps necessary, part of public policy making in the United States. For some, lobbying has a reputation as a sort of sinister practice involving people who pursue special interests in not quite legitimate ways. Some people believe that lobbyists use bribery and other kinds of inappropriate influences to win their organizations' objectives.

Although it is true that lobbying is always about the pursuit of specialized interests, the use of inappropriate lobbying techniques or bribery is unusual. It is not well understood in American life that special interests include a range of concerns and that not all of them are selfish. In fact, all lobbyists pursue their objectives from some sort of idealistic point of view. Most organizations sincerely believe in their purposes and pursue their legislative objectives hoping the result will be beneficial to the people they represent. The National Rifle Association, whose activities many in the social services community would consider in negative terms, believes it is pursuing an important social goal by making it possible for citizens to purchase and own weapons for personal defense, sports, and hunting with a minimum of governmental interference. The defense industry, too, believes in its efforts to protect the American people from foreign enemies. The tobacco industry believes that its lobbying preserves the rights of tobacco users as well as the economic well-being of tobacco farmers and tobacco product manufacturers. So all lobbyists, including those who pursue social welfare goals, view themselves as pursuing worthy goals on behalf of citizens.

Most Americans are members of organizations that lobby, although they may not know it. Churches, the American Automobile Association, conservation groups, professional and trade associations, and most other large national organizations lobby. Being able to join organizations and help them finance their lobbying is a basic right having to do with free speech and freedom of association.

Methods of Lobbying. The methods and techniques used by lobbyists are not as self-serving or pecuniary as is often supposed. Many times the primary task of the lobbyist is to draft or analyze legislation so that lawmakers can best introduce it or to explain legislation that has been proposed by others. Much of the legislation that is ultimately passed in the United States, in both Congress and state legislatures, is originally drafted by lobbyists. The lobbyists for the American Association of Retired Persons (AARP), for example, propose specific changes in Social Security which would benefit older adults. That legislation is received by members of Congress who are interested in Social Security legislation and who, in turn, incorporate the AARP ideas into bills that are introduced into Congress. Often the member of Congress or a committee of Congress will modify the bill that has been drafted by the lobbyist, but, in some cases, the bill is introduced, acted upon, and made law without many changes at all.

In other circumstances, lobbyists testify before legislative committees on the impact of a given policy proposal or law. Often, because of his or her deep involvement in the specific area, the lobbyist has more detailed information on the consequences of a piece of legislation than do the members of Congress or others who must act on the legislation.

In other cases lobbyists mobilize support for or opposition to a piece of legislation which involves their organization's interests. They do so by asking their members to telephone, telegraph, and write to their representatives in Congress or the state legislatures opposing legislation that could be detrimental to their organization's interests or in support of legislation that pursues those interests.

Lobbyists have other methods, including those that win support from legislators, such as inviting legislators for meals and receptions, helping to obtain campaign support for legislators who are facing re-election campaigns, and inviting legislators to speak at organizational conferences, which may help them gain votes and may also earn them honoraria. Many groups also sponsor receptions and banquets to which legislators are invited. These are methods commonly used by lobbyists, including those who represent social welfare organizations.

Special interest groups for which lobbyists work are not always private organizations, and not all lobbyists are representatives of nonprofit associations of people with legislative concerns. Although they are not usually called lobbyists, the executive branch agencies also have employees who carry out extensive lobbying activities. Every department of government at the federal or state level has an interest in the activities of legislatures. In fact, their interests may be greater in some cases than those of any voluntary association or organization. Federal executive branch agencies have official designated legislative liaisons who are, in many ways, lobbyists. Their full-time job is to answer questions from legislative bodies, testify to their legislative committees, and pursue the legislative objectives of their agencies. Many state government executive branch agencies have similar personnel with similar responsibilities. The programs, budget, and even the survival of executive branch agencies depend, in large measure, on their ability to influence their legislative bodies. Therefore, most agencies actively press for their points of view and their programs.

It is important to point out, parenthetically, that the use of the general term *lobbyist* and the legal definition of a lobbyist may differ. Most legislatures do not define executive branch personnel as lobbyists and do not require them to register as such, which they do require of private organization lobbyists.

As suggested, most of the lobbying in the United States is carried on by voluntary associations representing specific interests or activities. There are public policies dealing with how extensive lobbying activities may be. There are also public policies dealing with the tax status of organizations that lobby. Whether or not an organization lobbies has some impact on its tax-exempt status. For example, a tax-exempt voluntary national human services organization is limited in the amount of its resources it may use for lobbying purposes.

Many organizations do not lobby directly but, instead, organize specialized subsidiary groups that have lobbying as a primary purpose. In the same way organizations that lobby often cannot make contributions to political candidates, corporations cannot make political contributions either. Therefore, there are many political action committees (PACs) which have the solicitation and distribution of political contributions as their primary purpose. Such organizations collect money from the members of the specialized group. They have boards of directors which determine how the contributions they collect are distributed to candidates. PACs are important in influencing elections and, in fact, in the legislative process. Legislative and executive branch members who receive funds from PACs are assumed to be more likely than others to support legislation favored by the organizations or industries that have supported them financially.

Lobbying the Executive Branch. Not all lobbying is carried on in the legislative branch of government. In fact, some observers think that the most effective kind of lobbying takes place within the executive branch instead. The executive branch has great influence over the legislation that is ultimately passed by legislative bodies, their primary influence being in the kinds of legislation they propose. Much of the legislation that is ultimately passed by these bodies originates in the executive branch. Therefore, the priorities and specific policies of the executive branch greatly influence what is ultimately passed. Lobbyists who want to have an impact on legislation often start by attempting to influence the executive branch proposals that are made to legislatures. The weight of the opinion of the executive branch agency has great significance for any legislative body, as does the work of the executive branch lobbyists, who are often consulted by the legislative bodies and their committees.

Persuading the executive branch agency to propose or support the legislative priorities of an interest group is often the most useful expenditure of that group's time and resources. If the group can persuade the commissioner, director, any chief executive officer, or any others with the ability to influence the organization's policy to support the organization's priorities, they may accomplish what they want much more readily than if they tried to influence the legislature directly. Such lobbying activities are not always difficult; in many cases the interest group's and the executive branch agency's priorities may coincide. It is also not unusual for a lobbying group to prepare legislation for an executive branch agency to modify and introduce as its own contribution to solving a social problem.

IMPLEMENTING LEGISLATION

Often the most important element of the practice of social policy is the implementation of policies by executive branch agencies, Again, there are thousands of human services workers around the country whose job it is to translate legislation into operational rules and regulations for the executive branch agencies that employ them.

Legislation is often not extensively detailed or concrete and, therefore, cannot easily be used to implement a policy or carry out a program. The legislation may be broad in scope and only suggestive of specific activities in which executive agencies will engage, though this is not always true. Some legislation is highly specific and detailed and, therefore, is easier to implement.

For the most part, legislation, to be implemented, needs at least some fine-tuning and often much hard work, and this requires policy specialists in executive branch agencies. Assume, for example, that a legislative body has passed a statute that deals with the requirement to provide services such as food and shelter to the homeless. How will the program be operated? If voluntary organizations are to receive contracts from the government to provide such services, what organizations are eligible? How will they be paid? Who will handle their payments? What kinds of statistics will they keep, and what forms will they use for keeping these statistics? What health and safety standards will shelters be required to maintain if they are to receive public funds for caring for the homeless? These are only some of the issues that would arise out of the passage of such legislation.

As B. S. Jansson (1990, 380) says, "Enacted policies are merely paper directives, that is, abstract guidelines and objectives that reflect the preferences of the framers of policies, who have often balanced value, political, and analytic consideration when constructing them."

In a later edition of his book on the practice of social policy, Jansson (1998) explains some of the complexities of implementing policies, including the ways in which the beliefs and actions of staff influence them.

246

He also points out that the beneficiaries of policies also have great influence over the ways in which they are implemented and carried out.

Rules and Regulations

In many cases state legislatures require specific procedures for the development of the rules and regulations that implement the statutes they have passed. In the federal government that is also true, and there is a special procedure used by the federal government to develop such rules and regulations.

For example, the full impact, if any, of the 1994 Contract with America could be determined, in part, by the implementation of any new legislation. It is only when federal legislation is specifically translated into operational rules and regulations, forms, and procedures that the impact can be fully measured. Executive branch implementation can moderate, enhance, and at times even thwart—which could be challenged in the courts—the objectives of Congress.

The Federal Register. For federal social policies, executive agencies must print their rules and regulations in the *Federal Register,* a document published daily by the government which includes the rules and regulations for all federal government agencies on all subjects. When the executive branch agency makes the rules and regulations that implement legislation, and when it changes its own policies, it is required to publish those changes as proposed modifications in the *Federal Register.* Usually the rules or regulations are outlined in detail. A comment period is also announced. Those who want to comment on the proposed rules or regulations are invited to make written remarks to a specific address within a specified time frame, usually a matter of several months. The agency then collects and analyzes these remarks. The analyses are published later in the *Federal Register,* along with an announcement that the agency has made some final rules or regulations on the policy. These are typically the rules and regulations that are first announced, with, in some cases, modifications based upon the comments that have been received.

All sorts of groups and individuals make comments on rules and regulations. Industries, interest groups, corporations, state government officials, and any other group or individual with an interest in the proposed rules can do so. The agency analyzes the comments and reports on the number and kinds of them it has received (again, this is in a later edition of the *Federal Register,* when the rules are made final).

Human services workers who are practitioners of social policy in the federal government play a large role in proposing rules and receiving comments on them following their publication in the *Federal Register.* Their first task to move (effectively translate) legislation into operational rules and regulations that conform to the intentions of Congress. Doing so often requires practitioners to study the *Congressional Record,* a daily journal of everything that is said in Congress, to examine minutes of committee meetings and committee hearings, and to pay particular attention to the debate on the bill and the points of view of those who support the legislation. Again, the rules and regulations that are developed must follow the intentions of Congress. If they do not, they can lose a court challenge in which the courts might decide that the executive branch agency's rules and regulations do not fulfill Congress's objectives in passing the legislation. Being accurate about the intentions of Congress requires research into the congressional debates, committee hearings, and speeches made by those who proposed and support the legislation.

Of course, effective practitioners of social policy must also write rules and regulations that reflect the wishes of their bosses—the governor, president, secretary, or commissioner. There is usually some latitude in the way legislation is written which allows it to be interpreted in ways that will satisfy executive branch officials as well as support the intentions of the legislative body.

As suggested, many state governments have procedures for executive rule making and legislative implementation that are similar to those used by the federal government. Some states publish comprehensive documents like the *Federal Register;* others require some kind of publication of rules and regulations before they are made final; others require public hearings on rules and regulations. Yet others use a special kind of legislative committee to monitor and approve or disapprove of executive branch rules and regulations. Such committees receive the rules and examine them before they become final. After the rules and regulations are approved by the legislative committee, they become law for the state.

It is perhaps obvious that much of the lobbying that takes place occurs at the time rules and regulations are made. Lobbying to have legislation passed is one matter. Making sure that the executive branch implements the law in the way one's organization wants it to be implemented is yet another. The latter is as important, in many cases, as the former. Some would suggest that it is not so much a matter of what the law says as what the implementing agency says the law says.

In addition to writing the rules and regulations and to carrying them through the necessary processes, it is also a function of human services professionals who are practicing policy to conduct public hearing and comment periods, to tabulate and analyze comments, and to write about the results of those comments for later publication.

To sum up, the tasks of the social policy practitioner include writing proposed policies, lobbying for the passage of those policies by legislative bodies or the implementation of them by executive branch agencies, preparing rules and regulations to implement social policies, conducting public comment periods, including public hearings, and writing about the results of those public comment periods. In addition, the policy practitioner who works for an association, organization, or state government may also lead constituents in their comments on proposed policies. Thus, policy practitioners function at every level of the policy process.

POLICY INTERPRETATION

There is another role in which policy practitioners function, and that is as interpreters of policies that already exist. Most large human services organizations, especially those that are connected with government, employ full-time units that answer policy questions for workers in the field. In programs such as TANF and Medicaid, for example, which have very complicated rules that may not clearly cover every possible situation, policy experts are available to answer questions from workers about the applicability of certain policies. How much of the incomes of all the family members has to be considered as part of the resources available to a family applying for family assistance? How does one determine the actual value of a collection of guns, which might be considered a resource in calculating eligibility? What are the employment requirements for a mother with a child who is chronically ill and whose family is receiving TANF? Questions such as these are asked and answered every day in public social services agencies and in large voluntary agencies as well. Many human services professionals practice their professions as policy experts. Because TANF is different in each state, the roles of public agency employees in developing and interpreting regulations are more important than ever. The federal rules have largely been dropped, so the states must fill in the gaps with their own clear and legal rules and regulations.

Policy units in large public agencies also analyze and evaluate legislation as it develops. Typically, during a legislative session, or even between sessions, when bills are being proposed for introduction, the policy unit of the department analyzes how much the bill will cost, what impact it will have on other services, and how it might be implemented by the agency. It also makes suggestions about the reactions of the agency to the legislation, sometimes going so far as to "oppose" or "support" bills, an action that does not fit most agencies, in which the chief executive officer is appointed by the governor. By definition, the agency supports the governor's program, whatever that program happens to be, even if the staff or the leadership of the agency might generally support or oppose the legislation. In other situations, in which the agency is controlled by a commission and is not directly under gubernatorial authority, the agency may be freer to take specific policy positions on legislation.

CONCLUSION

This chapter has shown the ways in which social policy is more than a single subject of study. It is a whole field of human services practice—what some human services workers do as their primary employment.

Policy practice will likely continue to expand as a field because of the growing importance of policy in the creation and delivery of human services. The practice roles for human services workers in policy range from simple tasks of explaining to coworkers what policy means to drafting new policies. It is likely that in the future, increasing numbers of those employed in the areas of social services and human services will be policy practitioners.

DISCUSSION QUESTIONS

1. Visit a library and look at a proposed human services policy in a current issue of the *Federal Register.* Note some of the proposed regulations and summarize them in a three-page essay.
2. Describe three roles of the policy practitioner. Are these roles totally different from the historic roles of social workers described in chapter 4, or do they seem to have some connection with them?
3. What are some of the roles that policy practice plays in the public

policy component of social policy? Review chapter 2 in answering this question.

4. Visit a government agency—either state or federal—and look at some of its policy manuals. Describe them in a two- or three-page essay. What are their characteristics? Do they show how they were developed? Would you make any observations about their clarity?

REFERENCES

Einbinder, S. D. (1995). Policy analysis. In R. L. Edwards et al. (Eds.), *Encyclopedia of social work,* 19th ed., 1849–1855. Washington, DC: NASW Press.

Figueira-McDonough, J. (1993, March). Policy-practice: The neglected side of social work intervention. *Social Work* 38 (2), 179–188.

Iatridis, D. (1995). Policy practice. In R. L. Edwards et al. (Eds.), *Encyclopedia of social work,* 19th ed., 1855–1866. Washington, DC: NASW Press.

Jansson, B. S. (1990). *Social welfare policy: From theory to practice,* 2d ed. Belmont, CA: Wadsworth. 1994.

Jansson, B. S. (1999). *Becoming an effective policy advocate: From policy practice to social justice,* 3d ed. Pacific Grove, CA: Brooks-Cole.

Kahn, A. J. (1993). *Issues in American social policy: The substantive and research challenges for social work doctoral education.* Paper presented at Group for the Advancement of Doctoral Education Annual Conference, St. Louis, MO, October 15, 1993.

Tropman, J. E. (1987). Policy analysis: Methods and techniques. In A. Minahan et al. (Eds.), *Encyclopedia of social work,* 18th ed., 268–283. Silver Spring, MD: NASW Press.

Wyers, N. (1991, Fall). Policy-practice in social work: Models and issues. *Journal of Social Work Education* 27 (3), 241–250.

Appendix 1

An Annotated Bibliography of Social Policy Journals in Human Services Professions

Compiled by David P. Fauri and Barbara J. Ettner

MULTIDISCIPLINARY JOURNALS OF SOCIAL POLICY

American Behavioral Scientist (ABS)

Sage Publications, Inc.
2455 Teller Road
Thousand Oaks, CA 91320

A multidisciplinary journal of social science, ABS is published six times annually and contains scholarly articles on broad areas of concern to social science professionals. Selected issues are devoted to topics of interest to social workers and to policy analysts and researchers interested in social work theory, program planning, and practice.

Daedalus

Norton's Woods
136 Irving Street
Cambridge, MA 02138

Published quarterly as the proceedings of the American Academy of Arts and Sciences, this journal focuses each issue on a single topic, with essays from various disciplines on a common theme. Some issues are devoted to health, family, mental health, and social policy topics, which are examined from different perspectives.

Evaluation and Program Planning
Industrial Technology Institute

P.O. Box 1485
Ann Arbor, MI 48106

Each journal issue contains articles of general interest and on special topics and book reviews dealing with broad social policy concerns. This is a highly policy-practice–oriented journal which provides added substance to policy analysis in the social arena.

Evaluation Review

Sage Publications
2455 Teller Road
Thousand Oaks, CA 91320

This journal of applied social research, which is directed toward researchers, planners, and policy makers, reports the findings of evaluation studies in such fields as child development, health, education, income security, personnel, mental health, and criminal justice. There is an emphasis on the application of evaluation results to policy and planning.

Journal of the American Institute of Planners

1776 Massachusetts Avenue, NW
Washington, DC 20036

Published quarterly by the American Institute of Planners, this journal encourages articles which represent significant contributions to knowledge about planning and urbanism. Included are articles on social policy and planning. This publication is useful for information on urban problems such as housing policies.

Journal of Social Issues

Plenum Publishing Corporation
233 Spring Street
New York, NY 10013

This is the journal of the Society for the Psychological Study of Social Issues of the American Psychological Association. Its primary audiences are psychologists and social scientists who are concerned about the impact of important social issues. It seeks to publish scientific findings regarding theory and practice about human problems of individuals, communities, groups, and nations. Quarterly issues often focus on a particular problem, such as child care policy research, in varied contexts.

Journal of Social Policy

Pitt Building
Trumptington Street
Cambridge, CB21RP
England
or
40 West 20th Street
New York, NY 10011–4211

This international journal of the Social Administration Association is published quarterly. Included are scholarly papers which analyze any aspect of social policy and administration. The policy-oriented articles discuss social problems in England and the rest of the world. Each issue includes a section of twelve to twenty book reviews on social policy.

Journal of Social Service Research

Haworth Press, Inc.
10 Alice Street
Binghamton, NY 13904–1580

This quarterly publication contains articles on clinical research in the behavioral and social sciences and empirical policy studies, particularly from the international social policy perspective. The articles in the *Journal of Social Service Research* are characterized by careful methodological design and rigorous data analysis.

Policy Review

214 Massachusetts Avenue, NE
Washington, DC 20002

This is a quarterly publication of the Heritage Foundation. Articles in each issue cover a wide range of social policy topics. The authors have diverse viewpoints that do not necessarily reflect the conservative philosophies of the Heritage Foundation. A major goal of the journal is to expand discussion and debate on contemporary social policy issues.

Policy Sciences

Institute of Policy Sciences and Public Affairs
Duke University
4875 Duke Station
Durham, NC 27706

This international journal, devoted to the improvement of policy making, focuses on an integrated, interdisciplinary, analytic approach to policy with contributors from many disciplines. Emphasis is on the process of policy development and analysis.

Policy Studies Journal

Department of Political Science
Iowa State University
Ames, IA 50011

This is a quarterly publication of the Policy Studies Organization, the Institute for Public Policy and Business Research, the University of Kansas, and the Maxwell School of Citizenship and Public Affairs, Syracuse University. Contributors come from the fields of economics, public administration, social welfare, and other areas. A wide range of public policy topics are included, and articles demonstrate application of political and social sciences to important public policy problems. Emphasis is on formal policy design and analysis.

Policy Studies Review

University of Illinois
361 Lincoln Hall
702 S. Wright Street
Urbana, IL 61801

This is a journal of the Policy Studies Organization and the Morrison Institute for Public Policy, Arizona State University. The journal is devoted to the substance (the nature of public policy, its causes and effects) and procedures (methods of arriving at societal decisions that maximize benefits, reduce costs) of policy studies. Articles on social policy issues such as health, education, welfare, and unemployment are included.

Prevention in Human Services

Haworth Press, Inc.
10 Alice Street
Binghamton, NY 13904

The editors of *Prevention in Human Services,* a biannual publication, are committed to producing a multidisciplinary journal with articles and special issues on aspects of prevention programming for various populations (elderly, children, mentally ill, etc.). This journal overlaps other specialized areas such as mental health, health, families, and gerontology, and it is the successor to *Community Mental Health Review.* It stresses the preventative aspects of policies and programs in various disciplines.

Public Administration Review

1120 G Street, NW
Washington, DC 20005

This journal is published by the American Society for Public Administration. It is dedicated to improved management in public service. The articles are addressed to government administrators, teachers, researchers, consultants, students, and civic leaders. Some are related to management issues, but many articles address public policy issues. The topics tend to be general, as the contributors are encouraged to communicate with readers who have varied interests and specializations.

Public Interest

National Affairs, Inc.
10 East 53rd Street
New York, NY 10022

In an effort to seek solutions to social problems of our time, this journal publishes articles on a wide variety of social issues. Contributors are from various disciplines such as political science, law, sociology, and health. Social policy issues such as poverty, aging, education, and crime are included.

Social Forces

University of North Carolina Press
Box 2288
Chapel Hill, NC 27514

An international journal of social research associated with the Southern Sociological Society, the journal publishes research on social problems. The contributors are primarily sociologists who present research studies on broad social issues which have policy implications.

Social Policy

33 West 42nd Street, Room 1212
New York, NY 10036

This journal, which advocates fundamental social change, publishes articles on issues in the human services areas of health, education, welfare, and community development. Emphasis is given to major institutional change and issues involving equality and discrimination.

Social Thought

Catholic Charities USA
1319 F Street, NW
Washington, DC 20004

Publication of *Social Thought* is cosponsored by the School of Social Service of the Catholic University of America and Catholic Charities USA. The journal offers a multidisciplined perspective on issues and problems in social welfare and social work practice with particular emphasis on the development of a society in which the principles of social justice and charity are incorporated. Included are articles that integrate social work theory, policy, and practice with ethical, philosophical, and theological principles.

JOURNALS OF POLICY ANALYSIS AND POLITICS

Evaluation & Program Planning

Pergamon Press, Inc.
395 Saw Mill River Road
Elmsford, NY 10523

The primary goals of this journal are to improve evaluation and planning practice and to add to the knowledge base of this profession. The journal contains articles concerning planning efforts in organizational, public health, mental health, social service, corrections, education, and substance abuse settings. Fiscal, legal, and ethical perspectives are presented on various policy problems.

Journal of Policy Analysis and Management (JPAM)

Graduate School of Public Policy
University of California at Berkeley
2607 Hearst Avenue
Berkeley, CA 94720

JPAM's major purpose is to promote communication regarding social policy issues among public policy analysts and public administrators. Areas of interest and journal topics are diverse, and the editors strive to include articles of interest to a diverse group of professionals, academics, and students in the policy sciences and management sciences.

Journal of Policy Modeling

Elsevier Science Publishing Co., Inc.
655 Avenue of the Americas
New York, NY 10010

The *Journal of Policy Modeling* is published five times each year by the Society for Policy Modeling. Its major goal is to provide a forum for debate concerning international policy issues. The fundamental theoretical framework of the journal is that methodological understanding and development of policy modeling techniques will lead to a better understanding of socioeconomic environments. Understanding and sharing ideas are seen by the editors as being necessary for solving social problems, and the subject matter reflects this view.

Law and Policy Quarterly

Baldy Center for Law and Social Policy
511 O'Brian Hall
Buffalo, NY 14260

This journal publishes research papers which analyze the role of legislative process in public policy. Theoretical and empirical works are presented, and topics include social welfare, criminal justice, economic analysis, and government regulation. Particular attention is given to the relevance of legal issues in the policy process and to the use of appropriate methodology to address issues.

Policy and Politics

School for Advanced Urban Studies
Rodney Lodge
Grange Road
Bristol, BS84EA
England

Policy and Politics is a quarterly journal that provides an overview of contemporary policy issues in Europe and Great Britain. It presents broadly ranging articles on social, housing, education, health, transportation, and environmental policies. Particular themes of interest to the journal editors are theories, implementation, and effectiveness.

Public Productivity and Management Review

National Center for Public Productivity
Hill Hall, 7th floor
Rutgers University
Newark, NJ 07102

This journal is devoted to publishing articles on administrative, technical, legal, economic and social factors that influence productivity in public and private sectors. Its publication is cosponsored by the Section on Management Science and Policy Analysis of the American Society for Public Administration and the National Center for Public Productivity. The underlying theme of the journal is that improved productivity enhances policy-making and policy-implementing processes.

SOCIAL WORK/SOCIAL WELFARE JOURNALS

AFFILIA Journal of Women and Social Work

Sage Publications, Inc.
2455 Teller Road
Thousand Oaks, CA 91320

This is a quarterly journal publishing diverse forms of writing related to women and social welfare. Writing styles range from poetic to analytical, and topics are equally far-reaching along a broad continuum of social issues.

Administration in Social Work

Haworth Press, Inc.
10 Alice Street
Binghamton, NY 13904

This quarterly journal of human services management is written for executives and middle managers in social-service–providing organizations. The journal focuses on theory, research, and practice with special attention to the relationship between social administration and social policy planning. Included are articles that show administration as the link between social policy planning and social service delivery. Special issues address specific policy and practice topics.

Journal of Social Work Education

1600 Duke Street
Alexandria, VA 22314

Published three times a year by the Council on Social Work Education, this journal is concerned with education in the field of social work knowledge and social welfare. It serves as a forum for creative exchange on trends, developments, innovations, and problems relevant to social work professional education at the undergraduate, master's, and post-graduate levels. The journal includes articles relating to the teaching of social policy and policy practice with emphasis on the educational response to social policy issues and social policy as part of the social work curriculum.

Journal of Sociology and Social Welfare (JSSW)

School of Social Work
Western Michigan University
Kalamazoo, MI 49008

JSSW is a journal devoted to publishing articles that bridge the gap between theory and practice in social work. The articles included in the journal deal with diverse areas, including social welfare institutions, policies, and problems.

Policy and Practice

810 First Street, NE, Suite 500
Washington, DC 20002–4267

Published quarterly by the American Public Human Services Association, this journal covers every aspect of the public welfare and related fields with articles directed toward human services practitioners. Included are reports of significant work in the field, national policy issues, and social legislation.

Social Service Review

969 East 60th Street
Chicago, IL 60637

Edited by the faculty of the School of Social Service Administration at the University of Chicago, this quarterly journal is written for social workers and others concerned with social welfare issues. Included are research-based articles on social welfare research, practice, policy, and history.

Social Work

NASW
750 First Street, NE
Washington, DC 20002–4241

This official publication of the National Association of Social Workers is published six times each year. The purpose is to improve practice and extend knowledge in social work and social welfare. Articles on practice, research, social problems, and the social work profession are included. While only a few articles present true policy issues, and there is little on policy methodology, policy issues presented are directly related to social work and are of particular interest to the social work professional.

JOURNALS ADDRESSING SPECIALIZED AREAS OF INTEREST

Children and Families

Child Abuse and Neglect

Elsevier Science, Inc.
655 Avenue of the Americas
New York, NY 10010

This journal concerns itself with all issues relating to child maltreatment on all levels, from family to society. The articles are descriptive and evaluative of child welfare topics that have important implications for policy analysts and program planners.

Child Abuse and Neglect: The International Journal

Pergamon Press, Inc.
395 Saw Mill River Road
Elmsford, NY 10523

This journal provides an international, multidisciplinary forum on diverse topics concerning child abuse and neglect. The editors are especially interested in publishing articles that deal with treatment and prevention and articles describing factors that facilitate or negate family cohesiveness. Articles are contributed from diverse fields—law, medicine, psychology, nursing, education, anthropology, and social work.

Child and Youth Services

Haworth Press, Inc.
10 Alice Street
Binghamton, NY 13904–1580

This biannual publication contains articles on diverse topics concerning child welfare and service delivery to children and youths. Relevant policy implications concerning youth issues are treated in depth in selected articles.

Child Welfare

440 First Street, NW
Washington, DC 20001–2085

The Child Welfare League of America publishes articles which extend knowledge in child-family welfare and related services. Topics include any aspect of administration, supervision, casework, group work, community organization, teaching, and research as well as issues of social policy that bear on the welfare of children and their families. The journal is a good source on child welfare policy.

Children and Youth Services Review

Department of Social Welfare
School of Public Policy and Social Research
University of California, Los Angeles
Box 951452
Los Angeles, CA 90095–1452

An international quarterly review, this journal is concerned with a multidisciplinary approach to improving the quality and effectiveness of services to children and youth. The emphasis is on the problems of children and youth and on the service programs designed to address these problems. Policy issues are confined to those affecting this segment of the population.

Families in Society: The Journal of Contemporary Human Services

Families in Society
11700 W. Lake Park Drive
Milwaukee, WI 53224

This publication, a continuation of Social Casework, is dedicated to presenting practice- and issue-related articles for human services professionals. Subject matter of this journal includes public policy issues as well as family theory and questions of practice and management. The journal contains sections with viewpoints, essays, questions and answers, letters and comments, feature articles, research, special reports, and book reviews.

Family Relations

National Council on Family Relations
3989 Central Avenue, NE
Minneapolis, MN 55421

This journal of applied family and child studies is directed toward practitioners serving the family field through education, counseling, and community services. There is an emphasis on innovative methods and the application of research and theory to practice and policy.

Journal of Family Issues

Sage Publications, Inc.
2455 Teller Road
Thousand Oaks, CA 91320

This quarterly journal concerns theory, research, and practice regarding marriage and family life. Two issues each year are devoted to topics of current interest, and two issues are devoted to articles, commentary, and advocacy pieces concerning family matters in contemporary society. The journal editors seek to serve those who work with and those who study families.

Journal of Marriage and the Family

National Council on Family Relations
3989 Central Avenue, NE
Minneapolis, MN 55421

A quarterly journal of the National Council on Family Relations, this journal seeks to reach persons working in family research, teaching, and social welfare. There is an emphasis on promoting family welfare and influencing family policy.

Gerontology

The Gerontologist

Gerontological Society of America
1275 K Street, NW, Suite 350
Washington, DC 20005–4006

A bimonthly publication of the Gerontological Society of America targeted at practitioners, this journal draws on all areas of gerontology that pertain to practice, policy, and applied research. Included are articles with a multidisciplinary focus and editorials that highlight policy implications of articles in the current issue. The journal seeks to enhance understanding of human aging.

Journal of Applied Gerontology

Sage Publications, Inc.
2455 Teller Road
Thousand Oaks, CA 91320

This journal contains articles on diverse issues related to aging and the field of gerontology. Long-term care, daily living, senior centers, and mental health services are some primary topics. Articles on research, theory, and practice are also published in this journal.

Journal of Gerontology

1275 K Street, NW, Suite 300
Washington, DC 20005–4006

Published bimonthly by the Gerontological Society of America, targeted to present research results, this journal promotes exchange among the various disciplines concerned with the study of aging and fosters the use of gerontological research in forming public policy. The content of the journal is divided into four sections: medical sciences, psychological sciences, social sciences, and biological sciences.

Health Policy

AIDS and Public Policy Journal
University Publishing Group
107 East Church Street
Frederick, MD 21701

This journal publishes original articles, case studies, and commentaries on legal, health, and social policy issues concerning AIDS. The articles come from diverse disciplines and intellectual perspectives and deal with theory, research, and practice.

AIDS Weekly
P.O. Box 830409
Birmingham, AL 35283–0409

This newsletter contains brief articles concerning AIDS legislation, regulation, litigation, and epidemiology. It is included here because it may contain information of assistance to policy analysts in various disciplines even though the articles do not meet the scholarly standards of the academic journals included in this annotated bibliography.

American Journal of Public Health
1015 Fifteenth Street, NW
Washington, DC 20005

Published monthly, this is the official journal of the American Public Health Association, which was organized to protect and promote personal and environmental health by exercising leadership in the development and dissemination of health policy. All disciplines and specialties in public health are represented. Many of the articles are research studies of public health problems which may have policy implications. The journal also makes position statements on health policy issues.

Health and Social Work
NASW
750 First Street, NE
Washington, DC 20002–4241

This quarterly journal of the National Association of Social Workers is committed to improving social work practice and extending knowledge in the field of health. Articles deal with all aspects of health that are of professional concern to social workers. Included are articles on practice, policy, planning, legislative issues, and research. This journal is a good resource for information on social work involvement in health policy.

Journal of Community Health

Human Sciences Press
233 Spring Street
New York, NY 10013–1578

This journal publishes peer-reviewed papers, original essays, reviews, editorial commentaries, and letters that relate to community health, preventive medicine, public health, medical ethics, and socioeconomic issues in health care.

Journal of Health Politics, Policy and Law

Duke University Press
6697 College Station
Durham, NC 27708

Sponsored by Duke University, this journal publishes papers from scholars, policy makers, and practitioners from any discipline concerned with health. All areas of health policy are addressed, but there is some emphasis on the economic perspective.

New England Journal of Medicine

10 Shattuck Street
Boston, MA 02115–6094

Published weekly, this medical journal is addressed primarily to physicians, but it is a good source for health policy issues closely watched by the media. Included are abstracts of articles which can be cut out and filed under key words.

Social Work in Health Care

Haworth Press, Inc.
10 Alice Street
Binghamton, NY 13904

This quarterly journal of medical and psychiatric social work is directed to social workers in all areas of health care. There is a focus on articles which reflect a commitment to the humanization of health care in practice and policy.

Social Science and Medicine

Elsevier Science, Inc.
655 Avenue of the Americas
New York, NY 10010

This international journal, which is published twenty-four times a year, focuses on the interrelationship between medicine and the social sciences. Included are articles on anthropology, economics, education, psychology, social work, and sociology which relate directly to mental and physical health practice and policy.

Mental Health Policy

Administration and Policy in Mental Health

Human Sciences Press, Inc.
233 Spring Street
New York, NY 10013–1578

Addressed primarily to administrators in mental health and human services programs, this journal publishes articles on organizational relationships, planning, policy, and administration. The journal publishes case reports and original articles on all aspects of these topics.

Community Mental Health Journal

Human Sciences Press
233 Spring Street
New York, NY 10013–1578

This official publication of the National Council of Community Mental Health Centers, Inc. is devoted to the broad fields of community mental health theory, practice, research, and policy. It is a multidisciplinary journal which includes contributions from psychology, the social sciences, and medicine.

Hospital and Community Psychiatry

1700 18th Street NW
Washington, DC 20005

Articles in this journal are directed toward staff members of facilities and agencies concerned with the care of the mentally disabled. A publication of the American Psychiatric Association, the journal seeks to improve care and treatment, to promote research and professional education in psychiatric and allied fields, and to advance the standards of psychiatric services and facilities.

Justice Policy

Crime and Delinquency

Sage Publications, Inc.
2455 Teller Road
Thousand Oaks, CA 91320

Published quarterly in cooperation with the National Council on Crime and Delinquency, this policy-oriented journal is directed toward professionals in the criminal justice field. Included are articles which fall into the following criminal justice areas: the social, political, and economic context; the victim and the offender; the criminal justice response; the setting of sanctions; and the implementation of sanctions.

Journal of Criminal Justice

Elsevier Science, Inc.
655 Avenue of the Americas
New York, NY 10010

Published bimonthly, this international journal is directed toward practitioners and academicians in the criminal justice area. The articles are related to crime and the criminal justice system with some emphasis on policy implications.

The Journal of Criminal Law and Criminology

357 East Chicago Avenue
Chicago, IL 60611

The journal publishes articles and book reviews of interest to justice policy analysts and practitioners. A legalistic approach is presented that is useful for the study of social policy in this important area.

Juvenile and Family Court Journal

University of Nevada
P.O. Box 8970
Reno, NV 89507

Published quarterly by the National Council of Juvenile and Family Court Judges, this journal includes articles on the juvenile justice system, juvenile and family courts, and the treatment and control of juvenile delinquency.

Future Policy

Futures

Elsevier Science, Inc.
The Boulevard
Langford Land
Kidington, Oxford OX51GB
England

This is a multidisciplinary journal concerned with forecasting the future of the earth and its inhabitants and with future policy making. Issues dealt with include economics, technology, politics, and the environment. Long-term policy-making issues are of particular interest to these editors.

Futurist

World Future Society
7910 Woodmont Avenue, Suite 450
Bethesda, MD 20814–6089

This journal, a publication of the World Future Society, includes articles concerned with future developments on this planet. Society, economics, technology, and politics are discussed from the particular perspective of the future. Implications of change in all these areas are debated and described.

Appendix 2

A Comparison of the Aid to Families with Dependent Children and Temporary Assistance to Needy Families Programs

The following summary was prepared by the American Public Welfare Association (now the American Public Human Services Association), National Conference of State Legislature, and the National Governor's Association in September 1996. It compares the Aid to Families with Dependent Children (AFDC) program to the Temporary Assistance to Needy Families (TANF) program that replaced it in 1997 under the provisions of the Personal Responsibility and Work Opportunity Reconciliation Act of 1996.

Some provisions were changed in 1997. For example, Title IV, which restricts welfare and public benefits for aliens, was modified so that noncitizens who were living in the United States on August 22, 1996, the day the bill became law, were restored to eligibility for benefits under the 1997 Balanced Budget Act. Under the Title VIII food stamp provisions, the law originally barred food stamp assistance to able-bodied adults who had no dependent children after three months every three years if they were not employed or in a work or training program.

This summary shows the details that go into social welfare policy and the extent of the changes that were made in almost every element of the federal public assistance and social service programs. The complexity also shows the importance of executive implementation of statutes and the wide latitude that may be exercised in dealing with the day-to-day meaning of complicated legal and programmatic changes.

Comparison of PRIOR LAW and the PERSONAL RESPONSIBILITY AND WORK OPPORTUNITY
RECONCILIATION ACT OF 1996 (P.L. 104–193)

PROVISION	PRIOR LAW	P.L. 104–193
Title I: Block Grants for Temporary Assistance for Needy Families		
AFDC, EA, and JOBS	Aid to Families with Dependent Children (AFDC) provided income support to families with children deprived of parental support. JOBS was an employment and training program for AFDC recipients. Emergency Assistance (EA) provided short-term emergency services and benefits to needy families. The federal government established eligibility criteria for AFDC and EA benefits and guidelines for the JOBS program. States determined benefit levels, which were required to be applied uniformly to all families in similar circumstances.	The law block grants AFDC, EA, and JOBS into a single capped entitlement to states—Temporary Assistance to Needy Families (TANF).

States are required to implement their block grants program by July 1, 1997. States have the option to submit plans immediately subsequent to the President's signing of the bill (August 22, 1996). The Department of Health and Human Services (HHS) reviews the plan for completeness. |
| **Funding** | Open-ended funding was on a matching basis for AFDC benefits and administration and EA. JOBS was an entitlement requiring state match and was capped at $1 billion in FY 1996. | The total cash assistance block grant is estimated to be $16.4 billion for each year from FY 1996 to FY 2003. Each state receives a fixed amount—based on historical expenditures for AFDC benefits and administration, EA, and JOBS—equal to the greater of: (1) the average of federal payments for these programs in FYs 1992–1994; (2) federal payments in FY 1994, plus additional EA funding for some states; or |

	(3) estimated federal payments in FY 1995. States can carry over unused grant funds to subsequent fiscal years.	
AFDC Entitlement	AFDC was an entitlement to states. Recipients of SSI and Foster Care payments were not eligible for AFDC. Eligible individuals were guaranteed aid at state-established benefit levels. Certain individuals also received guaranteed child care benefits. States received federal matching dollars for expenditures, without a cap. Benefits were guaranteed to eligible individuals even in recessions and fiscal downturns.	No individual guarantee of benefits, but the state plan must have "objective criteria for delivery of benefits and determining eligibility" and provide an "explanation of how the state will provide opportunities for recipients who have been adversely affected to be heard in an appeal process."
Time Limits for Cash Assistance	Recipients remained eligible for benefits as long as they met program eligibility rules.	Families who have received federally funded assistance for 5 cumulative years (or less at state option) would be ineligible for federally funded cash aid. States are permitted to exempt up to 20% of the caseload from this time limit. Months spent living on Indian reservations with populations of at least 1,000 and unemployment rates of at least 50% do not count against the time limit. Block grant money transferred to Title XX can be used to provide noncash assistance to families after the federal time limit. State funds that are used to count toward the maintenance of effort require-

273

ments may be used to provide assistance to families beyond the federal time limit.

General Requirements: As part of their state plan, states must demonstrate that they will require families to work after two years on assistance.

Work Rates: A state's required work participation rate for all families is set at 25% in FY 1997, rising to 50% by FY 2002 (states will be penalized for not meeting these rates). The rate for two-parent families increases from 75% to 90% by FY 1999. The law provides pro rata reduction in the participation rate for reductions in caseload levels below FY 1995 that are not due to eligibility or federal law changes.

Work Hours: Single-parent recipients are required to participate 20 hours per week upon implementation of the law, increasing to at least 30 hours per week by FY 2000. Single parents with a child under age 6 are deemed to be meeting the work requirements if they work 20 hours per week. Two-parent families must work 35 hours per week.

Work Requirements

For FY 1994, 15% of nonexempt caseloads was required to participate in JOBS activities for at least 20 hours per week. This increased to 20% in FY 1995. (There were no statutory single-parent standards after FY 1995). For FY 1994, 40% of two-parent families were required to participate in work activities for as least 16 hours per week. This was scheduled to increase to 75% by FY 1997. Matching rate on JOBS dollars could have been reduced for failing to meet general or AFDC-UP participation rates.

Individuals were exempt from JOBS if they were ill, incapacitated, or aged; had a child under age 3 (or 1 at state option); were under age 16 or in school full-time; were in 2d or 3d trimester of pregnancy; were needed in the home to care for an ill or incapacitated family member; were employed 30 hours or more per week; resided in an area where the program was not available; or were providing care to a child under 6 and child care would not be guaranteed.

Exemptions: Single parents of children under age 6 who cannot find child care cannot be penalized for failure to meet work requirements. States can exempt from the work requirement single parents with children under age 1 and disregard these individuals in the calculation of participation rates for up to 12 months.

Other: For two-parent families, the second spouse is required to participate 20 hours per week in work activities if they receive federally funded child care (and are not disabled or caring for a disabled child). Individuals who receive assistance for 2 months and are not working or exempt from the work requirements are required to participate in community service, with the hours and tasks to be determined by the state (states can opt out of this provision).

To count toward the work requirement, single-parent families are required to participate at least 20 hours per week and two-parent families 30 hours per week in unsubsidized or subsidized employment, on-the-job training, work experience, community service, up to 12 months of vocational training, or provide child care services to individuals who are participat-

Work Activities

States were required to provide basic and secondary education, ESL, job skills training, job development and placement and job readiness. States were required to offer two of the following work activities: job search, on-the-job-training, work supplementation, or the community work experience program. Postsecondary education was optional. Twoing in community service. Up to 6 weeks of job search (no more than 4 consecutive weeks) counts toward the requirement, except that states with unemployment rates at least 50% above the national average may count up to 12 weeks of job search. Beyond 20 hours per week for single-parent families (or 30 hours per week for two-parent families), participation may also include job skills training related to employment, education directly related to employment (for someone without high school or Graduate Equivalency Degree [GED]), and secondary school or GED (for someone without high school or GED). Teen heads of household (up to age 19) in secondary school also count toward work requirement. However, no more than 20% of the caseload can count vocational training toward meeting the work requirement (including teen parents in secondary school). Individuals who had been sanctioned (for not more than 3 of 12 months) are not included in the denominator of the rate.

parent families were required to participate in work activities.

Supplemental Funds

For AFDC and EA, open-ended funds were available as needed. No provision for JOBS.

Establishes a $2 billion contingency fund. For eligible states, state TANF spending in excess of FY 1994 levels of AFDC-related spending is matched to draw down contingency fund dollars. If a state draws down matching child care funds (for which it must exceed its FY 1994 level of child care spending), its child care spending under TANF would not be eligible for a contingency fund match, and AFDC-related child care would be subtracted from the FY 1994 base. States can meet one of two triggers to access the contingency fund: (1) an unemployment rate for a 3-month period that was at least 6.5% and equal to 110% of the rate for the corresponding period in either of the two preceding calendar years; or (2) a trigger based on food stamps. Under the second trigger, a state is eligible for the contingency fund if its food stamp caseload increased by 10% over the FY 1994 or 1995 level (adjusted for the impact of the law's immigrant and food stamp provisions on the food stamp caseload). Payments from the fund for any fiscal year are limited to 20% of the state's base grant for that year. A state can be drawn down no more than one-twelfth of its maximum annual contingency fund amount in a given month. The match rate for the contingency fund is the state's Medicaid match rate, times the number of months the state received contingency funds in a fiscal year, divided by 12. The law also includes: (1) an $800 million grant fund

		for states with exceptionally high population growth, benefits lower than 35% of the national average, or above-average growth and below-average AFDC benefits (no state match); and (2) a $1.7 billion load fund.
Maintenance of Effort (MOE)	States were required to match the federal dollars provided for AFDC, EA, and JOBS. There was no maintenance of effort requirement in AFDC and EA. For JOBS, states were required to spend no less than total state and local expenditures for FY 1986 for training, employment, and education programs whose purpose was preventing welfare dependency.	Each state is required to maintain 80% of FY 1994 state spending on AFDC and related programs, including JOBS, EA, and child care. For states who meet the work participation requirements, the maintenance of effort provision may be reduced to 75%. States must maintain 100% maintenance of effort (MOE) for access to the contingency fund.
Transfers	No provision.	A state is permitted to transfer up to 30% of the cash assistance block grant to the child care block grant and/or the Title XX block grant. No more than one-third of transferred amounts can be transferred to Title XX, and all such funds transferred must be spent on children and their families whose income is less than 200% of the poverty line.
Persons Convicted of Drug-Related Crimes	No provision.	Individuals who after the date of enactment are convicted of drug-related felonies are prohibited for life from receiving benefits under the TANF and food stamp programs. States

may opt out of this provision or limit the length of the sanction.

Federal benefits specifically exempted: emergency medical services: short-term, noncash disaster; public health for immunizations and communicable diseases; prenatal care; job training programs; and drug treatment programs.

The following penalties can be imposed on states: (1) for failure to meet the work participation rate, a penalty of 5% of the state's block grant in the first year increasing by 2 percentage points per year for each consecutive failure (with a cap of 21%); (2) a 4% reduction for failure to submit required reports; (3) up to a 2% reduction for failure to participate in the Income and Eligibility Verification System; (4) for the misuse of funds, the amount of funds misused (if the secretary of HHS was able to prove that the misuse was intentional, an additional penalty equal to 5% of the block grant will be imposed); (5) up to a 5% penalty for failure, by the agency administering the cash assistance program, to impose penalties required by the child support enforcement agency; (6) escalating penalties of 1% to 5% of

Penalties

Penalties could have been imposed for JOBS and AFDC.

If a state failed to achieve general and two-parent participation rates, the federal matching rate for JOBS spending (which generally ranged from 60% to 79% among states) was to be reduced to 50%. In addition, states faced a reduced federal match unless 55% of JOBS funds was spent on long-term recipients, those under age 24 with no high school diploma, or those who were within two years of becoming ineligible for aid because of the age of their child.

A state could also have been penalized if its AFDC payment error rate (based on quality control) exceeded national standards.

		block grant payments for poor performance with respect to child support enforcement; (7) a 5% penalty for failing to comply with the 5-year limit on federally funded assistance; (8) a 5% penalty for failing to maintain assistance to a parent who cannot obtain child care for a child under age 6; and (9) penalties for failure to meet conditions for loan and contingency funds received. States that are penalized must expend additional state funds to replace federal grant penalty reductions.
Individual Responsibility Plans	An employability plan was required in JOBS.	States are required to make an initial assessment of recipients' skills. At state option, Individual Responsibility Plans can be required.
Teen Parents Provisions	AFDC benefits were available to each eligible dependent child and parent, regardless of whether the mother was under age 18. States were given the option to require minor parents to reside in their parents' household, with a legal guardian, or in another supervised living arrangement, with certain exceptions. Teens over 16 who were not in school were required to participate in educational activities.	Unmarried minor parents are required to live with an adult or in an adult-supervised setting and participate in educational and training activities in order to receive federal assistance.
	No provision to locate adult-supervised homes.	States are responsible for locating or assisting in locating adult-supervised settings for teens.

280

Performance Bonus to Reward Work	No provision.	The secretary of HHS, in consultation with the National Governor's Association and the American Public Welfare Association, is required to develop a formula measuring state performance relative to block grant goals. States will receive a bonus based on their score on the measure(s) in the previous year, but the bonus cannot exceed 5% of the family assistance grant. $200 million per year is available for performance bonuses (in addition to the block grant), for a total of $1 billion between FYs 1999 and 2003.
		The Secretary of HHS is required to establish and implement a strategy to: (1) prevent nonmarital teen pregnancies; and (2) assure that at least 25% of communities have teen pregnancy prevention programs. The department will report to Congress annually on progress in these areas. No later than January 1, 1997, the attorney general shall establish and implement a program that provides research, education, and training on the prevention and prosecution of statutory rape.
Family Cap	Families on welfare received additional AFDC benefits whenever they had another child.	No provision, no state option.
Illegitimacy Bonus	No provision for Illegitimacy Bonus; however, states were required to provide family planning	The law establishes a bonus for states who demonstrate that the number of out-of-wed-

281

services (to prevent/reduce the incidence of births out of wedlock) to any AFDC recipient who requested the services. The law required a reduction of 1% in AFDC matching funds if a state failed to offer and provide family planning.

lock births and abortions that occurred in the state in the most recent two-year period decreased compared to the number of such births in the previous period. The top five states will receive a bonus of up to $20 million each. If fewer than five states qualify, the grant will be up to $25 million each. Bonuses are authorized in FYs 1999 through 2002.

Waivers

The secretary of HHS had the authority under Section 1115 of the Social Security Act to waive specified provisions of the act in the case of demonstration projects that were likely to promote the objectives of the act. Such demonstration projects were required to be cost-neutral to the federal government and rigorously evaluated.

Under the new law, states which receive approval for welfare reform waivers before 7/1/97 have the option to operate their cash assistance program under some or all of these waivers. For states electing this option, provisions of the new law which are inconsistent with the waivers will not take effect until the expiration of the applicable waivers in the geographical areas covered by the waivers.

Medicaid Guarantee

These policies remain in effect in P.L. 104–193.

Federal Medicaid law mandates that state Medicaid programs cover specified categories of individuals, including members of families receiving AFDC; other low-income families, children and pregnant women; low-income Medicare beneficiaries; and, in general, recipients of SSI. Federal law also specifies numer-

Regardless of a state's TANF eligibility requirements, for purposes of Medicaid eligibility the new law requires states to provide medical assistance to individuals based on AFDC income and resource eligibility requirements they had in place on July, 16 1996; however, states may terminate Medicaid eligibility for adults who are terminated from TANF for failure to work. (The new law does not change other Medicaid

	ous groups whom states could, at their option, have made eligible for Medicaid. These groups include those whose medical costs impoverish them ("medically needy") as well as persons who are in nursing facilities or other institutions, or who required institutional care if they were not receiving care in the community.	eligibility categories.) States have the option of using more liberal income and resource standards or methodologies for Medicaid eligibility. States are not permitted to reduce income standards below those in place on May, 1 1988. States are not permitted to increase the income standard above that of July, 16 1996 by more than the percentage increase in the consumer price index for all urban consumers over the same period.
Transitional Medicaid	*These policies remain in effect in P.L. 104–193.* AFDC recipients are entitled to one year of transitional Medicaid when they lose welfare due to increased earnings from work. This provision sunsets September, 30 1998. Families who lose welfare due to collection of child or spousal support are entitled to 4 months of transitional Medicaid.	Families losing Medicaid benefits due to increased earnings from work, child support, or spousal support will receive transitional Medicaid benefits as under prior law. The sunset has been extended to Septmeber, 30 2001.
Reductions in Federal Government	No provision.	The secretary of HHS is required to reduce the number of positions at HHS related to the conversion of AFDC, JOBS, and EA into the TANF block grant by 75% or by 245 full-time equivalent program positions and 60 managerial positions.

283

Title II: Supplemental Security Income
SSI for Children

Children with disabilities who did not meet or equal the Listing of Medical Impairments were determined to be disabled (thereby eligible for cash benefits if all other criteria were satisfied) if they suffered from any medically determinable physical or mental impairment of comparable severity to an adult. Comparable severity was found if the child was not functioning at an age-appropriate level as measured by the Individual Functional Assessment (IFA) and evaluated by the Social Security Administration (SSA).

Provides a new definition of disability for children. Under this new definition, a child will be considered to be disabled if he or she has a medically determinable physical or mental impairment which results in marked and severe functional limitations, which can be expected to result in death, or which has lasted or can be expected to last for at least 12 months. In addition, this law instructs SSA to remove references to maladaptive behavior as a medical criteria in its listing of impairments used for evaluating mental disabilities in children. All of these provisions will apply to new claims filed on or after enactment and to all claims that have not been finally adjudicated (including cases pending in the courts) prior to enactment. SSA is also required to redetermine the cases of children currently receiving SSI to determine whether they meet the new definition of disability.

Redeterminations of current recipients must be completed during the year following the enactment. The earliest that a child currently receiving SSI can lose benefits is July, 1 1997. If the redetermination is made after that date, then benefits will end the months following

284

the month in which the redetermination is made. SSA is required to notify all children potentially affected by the change in the definition by January, 1 1997. An additional $150 million for FY 1997 and $100 million for FY 1998 are authorized for continuing disability reviews and redeterminations.

For privately insured, institutionalized children, cash benefits will be limited to $30 per month. The law requires that large retroactive SSI payments due to child recipients be deposited into dedicated savings accounts, to be used only for certain specified needs appropriate to the child's condition.

The law provides that large retroactive benefit amounts will be paid in installments (applies to children and adults).

SSI Continuing Disability Reviews (CDRs)

Required the SSA to conduct a specified number of CDRs on SSI cases (including both adults and children) in each of FYs 1996 to 1998.

Requires CDRs once every 3 years for recipients under age 18 with nonpermanent impairments and not later than 12 months after birth for low-birth-weight babies.

Requires that the representative payee of a recipient with continuing eligibility is being reviewed to present evidence, at the time of the

		review, that the recipient is receiving medical treatment, unless the commissioner of SSA determines that such treatment would be inappropriate or unnecessary. The commissioner may change the payee if he or she refuses to cooperate. Applies to benefits for months beginning on or after enactment.
SSI Redetermination upon Attainment of Age 18	Required redeterminations, using adult initial eligibility criteria, of the eligibility of one-third of the recipients who attain age 18 in or after May 1995 in each of the FYs 1996 through 1998.	Requires eligibility determinations, using adult initial eligibility criteria, during the one-year period beginning on a recipient's eighteenth birthday.
	Required SSA to submit a report regarding these reviews to Congress not later than October 1 1998.	No provision for reports to Congress regarding these reviews.
Title III: Child Support		
Child Support	The state was required to establish paternity and establish and enforce child support orders for AFDC, Medicaid, IV-E recipients, and all others upon request.	States must operate a child support enforcement program meeting federal requirements in order to be eligible for the Family Assistance Program. Recipients must assign rights to child support and cooperate with paternity establishment efforts. Distribution rules are changed so that families no longer on assistance have priority in receipt of child support arrears. With the current law, $50 pass-through is not required.
	States were required to disregard the first $50 a month in child support payments collected by the state and pass that amount through to the family.	

Individuals who fail to cooperate with paternity establishment will have their monthly cash assistance reduced by at least 25%.

Streamlines the process for establishing paternity and expands the in-hospital voluntary paternity establishment program.

The law requires states to establish central registries of child support orders and centralized collection and disbursement units. Requires states to have expedited procedures or child support enforcement.

Establishes a Federal Case Registry and National Direction of New Hires to track delinquent parents across state lines. Requires that employers report all new hires to state agencies and new hire information to be transmitted to the National Directory of New Hires. Expands and streamlines procedures for direct withholding of child support from wages.

Provides for uniform rules, procedures, and forms for interstate cases.

Requires states to have numerous new enforcement techniques, including the revoking of driver's and professional licenses for delinquent obligors, expanding wage garnishment, and allowing states to seize assets.

Provides grants to states for access and visitation programs.

Title IV: Restricting Welfare and Public Benefits for Aliens Immigrants

Aliens permanently residing under color of law (PRUCOL) were eligible for SSI benefits (subject to deeming); aliens who were not PRUCOL were not eligible.

Aliens who were PRUCOL were eligible for AFDC, Medicaid, food stamp, and Social Services benefits (subject to deeming in AFDC and food stamps); aliens who were not PRUCOL were not eligible, except for emergency Medicaid services. The Social Services Block Grant did not take immigration status into account.

A portion of a sponsor's income and resources was "deemed" available to a sponsored immigrant for 3 years after the individual's entry into the United States under AFDC, food stamps, and SSI (although deeming was temporarily extended from 3 to 5 years in SSI

Most legal immigrants (both current and future, and including current recipients) will be ineligible for SSI until citizenship. Exemptions are made for refugees for first 5 years in country; asylees and persons whose deportation has been withheld under section 243(h) of the Immigration and Naturalization Act until 5 years after granting of status; Active Armed Forces personnel, veterans, and their spouses and unmarried dependent children; and legal permanent residents with 40 qualifying quarters of work. Eliminates eligibility of legal immigrants for SSI and food stamps immediately at the time of recertification (no later than one year after enactment).

Medicaid, TANF block grants, Title SS Social Services, state-funded assistance: States have the option to make most current legal immigrants already in the United States ineligible for Medicaid, TANF, Title XX Social Services,

288

and state-funded assistance until citizenship (with same refugee/asylee and other exemptions as described above). Current recipients are eligible to continue receiving benefits until January, 1 1997.

Qualified aliens entering on or after enactment will be ineligible for 5 years for certain federal means-tested programs, including Medicaid (except emergency Medicaid), with most of the same refugee/asylee and other exemptions as described above.

Applicants for federal public benefit programs would be subject to new verification requirements (with certain exceptions) to determine if they are qualified and eligible for benefits. Not later than 18 months after enactment, the attorney general, in consultation with the secretary of HHS, shall issue regulations requiring verification for certain federal public benefit programs. States that administer a program that provides a federal public benefit have 24 months after such regulations are issued to implement a verification system that complies with the regulations. Nonprofit charitable organizations are exempt from verification requirements.

(from January, 1 1994 to October, 1 1996).

Some immigrants were required to satisfy State Department or Immigration and Naturalization Service that they were not likely to become a public charge by obtaining an affidavit of support from a sponsor. Courts ruled affidavits of support (which were used by AFDC, SSI, and food stamps to determine when sponsor deeming was applied) to be morally, rather than legally, binding.

States were generally determined to be constitutionally prohibited from denying benefits to legal immigrants, due primarily to the equal protection clauses of the 14th Amendment to the Constitution.

Aliens who were not permanently residing under color of law were ineligible for major means-tested entitlement benefits (except emergency Medicaid). Immigration status was required to be verified. Eligibility criteria for many discretionary-funded programs (e.g., Head Start, public health clinics) did not take immigration status into consideration.

Health and welfare workers were generally prohibited from reporting illegal immigrants to law enforcement agencies.

Title V: Child Protection
Child Protection and Adoption

States received entitlement funds under several programs for a variety of purposes. Most funds were reimbursements to states for a portion of their costs incurred in maintaining eligible children in foster care or assisted adoptions, as well as related administrative and child placement services. States also received funds from formula grants for the provision of

Future sponsors/immigrants will be required to sign new, legally binding affidavits of support (which will be available sometime mid-1997). For immigrants who have executed these new legally binding affidavits of support, the law extends deeming to citizenship or 40 qualifying work quarters; 100% of a sponsor's and the sponsor's spouse's income and resources are deemed; deeming is required for federal means-tested public benefit programs, including Medicaid (except emergency Medicaid). Certain battered and indigent immigrants are exempt from these new deeming rules.

Provisions include: (1) authority for states to make foster care maintenance payments using IV-E funds on behalf of children in for-profit child care institutions; (2) extension of the enhanced federal match for statewide automated child welfare information systems through 1997; (3) appropriation of $6 million per year in each of FYs 1996 through 2002 for a na-

child welfare services, family preservation and support services, independent living services, and child abuse prevention and treatment services. Some of these programs were capped entitlements while others were appropriated funds. Several demonstration authorities were aimed at providing funds for innovative programs through which new knowledge may be developed.

tional random sample study of abused and neglected children or children at risk of abuse and neglect; and (4) a requirement that states consider giving preference for kinship placements, provided that the relative meets state standards for child protection.

The states were required to have in place approved plans with regard to funds provided under IV-B (Child Welfare Services and Family Preservation and Support Services) and IV-E (Foster Care and Adoption Assistance). Eligibility for CAPTA state grant program was tied principally to the existence of laws and procedures regarding child abuse and neglect reports and investigations.

States were required to comply with a series of protections designed to assure children were not removed from their parents unnecessarily and that efforts were made to assure that children in the state's care were quickly placed in a permanent home through either reunification or adoption. Every child was required to have a case plan, the child's status was to be reviewed periodically, and reasonable efforts must have been made to reunify the family.

Title VI: Child Care
Child Care

There are two child care funding types:

(1) Title IV-A welfare-related child care entitlement—AFDC/JOBS, Transitional (TCC), and At-Risk Child Care.

(2) Discretionary Child Care and Development Block Grant (CCDBG).

Open-ended entitlement funding for AFDC and TCC in FY 1995 equaled approximately $893 million. At-Risk was capped at $300 million per year. $935 million was authorized in FY 1995 for CCDBG.

Child care was guaranteed for working AFDC recipients, those participating in JOBS or state-approved training or education programs, as well as for up to one year during transition off welfare due to employment. Provided good-cause exception from participation in JOBS to parents who did not have child care.

There is a separate allocation specifically for child care. The law authorizes $13.9 billion in mandatory funding for FYs 1997–2002. States receive approximately $1.2 billion of the mandatory funds each year. The remainder is available subject to state match (at the 1995 Medicaid rate). Also, states must maintain 100% of FY 1994 or FY1995 child care expenditures (whichever is greater) to draw down the matching funds. Also authorizes $7 billion in discretionary funding for FYs 1996–2002.

The law provides no child care guarantee, but single parents with children under 6 who cannot find child care may not be penalized for failure to engage in work activities.

Child Care—

Child care providers receiving federal child

Extends current law requirement that all states

292

Health and Safety/Quality and Supply	care subsidy were required to meet health and safety standards set by the states. Under CCDBG, states were required to protect health and safety of children in child care by setting standards in three areas: (1) building and physical premises safety; (2) control of infectious disease; (3) health and safety training for providers. Required states to use 25% of CCDBG funds to improve the quality of child care and to increase the availability of early childhood development and before- and after-school programs. Appropriate quality expenses included: (1) resource and referral; (2) grants or loans to assist in meeting state standards; (3) monitoring of compliance with licensing and regulatory requirements; (4) training; and (5) compensation.	establish health and safety standards for prevention and control of infectious diseases, including immunizations, building and physical premises safety, and minimum health and safety training. Extends health and safety protections to all federally funded child care (including mandatory funding). Requires states to use not less than 4% of total federal (mandatory and discretionary) child care funds to provide consumer education to parents and the public, to increase parental choice, and to improve the quality and availability of child care (such as resource and referral services).
Title VII: Child Nutrition Programs **Child Nutrition**	Eligibility criteria did not take into account immigration/citizenship status.	The law makes individuals who are eligible for free public education benefits under state or local law not ineligible for school meal benefits under the National School Lunch Act and the Child Nutrition Act of 1966, regardless of citizenship or immigrant status. States have the option to determine whether to provide WIC and other child nutrition benefits to illegal aliens and certain other noncitizens.

Prior law rates were $2.235 for each lunch/support, $1.245 for each breakfast, and $.5875 for each snack. Rates were rounded to the nearest quarter-cent.

All meals served in family or group day care homes received the same reimbursement rates of $1.625 for each lunch/supper, $.8875 for each breakfast, and $.485 for each snack.

Reimbursement rates for full-price meals rounded down to the nearest quarter-cent.

Effective for the summer of 1997, reduces maximum reimbursement rates for institutions participating in the Summer Food Service Program to $1.97 for each lunch/supper, $1.13 for each breakfast, and 46 cents for each snack/supplement. Rates are adjusted each January and rounded to the nearest lower cent.

Restructures reimbursements for family or group day care homes under the Child Care Food Program to better target benefits to homes serving low-income children and reduces reimbursement rates for higher income children to 95 cents for lunches/suppers, 27 cents for breakfasts, and 13 cents for supplements.

Rounds down to the nearest cent when indexed to the reimbursement rates for full-price meals in the school breakfast and school lunch programs and in child care centers.

Eliminates School Breakfast start-up and expansion grants. Makes funding for the Nutrition Education and Training (NET) Program discretionary.

Title VIII: Food Stamps and Commodity Distribution
Food Stamps

Six categories of legal aliens were allowed to receive food stamp benefits if they met eligibility criteria.

Most legal immigrants (both current and future, and including current recipients) will be ineligible for food stamps until citizenship (exemptions for refugees/asylees, but only for the first five years in the United States; veterans; and people with 40 qualifying quarters of work). Eliminates eligibility of legal immigrants at the time of redetermination. (Implementation of this provision was delayed until April, 1 1997 by the subsequently passed immigration provisions in the 1997 appropriations law.) Redeterminations must take place by August, 1 1997. Future immigrants entering after enactment will be ineligible for five years (same exemptions as noted earlier).

The income and resources of an alien's sponsor and the sponsor's spouse, less a prorated share for the sponsor and spouse, were attributed to aliens for 3 years.

For sponsors/immigrants signing new legally binding affidavits of support: extends deeming until citizenship and changes deeming to count 100% of sponsor's income and resources.

Maximum benefit levels were based on 103% of the cost of the Thrifty Food Plan and were indexed annually.

Reduces maximum benefit levels to the cost of the Thrifty Food Plan and maintains indexing.

The shelter deduction cap was $247; it would

Retains the cap on the excess shelter deduc-

Food Stamps, continued

have increased October, 1 1996 and each October 1 thereafter. The standard deduction was $134; it would have increased October, 1 1996 and each October 1 thereafter. All governmental energy assistance was excluded as income. Earnings of elementary and high school students under 22 were excluded as income. Individuals under 22 who lived with their parents could be certified as separate households if they also lived with their spouse and/or children.

Able-bodied adults between 16 and 60 were expected to register for and accept jobs or participate in the Employment and Training Program unless they were already working, subject to the requirements of other work programs, students, or responsible for dependents under age 6 or incapacitated people.

tion and sets it at $247 through December, 31 1996; $250 from January, 1 1997 through September, 30 1998; $275 for FYs 1999 and 2000; and $300 from FY 2001 and thereafter. Freezes the standard deduction at the FY 1995 level of $134 for 48 states and DC, and makes similar reductions for other areas. Includes as income for the food stamp program energy assistance provided by state and local government entities. Lowers the age for excluding from income the earnings of elementary and secondary students to those who are 17 and under.

Establishes a new work requirement under which nonexempt 18 to 50-year-olds without dependent children or not responsible for dependent children will be ineligible to continue to receive food stamps after the first 3 months of 36 unless they are working or participating in a workfare, work, or employment and training program. Individuals may qualify for three additional months in the same 36-month period if they have worked or participated in a work or workfare program for 30 days and lose that placement. Permits states with waiver requests denied by August, 1 1996 to lower the

Food Stamps, continued

age at which a child exempts a parent/caregiver from food stamp work rules for 6 years to 1 to 3-year-old.

Disqualified recipients for 6 months for first intentional violations; 1 year for second violations or first drug violations, second drug violations, or first violations involving firearms. States were required to collect claims resulting from overissuances to households but could not require households whose claims were due to state errors to repay claims through allotment reductions; states could retain 50% of amounts recovered from fraud claims and 25% of nonfraud recoveries.

Program Integrity and Additional Retailer Management Controls: Doubles recipient penalties for fraud violations to 1 year for first offense and 2 years for second offense; permanently disqualifies individuals convicted of trafficking in food stamp benefits of $500 or more; disqualifies for 10 years those convicted of fraudulently receiving multiple benefits; mandates that states collect claims by various means including the Federal Tax Refund Offset Program (FTROP); allows retention of 35% of collections for fraud claims and 20% for other client error claims; and allows allotment reductions for claims arising from state agency errors.

The law also requires a waiting period for retailers denied approval; permits disqualification of retailers disqualified under the Women, Infants, and Children (WIC) Program; expands criminal forfeiture; disqualifies up to permanently retailers who intentionally submit falsified applications; and improves USDA's ability to monitor authorized stores.

USDA had limited tools for insuring that only qualified stores were authorized to accept and redeem food stamps, monitoring their participation, and deterring violations.

Food Stamps, continued

The Food Stamp Act contained many prescriptive requirements related to states' administration of the FSP, particularly in the areas of client services, but also related to verification methods and training of states' employees. Demonstration project waiver authority prohibited approving projects that would lower or further restrict FSP income or resource standards or benefits levels. A few demonstration projects cashed out food stamp benefits to specific populations (SSI, elderly) to provide benefits in the form of wages or provided cash benefits as part of welfare reform.

Simplifies program administration by expanding states' flexibility. Allows states to submit standard cost allowances to use in calculating self-employment income; deletes detailed federal requirements over application form; deletes detailed federal customer service requirements over areas such as toll-free telephone numbers; extends expedited service processing period to 7 days and eliminates requirement to provide expedited service to homeless persons; makes use of the income and eligibility verification system (IEVS) and the immigration status verification system (SAVE) option; permits states to determine their own training needs; and authorizes the Simplified food stamp program, through which states can employ a single set of rules for their state cash assistance programs and the food stamp program. Expands food stamp waiver authority to permit projects that reduce, within set parameters, benefits to families. New demonstration projects testing cash-out of benefits are prohibited under the new waiver authority.

The Fair Market Value of most licensed vehicles was counted toward household's resource limit to the extent that the value exceeded

Sets and freezes the Fair Market Value for the vehicle allowance at $4,650.

$4,600. This amount would have increased to $5,000 10/1/96 and was indexed thereafter.

Requires EBT implementation by all states by October, 1 2002 unless waived by USDA. Exempts Food Stamp EBT from the requirements of Regulation E.

USDA has been moving expeditiously to implement electronic benefit issuance.

Consolidates the Emergency Food Assistance Program and the Soup Kitchen/Food Bank Program; provides for $100 million in mandatory spending in the Food Stamp Act to purchase commodities. Provides for state option to restrict benefits to illegal aliens.

Title IX: Miscellaneous
Title XX: Social Services Block Grant

Title XX Social Services Block Grant (SSBG) program provided assistance to states to enable them to furnish services directed at : (1) achieving or maintaining economic self-support to prevent, reduce, or eliminate dependency; (2) achieving or maintaining self-sufficiency, including reduction or prevention of dependency; (3) preventing or remedying neglect, abuse, or exploitation of children and adults unable to protect their own interests, or preserving, rehabilitating, or reuniting families; (4) preventing or reducing inappro-

Annual funding for the SSBG is $2.38 billion in FYs 1996 through 2002 and $2.8 billion in FY 2003 and each succeeding fiscal year. (The omnibus spending bill changed the FY 1997 spending level for the SSBG and appropriated $2.5 billion for that year.) Noncash vouchers for families that become ineligible for cash assistance under family caps or Title IV-A time limits are authorized as an allowable use of Title XX funds.

priate institutional care by providing for community-based care, home-based care, or other forms of less intensive care; and (5) securing referral or admission for institutional care when other forms of care were not appropriate, or providing services to individuals in institutions. Funding for the SSBG was capped at $2.8 billion a year. Funds were allocated among states according to the state's share of its total population.

Drug Testing	No provision.	Nothing in federal law prohibits states from performing drug tests on recipients or from sanctioning recipients who test positive for controlled substances.
Abstinence Education	No provision.	Starting in FY 1998, $50 million a year in mandatory funds will be added to the appropriations of the Maternal and Child Health (MCH) Block Grant. The funds will be allocated to states using the same formula used for Title V MCH Block Grant funds. Funds will enable states to provide abstinence education with the option of targeting the funds to high risk groups (i.e., groups most likely to bear children out of wedlock). Education activities are explicitly defined.

Index